Teleology

OXFORD PHILOSOPHICAL CONCEPTS

[OXFORD PHILOSOPHICAL CONCEPTS]

Christia Mercer, Columbia University

Series Editor

PUBLISHED IN THE OXFORD PHILOSOPHICAL CONCEPTS SERIES

Efficient Causation
Edited by Tad Schmaltz

Sympathy
Edited by Eric Schliesser

The Faculties
Edited by Dominik Perler

Memory
Edited by Dmitri Nikulin

Moral Motivation
Edited by Iakovos Vasiliou

Eternity
Edited by Yitzhak Melamed

Self-Knowledge
Edited by Ursula Renz

Embodiment
Edited by Justin E.H. Smith

Dignity
Edited by Remy Debes

Animals
Edited by G. Fay Edwards and Peter Adamson

Pleasure
Edited by Lisa Shapiro

Health
Edited by Peter Adamson

Evil
Edited by Andrew Chignell

Persons
Edited by Antonia LoLordo

Space
Edited by Andrew Janiak

Teleology
Edited by Jeffrey K. McDonough

FORTHCOMING IN THE OXFORD PHILOSOPHICAL CONCEPTS SERIES

The Self
Edited by Patricia Kitcher

Modality
Edited by Yitzhak Melamed

The World-Soul
Edited by James Wilberding

Powers
Edited by Julia Jorati

Human
Karolina Hubner

Love
Edited by Ryan Hanley

OXFORD PHILOSOPHICAL CONCEPTS

Teleology
A HISTORY

Edited by Jeffrey K. McDonough

OXFORD
UNIVERSITY PRESS

OXFORD
UNIVERSITY PRESS

Oxford University Press is a department of the University of Oxford. It furthers
the University's objective of excellence in research, scholarship, and education
by publishing worldwide. Oxford is a registered trade mark of Oxford University
Press in the UK and certain other countries.

Published in the United States of America by Oxford University Press
198 Madison Avenue, New York, NY 10016, United States of America.

© Oxford University Press 2020

All rights reserved. No part of this publication may be reproduced, stored in
a retrieval system, or transmitted, in any form or by any means, without the
prior permission in writing of Oxford University Press, or as expressly permitted
by law, by license, or under terms agreed with the appropriate reproduction
rights organization. Inquiries concerning reproduction outside the scope of the
above should be sent to the Rights Department, Oxford University Press, at the
address above.

You must not circulate this work in any other form
and you must impose this same condition on any acquirer.

Library of Congress Cataloging-in-Publication Data
Names: McDonough, Jeffrey K., editor.
Title: Teleology : a history / edited by Jeffrey K. McDonough.
Description: New York, NY, United States of America : Oxford University Press, 2020. |
Series: Oxford philosophical concepts |
Includes bibliographical references and index. |
Identifiers: LCCN 2019048675 (print) | LCCN 2019048676 (ebook) |
ISBN 9780190845711 (hardback) | ISBN 9780190845704 (paperback) |
ISBN 9780190845735 (epub) | ISBN 9780190845742 (online)
Subjects: LCSH: Teleology—History.
Classification: LCC BD541 .T44 2020 (print) | LCC BD541 (ebook) |
DDC 124—dc23
LC record available at https://lccn.loc.gov/2019048675
LC ebook record available at https://lccn.loc.gov/2019048676

1 3 5 7 9 8 6 4 2

Paperback printed by Marquis, Canada
Hardback printed by Bridgeport National Bindery, Inc., United States of America

Contents

SERIES EDITOR'S FOREWORD vii

CONTRIBUTORS ix

Introduction 1
JEFFREY K. MCDONOUGH

1 Plato's Teleology 14
THOMAS KJELLER JOHANSEN

2 Teleology in Aristotle 39
MARISKA LEUNISSEN

Reflection I Teleology and Function in Galenic Anatomy 64
PATRICIA MARECHAL

3 Avicenna on Teleology: Final Causation and Goodness 71
KARA RICHARDSON

4 Teleology in the Later Middle Ages 90
ROBERT PASNAU

Reflection II Teleology in Cimabue's Apocalypse Murals at Assisi 116
HOLLY FLORA

5 Teleology in Jewish Philosophy: Early Talmudists to Spinoza 123
YITZHAK Y. MELAMED

6 Not Dead Yet: Teleology and the "Scientific Revolution" 150
JEFFREY K. MCDONOUGH

Reflection III The End of Poetry: Teleology in Philip Sidney's Sonnets 180
KATHRYN MURPHY

7 "The Revised Method of Physico-Theology": Kant's Reformed Teleology 186
PAUL GUYER

8 Hegel: The Reality and Priority of Immanent Teleology 219
JAMES KREINES

Reflection IV Decoding the Teleology of Jazz 249
ANNA HARWELL CELENZA

9 Contemporary Teleology 255
PATRICK FORBER

BIBLIOGRAPHY 279

INDEX 297

Series Editor's Foreword

Oxford Philosophical Concepts (OPC) offers an innovative approach to philosophy's past and its relation to other disciplines. As a series, it is unique in exploring the transformations of central philosophical concepts from their ancient sources to their modern use.

OPC has several goals: to make it easier for historians to contextualize key concepts in the history of philosophy, to render that history accessible to a wide audience, and to enliven contemporary discussions by displaying the rich and varied sources of philosophical concepts still in use today. The means to these goals are simple enough: eminent scholars come together to rethink a central concept in philosophy's past. The point of this rethinking is not to offer a broad overview, but to identify problems the concept was originally supposed to solve and investigate how approaches to them shifted over time, sometimes radically.

Recent scholarship has made evident the benefits of reexamining the standard narratives about western philosophy. OPC's editors look beyond the canon and explore their concepts over a wide philosophical landscape. Each volume traces a notion from its inception as a solution to specific problems through its historical transformations to its modern use, all the while acknowledging its historical context. Each OPC volume is a history of its concept in that it tells a story about changing solutions to its well-defined problem. Many editors have found it appropriate to include long-ignored writings drawn from the Islamic and Jewish traditions and the philosophical contributions of women. Volumes also explore ideas drawn from Buddhist, Chinese, Indian, and other philosophical cultures when doing so adds an especially helpful new perspective. By combining scholarly innovation with focused and astute analysis, OPC encourages a deeper understanding of our philosophical past and present.

One of the most innovative features of Oxford Philosophical Concepts is its recognition that philosophy bears a rich relation to art, music, literature, religion, science, and other cultural practices. The series speaks to the need for informed interdisciplinary exchanges. Its editors assume that the most difficult and profound philosophical ideas can be made comprehensible to a large audience and that materials not strictly philosophical often bear a significant relevance to philosophy. To this end, each OPC volume includes Reflections. These are short stand-alone essays written by specialists in art, music, literature, theology, science, or cultural studies that reflect on the concept from their own disciplinary perspectives. The goal of these essays is to enliven, enrich, and exemplify the volume's concept and reconsider the boundary between philosophical and extraphilosophical materials. OPC's Reflections display the benefits of using philosophical concepts and distinctions in areas that are not strictly philosophical, and encourage philosophers to move beyond the borders of their discipline as presently conceived.

The volumes of OPC arrive at an auspicious moment. Many philosophers are keen to invigorate the discipline. OPC aims to provoke philosophical imaginations by uncovering the brilliant twists and unforeseen turns of philosophy's past.

Christia Mercer
Gustave M. Berne Professor of Philosophy
Columbia University in the City of New York

Contributors

ANNA HARWELL CELENZA is the Caestecker Professor of Music at Georgetown University. She is the author of numerous articles and scholarly books, the most recent being *Jazz Italian Style: From Its Origins in New Orleans to Fascist Italy and Sinatra* and the *Cambridge Companion to Gershwin*. She also serves as a writer/commentator for NPR and has published eight award-winning children's books.

HOLLY FLORA, Associate Professor of Art History at Tulane University, teaches and writes about art and religion in late medieval and early Renaissance Italy. She is the author of *The Devout Belief of the Imagination* (Turnhout: Brepols, 2009) and has just completed a book on Cimabue and his Franciscan patrons, for which she has received fellowships from the American Academy in Rome and the Harvard Center for Italian Renaissance Studies at Villa I Tatti.

PATRICK FORBER is Associate Professor of Philosophy and Core Faculty for the Science, Technology, and Society Program at Tufts University. He writes extensively on the nature of scientific evidence, evolutionary dynamics, and the origins of social behavior, publishing in both philosophical and scientific journals. For more details on his work, visit www.patrickforber.org.

PAUL GUYER is Jonathan Nelson Professor of Humanities and Philosophy at Brown University. He is the author of many books on the philosophy of Immanuel Kant, most recently *Virtues of Freedom: Selected Essays on Kant* (2016). For the Cambridge Edition of the Works of Immanuel Kant, of which he was co-general editor, he coedited the *Critique of Pure Reason* and edited the *Critique of the Power of Judgment* and Kant's *Notes and Fragments*. He has recently completed a monograph on the intertwined philosophical careers of Kant and Moses Mendelssohn, and is working on a book on the impact of Kant's moral philosophy on the subsequent history of philosophy.

THOMAS KJELLER JOHANSEN is Professor of Philosophy at the University of Oslo. He was previously Professor of Ancient Philosophy at the University of Oxford, and has also taught at Edinburgh and Bristol Universities. His publications include three monographs: *The Powers of Aristotle's Soul* (Oxford University Press, 2012), *Plato's Natural Philosophy: A Study of the "Timaeus-Critias"* (Cambridge University Press, 2004), and *Aristotle on the Sense-Organs* (Cambridge University Press, 1998).

JAMES KREINES is Professor of Philosophy at Claremont McKenna College. He is the author of *Reason in the World: Hegel's Metaphysics and its Philosophical Appeal* (Oxford University Press, 2015), and articles on Kant and Hegel. He is the co-editor of *Hegel on Philosophy in History* (Cambridge University Press, 2016). Future interests include responses to Spinoza during the period of German Idealism, Kant's account of reason, metaphilosophy, and a project titled *Hegel's Absolute Idealism and the Metaphysical Definitions of God*.

MARISKA LEUNISSEN is Professor in the Department of Philosophy at the University of North Carolina at Chapel Hill. She is the author of multiple papers on Aristotle's natural philosophy, his philosophy of science, and their intersections with his political science and theory of virtue, and has published two monographs, *Explanation and Teleology in Aristotle's Science of Nature* (Cambridge University Press, 2010) and *From Natural Character to Moral Virtue in Aristotle* (Oxford University Press, 2017). She also edited *Aristotle's Physics* for the Cambridge Critical Guides Series (Cambridge University Press, 2015).

PATRICIA MARECHAL is Assistant Professor in the Department of Philosophy at Northwestern University. Her research focuses on classical Greek philosophy, especially Aristotle's moral psychology, epistemology, and value theory. She has also taught and written on the history of medicine in antiquity, with an emphasis on Galen's works.

JEFFREY K. MCDONOUGH is Professor of Philosophy at Harvard University. His work focuses on the intersection of philosophy, science, and religion in the early modern era. He is currently working on two book projects, one on the history of the philosophy of religion and another on the philosophical implications of G. W. Leibniz's work in mechanics. For more on his work, visit scholar.harvard.edu/mcdonough.

YITZHAK Y. MELAMED is the Charlotte Bloomberg Professor of Philosophy at Johns Hopkins University. He works on early modern philosophy, German Idealism, medieval philosophy, and issues in contemporary metaphysics (time, mereology, and trope theory), and is the author of *Spinoza's Metaphysics: Substance and Thought* (Oxford University Press, 2013).

KATHRYN MURPHY is Fellow and Tutor in English Literature at Oriel College and Associate Professor in the English Faculty, University of Oxford. She is the author of several articles on the style, rhetoric, and philosophy of early modern prose and poetry. She is currently writing a book entitled *The Tottering Universal: Metaphysical Prose in the Seventeenth Century*.

ROBERT PASNAU is Professor of Philosophy at the University of Colorado, Boulder. He specializes in philosophy from the later Middle Ages and early modern period, and is the editor of the *Cambridge History of Medieval Philosophy* and *Oxford Studies in Medieval Philosophy*. His Isaiah Berlin Lectures, delivered at Oxford University in 2014, have been published by Oxford University Press under the title *After Certainty: A History of Our Epistemic Ideals and Illusions*.

KARA RICHARDSON is Associate Professor of Philosophy at Syracuse University. She is the author of several articles on causation in medieval metaphysics and psychology. She is currently writing a book entitled *Avicenna on Causation and Agency*.

Introduction

Jeffrey K. McDonough

At a first pass, the concept of teleology seems clear enough. Its central idea is that some things happen, or exist, for the sake of other things, that, for example, children go to zoos in order to see animals. Hippos lie in mud in order to cool themselves. Lions' teeth are for the sake of tearing flesh. It is closely related to a family of further notions including ends, goals, purposes, functions, and final causes. If some things happen or exist for the sake of other things, then the latter may be identified as the ends, goals, purposes, functions, or final causes of the former. Seeing animals is a goal for children visiting zoos. Tearing flesh is a function of a lion's teeth. The concept of teleology, seemingly clear in itself, also seems simple to apply. Supposing that hippos lie in mud in order to cool themselves, we find it easy to suppose that the goal of cooling themselves might explain why hippos lie in mud. Why is the hippo lying in mud? To cool itself. As my zoo-loving daughter likes to say: easy-peasy.

As we dig deeper into the concept of teleology, however, more and more questions arise. One set of questions centers around the issue of whether teleology is inherent in its subjects or imposed from the outside. Is teleology *intrinsic* or *extrinsic*? Take, for example, the box in my son's bedroom. It was once used to package, store, and transport shoes. That was its function, its purpose. It is now used to store Legos. Now, that's its function, its purpose. The function of the box in my son's bedroom seems extrinsic. The box has a function only because someone—a shoe company, a little boy—gives it a function. By itself—intrinsically—it has no function, no purpose, no end. But not so the activities of my son. When he goes to his bedroom in order to play with Legos, his action has a goal, namely, playing with Legos. But that goal isn't imposed from the outside. Whereas the shoebox seems to have only extrinsic teleology, my son, or his actions, seem to have intrinsic teleology. What else has extrinsic teleology? What else has intrinsic teleology? If we suppose that fire has an end, should we think that its end is extrinsic or intrinsic? If we suppose that hearts have functions, should we suppose that their functions are extrinsic or intrinsic? If we imagine that dogs and cats act teleologically, should we think that their actions are intrinsically teleological, like my son's, or extrinsically teleological, like the function of his Lego box?

Another set of questions centers around *intentionality*—the "aboutness" that is most familiar from our thoughts. When my daughter goes into the kitchen in order to get a cookie her action is teleological—it has the end or goal of getting a cookie. Her action is also intentional in the sense that it involves a thought about something, namely, a cookie. Does intrinsic teleology therefore presuppose intentionality? Could my daughter aim to get a cookie without having a thought about a cookie? What about extrinsic teleology? At first, one might suppose that my son's Lego box shows that there can be extrinsic teleology without intentionality. My son's Lego box is a fine box as far as boxes go, but it doesn't have thoughts of its own: by itself, it's not *about* anything. But, on a second pass, maybe even extrinsic teleology presupposes intentionality. Maybe my son's Lego box has a function only because *he* has thoughts about using it to store his Legos. Perhaps then teleology presupposes intentionality either directly—as when my daughter gets a cookie—or indirectly—as when my son gives a function to a box. That conclusion, however, might be difficult to square with intuitions about organs and lower organisms. For we might think that hearts can have the function of circulating blood without having thoughts about circulating blood and without having been explicitly designed to circulate blood. Likewise, we might think that flowers might open in the morning in order to increase pollination without having thoughts themselves and without being designed by an intentional creator.

Yet another set of questions concerns the *scope* of teleology. It should be uncontroversial that my daughter and son act for the sake of ends (at least much of the time!). But once we leave the bastion of intentional human action, controversy reigns. Does the world have a purpose? The seas? Fish? Gills? Water? Questions concerning the scope of teleology often intersect with our earlier questions. For example, should we ascribe teleology to artifacts and organs? How we answer this question may depend on how we answer questions about extrinsic and intrinsic teleology. If we think that teleology must be intrinsic, then we may be inclined to deny that artifacts may be genuinely teleological. If we think that teleology may be extrinsic, then we may be more willing to grant that shoes and shoeboxes can have functions. Should we ascribe teleology to lower animals and plants? How we answer this question may depend on how we answer questions about intentionality. If we think that teleology presupposes intentionality, we may be reluctant to ascribe teleology to slugs and hydrangeas. If we think that teleology does not presuppose intentionality, we may see no reason to deny that bugs look for food and that plants seek light. And, of course, all of these considerations cut both ways. If we think that artifacts have genuine functions, we should be more likely to insist that teleology may be extrinsic. If we are sure that slugs and hydrangeas are genuinely teleological, we should be less likely to insist that all teleology must involve intentionality.

A final set of questions concerns the *explanatory power* of teleology. Many philosophers have insisted that genuine explanations must give us information about causes. An explanation of why the car slid off the road must provide information about the causes that resulted in the car's sliding off the road. It must cite, for example, the car's bald tires, its speed as it rounded the corner, the icy road conditions, etc. Now suppose I know that my daughter went into the kitchen in order to get a cookie. Do I have an explanation of why she went into the kitchen? Is her getting a cookie a cause? Perhaps I do have an explanation and her getting a cookie is a cause. Or perhaps I have an explanation, but not all explanations involve causes after all. Or perhaps explanations do involve causes, her getting a cookie is not a cause, and—contrary to my first impression—I don't have an explanation of why my daughter went into the kitchen. (Perhaps a genuine explanation of her behavior would cite only efficient causes—brain states, metabolic processes, and the like.) Other explanatory puzzles abound. What if there are no cookies in the kitchen? Can my daughter's behavior be explained by something that doesn't exist? My son used to try to solve problems in what he called "superhero math." (What does Superman plus Batman equal? What is Gamora times Aquaman?) Assuming that it is not really possible to perform mathematical operations on fictional characters, can his behavior be explained by something that is, in fact, impossible? And, again, what about organs and artifacts? When I say that the function of hearts is to circulate blood, am I implicitly providing information about the causes of hearts? When I say that the function of my son's shoebox is to store Legos, am I offering a causal explanation, a noncausal explanation, or no explanation at all?

The concept of teleology—like most philosophically interesting concepts—is thus both clear at first pass and puzzling on reflection.

This collection of essays seeks to explore in greater depth how the concept of teleology has been understood and developed through different times and traditions. Each essay digs into the views of a particular philosopher, tradition, or genre, seeking to unearth a coherent picture of how that philosopher, tradition, or genre understood the concept of teleology, of how he, she, or it would answer questions such as those just raised:

> Was the concept of teleology understood to involve a commitment to intrinsic or extrinsic teleology?
> Was the concept of teleology understood to presuppose intentionality?
> What did the philosopher, tradition, or genre in question take to be the scope of teleology?
> To what extent did that philosopher, tradition, or genre take teleology to be explanatory?

The overarching ambition of the volume is to offer an overview of the concept of teleology that provides insight into its complexity, its evolution, and its unifying themes. That hope is, if you will, the telos of the volume itself.

Our collection begins, appropriately enough, with the place of teleology in Plato's philosophy. In the *Phaedo*, Plato relates Socrates's early disappointment in the natural philosophy of Anaxagoras. Evidently seeking a teleological account of the world, Socrates found in Anaxagoras instead "a man making no use of his Intelligence at all, nor finding in it any reasons for the ordering of things." To Socrates, it was as if Anaxagoras wanted to explain intentional behavior in terms of efficient causes while neglecting the reasons for the behavior. It was as if someone were to say:

> The cause of everything that Socrates does is mind—and then, in trying to account for my [i.e., Socrates's] several actions, said first

that the reason why I am lying here now is that my body is composed of bones and sinews . . . and since the bones move freely in their joints, the sinews by relaxing and contracting enable me to somehow bend my limbs, and that is the cause of my sitting here in a bent position. . . . and never troubled to mention the real reasons, which are that since Athens has thought it better to condemn me, therefore I for my part have thought it better to sit here, and more right to stay and submit to whatever penalty she orders. Because by dog, I fancy that these sinews and bones would have been in the neighborhood of Megara or Boeotia long ago—impelled by a conviction of what is best!—if I did not think that it was more right and honorable to submit to whatever penalty my country orders rather than to take to my heels and run away.[1]

In his chapter on Plato's teleology, Thomas Kjeller Johansen argues that in this passage and others from the *Phaedo*, we can discern Plato's view that any genuine causal account must be holistic and recognize the good as the only proper cause. A genuine causal account must thus not only identify an individual's good but must identify that individual's good in relation to the whole or larger system of which it is a part or element. With Plato's view properly in mind, we can then see, according to Johansen, that the teleological cosmology of Plato's *Timaeus* represents his own attempt to provide a genuine causal account of the world as a whole. Relying heavily upon craft analogies, Plato's teleology looks to be extrinsic, intentional, all encompassing, and explanatory.

In her chapter on Aristotle's teleology, Mariska Leunissen shows how close attention to Aristotle's views on nature sheds light on his views on teleology. Like Plato, Aristotle sees a tight connection between teleology and craft. And yet, in sharp contrast with Plato, Aristotle rejects the notion of an intelligent, intentional, extrinsic, divine craftsman.

---

[1] Plato, *Phaedo*, trans. Hugh Tredennick, in *Plato: The Collected Dialogues*, ed. Edith Hamilton and Huntington Cairns (Princeton, NJ: Princeton University Press 1989), 80–81.

Instead, Aristotle places teleology within the very natures of things. Natural beings, by Aristotle's lights, have innate, internal potentials that tend—unless impeded—to realization. The acorn has becoming a mighty oak among its ends. Unless it is hindered by, say, drought or disease, it will realize that potential under the guidance and force of its intrinsic "crafting" nature. Likewise the bunny rabbit has the perpetuation of its species among its ends. Unless it is impeded by, say, a premature death or the lack of a suitable mate, it will realize that potential under the guidance and force of its intrinsic nature. Leunissen illustrates how Aristotle's understanding of teleology is woven into the details of his accounts of animal generation and the explanation of the parts and features of animals. As she presents him, teleology for Aristotle is a scientific hypothesis verified by the sense it helps us to make of the natural world around us. In contrast to Plato's views, Aristotle's teleology is generally intrinsic and nonintentional. As with Plato, however, it is nonetheless pervasive and explanatorily essential.

On Aristotle's view—as well as on Plato's—there is a tight connection between teleology and goodness. Indeed, on one reading of Aristotle, for something to come about for the sake of an end is for that end to come about because it is, or appears to be, good. Focusing on the work of the tenth-century philosopher Avicenna (Ibn Sīnā), Kara Richardson argues that Avicenna develops an alternative picture of the relationship between final causation and goodness. On Richardson's telling, Avicenna agrees with Aristotle—as well as Plato—that all natural and rational actions are directed toward ends that are, or appear to be, good. Nonetheless, on Richardson's reading, for Avicenna there is no essential connection between ends and goodness. For Avicenna, what is essential about final causes is that they are required for agents to be causes. Although in Avicenna's providentially ordered world agents bring about ends that are good (or appear to be good), it would nonetheless be a mistake to see goodness (or the appearance of goodness) as being essential to ends themselves. Avicenna would maintain that when my daughter goes into the kitchen in order to get a cookie, the end of getting a cookie causes her action and appears good to her. However, it does the former essentially, the latter merely contingently. As Richardson presents him, for Avicenna, teleology is pervasive and explanatorily essential. It can also be intrinsic and nonintentional. In being agent-centered rather than good-centered, however, teleology is not essentially tied to an agent's own good.

The later medieval tradition is well known for its development of Aristotelian "Scholastic" philosophy. One might therefore expect philosophers working in that tradition to hew closely to Aristotle's own views on teleology. In his chapter on the later medieval tradition, however, Robert Pasnau argues that the reception of Aristotle's views on teleology during the late Middle Ages was in fact quite critical. Scholastic philosophers tended to agree with both Plato and Aristotle in seeing teleology as being ubiquitous—their commitment to a providentially ordered universe ensured at least that much continuity. Nonetheless, in spite of their Aristotelian credentials, Scholastics tended to side with Plato over Aristotle in seeing teleology as being extrinsic and intentional. Pasnau argues that as a result, the most interesting discussions of teleology in the period often took place in discussions of ethics rather than in natural philosophy, as philosophers of the period wrestled with questions concerning how the human will is related to ends. Are we naturally ordered to our own happiness? If so, how are we to account for acts directed to the goods of others, including God? Is the will naturally inclined to something besides happiness, like justice? Or is it perhaps the case—as William Ockham would boldly propose—that our wills are not naturally inclined to anything at all? On Pasnau's telling, teleology in the later medieval tradition is a concept under massive pressure, pressure that first led philosophers to revise their Aristotelian inheritance and later brought them to question the very legitimacy of teleology even in its most secure bastions. In the later medieval tradition, many philosophers agreed that foundational teleology is intrinsic, intentional, and explanatory, but they disagreed over teleology's scope and implications.

In his discussion of teleology in the Jewish medieval to early modern tradition, Yitzhak Melamed begins by offering a brief review of some rabbinic teachings on the purpose of the world. Those teachings—likely to be quite surprising to contemporary readers—show that rabbinic thinkers differed considerably in their views on the purpose of the world and felt little temptation to identify the natural with the good. Jewish philosophers in the Middle Ages nonetheless generally inclined to an anthropomorphic, teleological worldview—to the thought that the world and its parts were created for the sake of humankind. Initially embracing just such a view, the great medieval Jewish philosopher Maimonides came to reject anthropomorphic teleology, with important implications for his views on divine teleology. Engaged in debates over the eternity of the world, Maimonides denies that there can be nonintentional, natural teleology and argues that it makes no sense to speak of God's existence or actions as having ends. Melamed shows that similar questions concerning divine teleology arose in the Kabbalistic tradition. The Jewish medieval and Kabbalistic traditions in turn provide underappreciated context for Baruch Spinoza's much-discussed early modern critique of teleology. As Melamed demonstrates, Spinoza's attack on divine and anthropomorphic teleology can be seen as building on the foundations of his Jewish predecessors and setting the stage for his bold claim that even human desires and intentions are nothing more than efficient causes. As Melamed reads him, for Spinoza, my daughter's intending to get a cookie is the result of an inevitable series of efficient causes in which teleology plays no genuine role. For Spinoza, there simply is no teleology—extrinsic, intrinsic, intentional, natural, or otherwise. Teleology and teleological explanations are, for Spinoza, merely illusions fueled only by our "blind desire and insatiable greed."

The essays by Richardson, Pasnau, and Melamed may defy readers' expectations that teleology was widely and uncritically accepted during the Middle Ages. If so, the essay by Jeffrey McDonough may defy expectations in the other direction. It is often thought that the rise of early modern science undermined a widespread medieval commitment to teleology, that teleological explanations were widely accepted before, but not after, the so-called scientific revolution of the early modern era. But if medieval philosophers were far more critical of teleology and teleological explanations than many have supposed, McDonough argues that, conversely, teleology was frequently upheld and developed even by pioneers of the scientific revolution. He argues that teleological reasoning is inextricably woven into William Harvey's pioneering work in anatomy and physiology and that divine teleology receives an explicit and systematic defense at the hands of Robert Boyle, widely considered to be one of the founding fathers of modern chemistry. Finally, McDonough argues that, in the work of Pierre Maupertuis, we even find a bold attempt to establish a role for teleology in the heart of modern mathematical physics. If for Spinoza teleology is nowhere, for many leading figures of the scientific revolution it is (once again) everywhere. In Harvey, Boyle, and Maupertuis we find teleology that is, at turns, extrinsic, intrinsic, intentional, natural, and deeply explanatory.

In his discussion of the place of teleology in the thought of Immanuel Kant, Paul Guyer argues that for Kant teleology is both a philosophical method and a central topic for philosophy. From early in his career, Kant assumes that our natural ways of thinking, at least properly understood, cannot be in vain—they must have some point, some proper function. As Guyer argues, it is Kant's understanding of the teleology of human reason that structures the overarching argument of his famous *Critique of Pure Reason*, providing the foundation for both Kant's theoretical and practical philosophical programs. Kant's regulative principles for the conduct of theoretical inquiry and postulates of pure practical reason thus hinge on the assumption that there is a telos to human reasoning. Kant explores teleology, as a philosophical topic, in connection with a wide range of subjects, including scientific concepts and laws, aesthetic experiences and judgments, organisms, our understanding of nature, and our relation to nature. Perhaps no philosopher since Aristotle assigns such far-reaching and integral roles to teleology as Kant. And yet, what is most striking and distinctive about Kant's views on teleology is his characteristic suggestion that while we must take teleology for granted as a feature of human experience, we cannot establish it as a metaphysical certitude. As Guyer shows with a masterful command of the subtleties and details of Kant's complex thought and development, Kant ultimately insists that we must reason as if teleology were ubiquitous while admitting that it cannot be established with metaphysical certainty. We must, as it were, act as if Harvey, Boyle, and Maupertuis were right to suppose that teleology is extrinsic, intrinsic, intentional, natural, and deeply explanatory, while conceding to Spinoza that for all we know it doesn't exist at all.

In his engaging discussion of teleology in the thought of Georg Wilhelm Friedrich Hegel, James Kreines presents Hegel as deeply engaged with his predecessors' views on teleology, and, in particular, with the views of Aristotle, Spinoza, and Kant. As Kreines reads him, Hegel's interest in teleology is spurred by two considerations in particular. The first is what Hegel sees as an early modern tendency to grant extrinsic teleology even while denying immanent teleology—to allow, for example, that my son's shoebox has a function even while denying that plants and animals have innate, natural ends. The second is Kant's subjectivism about teleology, that is, Kant's view that we should act as if the world is teleologically structured while stopping short of assigning teleology to the world as it is independently of our ways of thinking about it. Kreines argues that the first point "raises the stakes" for Hegel with respect to debates over teleology. For, according to Hegel, there can be no extrinsic teleology without intrinsic teleology. If my son doesn't enjoy intrinsic teleology, then his shoebox can't enjoy extrinsic teleology. In short, for Hegel, if there is no intrinsic teleology, then there is no extrinsic teleology either, and thus no teleology at all. Kreines argues that the second point leads Hegel to offer a powerful argument to the effect that reflection on the concept of life shows that living creatures may enjoy immanent teleology even without the existence of an external designer. Provoked by early modern skepticism about immanent teleology and Kant's distinctive subjectivism, Hegel, on Kreines's reading, thus seeks to reestablish a teleology that is not necessarily intentional but that is nonetheless intrinsic, widespread, and explanatory.

In the final chapter of the volume, Patrick Forber explores contemporary accounts of teleology in the context of modern biology. Biological systems have countless well-adapted features that appear to be well designed. Lions have famously sharp teeth. Hippos have a remarkable reflex that allows them to sleep under water. But can genuine teleological functions be assigned to biological systems in a way that is consistent with contemporary views of evolution? After sharpening the challenge to teleological functions provided by Darwin's theory of natural selection, Forber considers two important contemporary approaches to biological functions, namely, etiological accounts and causal role accounts. Very roughly, etiological accounts ground functions in reasons for the presence of an adaptation. The lion has sharp teeth for tearing flesh if its sharp teeth evolved because they tear flesh. Causal role accounts ground functions in the roles parts play in contributing to the capacities of organized systems. The hippo's reflex functions to allow the hippo to sleep under water if that reflex contributes to the hippo's capacity to sleep under water. Forber points out that while etiological and causal role accounts differ in what they see as the deepest roots of teleology, both kinds of accounts share a common assumption that the ascription of biological functions should be closely tied to scientific explanations. As readers of earlier chapters will recognize, this is very much in keeping with many earlier philosophical accounts going back at least to Plato. Nonetheless, it is precisely in their commitment to tying biological functions to explanations that Forber sees a "devil's bargain." For, Forber argues, in linking biological functions to explanations, the etiological and causal role accounts inevitably make them hostage to our own perspectives, interests, and inquiries. On Forber's account, Kant was in many ways close to right.

Teleological ascriptions may be useful, and even subjectively irresistible, but we have no reason to think—indeed, we have good reason not to think—that the world has a teleological structure that is both useful and accessible to us.

Collectively, the main chapters of the volume from Plato to Darwin provide a sort of keepsake book for the history of the concept of teleology as it has been understood by a wide variety of philosophical thinkers and traditions. Those main chapters mark especially important accounts and events in the long life of the concept. But philosophical thinking about teleology never took place in an intellectual vacuum. The concept of teleology is woven into almost every facet of human life. Interspersed with the main chapters, the reader will therefore find a number of shorter "Reflection" pieces that point to a few of the many ways in which our thinking about teleology is entangled with other concepts and concerns. In her piece, "Teleology and Function in Galenic Anatomy," Patricia Marechal explains how Galen of Pergamum used a synthesis of Plato's and Aristotle's views on teleology to guide his pioneering working in dissection, anatomy, and physiology. Holly Flora explores the interpretation of Christian teleology present in a thirteenth-century cycle of murals by the renowned painter Cimabue at the church of San Francesco at Assisi. Kathryn Murphy shows how Sir Philip Sidney hoped to reconcile his Aristotelian theory of ends with poetical tropes of courtly love. Anna Harwell Celenza shows how the music critic Barry Ulanov—taking inspiration from Kant—sought, in the mid-twentieth century, to defend the artistic validity of bebop by offering a teleological account of jazz. If the main chapters of the volume aim to show how the concept of teleology endured and evolved in the thought of a wide variety of philosophical thinkers and traditions, the reflection pieces by Marechal, Flora, Murphy, and Celenza bear witness to the fact that teleology is a concept whose implications reach far beyond the purview of philosophers. The concept of teleology—if not teleology itself—is certainly everywhere.

CHAPTER ONE

Plato's Teleology

Thomas Kjeller Johansen

The task of this chapter is to bring out the basic features of teleology as Plato understands them. I shall also point to some of the ways in which Plato's teleology agrees with and differs from the Aristotelian.

1.1. THE *PHAEDO*: CAUSAL REQUIREMENTS

Plato does not use the Greek equivalent for "teleology," nor does Aristotle. However, he does present a theory of causation in which ends and purposes play the central role of cause. Our key text for this theory is the *Timaeus*. However, as is widely appreciated,[1] the

---

[1] See, e.g., F. M. Cornford, *Plato's Cosmology* (London: Routledge, 1937), 174–175; D. Sedley, "Teleology and Myth in the *Phaedo*," *Proceedings of the Boston Area Colloquium in Ancient Philosophy* 5 (1989): 359; J. Lennox, "Plato's Unnatural Teleology," in *Aristotle's Philosophy of Biology* (Cambridge: Cambridge University Press, 2001), 281.

Thomas Kjeller Johansen, *Plato's Teleology* In: *Teleology*. Edited by: Jeffrey K. McDonough, Oxford University Press (2020). © Oxford University Press.
DOI: 10.1093/oso/9780190845711.003.0002

Timaeus is the culmination of a concern with teleology that goes back to Plato's earlier works. The *Phaedo* in particular raises the prospect of accounting for the cosmos and its parts in terms of the good, insisting that the good of something is its true cause (*aitia*) and that other so-called causes should be viewed at most as necessary conditions of the good.

Since the *Phaedo* in this way tells us about the criteria for a teleological account, let us consider this work in a little more detail. We can then turn to see how the *Timaeus* attempts to meet those requirements. Socrates as a young man, we are told (*Phaedo* 96a ff.),[2] was interested in natural philosophy and wanted to know why things come into being, exist, and are destroyed. At first, he thought he could answer these questions by referring to material processes of combination and separation in the manner of the earlier cosmologists. So, for example, growth would be explained by the addition of matter, diminution by the removal of matter. But then these processes considered more abstractly as addition and subtraction puzzled Socrates. For you can generate something that is two both by adding and by subtracting, for example, you could make a pair of dogs either by adding one dog to another, or by removing one dog from three dogs. Two apparently opposite processes, then, can give rise to the same result. One requirement of a causal theory seems then to be:

R1 For x to be a cause of y, the opposite of x should not also be a cause of y.[3]

This problem led Socrates to give up this style of inquiry. When he came across Anaxagoras, however, he thought he'd found a better

---

2 References to Plato's texts are to the standard Stephanus pagination, while Aristotle is referred to by the standard Bekker page numbers. Translations in this chapter are from the works listed in "Primary Sources" in the bibliography.
3 See for the following D. Sedley, "Platonic Causes," *Phronesis* 43 (1998): 122–123.

account of causation. Anaxagoras stipulated Reason (*nous*)[4] as an all-governing principle. It is worth attending to Socrates's words:

> **T1** I thought, "If this is so, Reason in arranging things arranges everything and establishes each thing as it is best for it to be. So if anyone wishes to find the cause of the generation or destruction or existence of a particular thing, he must find out what sort of existence, or passive state of any kind, or activity is best for it." (*Phaedo* 97c, trans. H. Fowler)

Socrates's expectation then is that referring to Reason brings in the good as a cause. Socrates doesn't tell us why, but his thought seems to be that if a rational agency arranges things, then it will do so in order to make them as good as possible. Now this may seem to secure merely the conclusion that the *apparent* good is the cause of the cosmos, not necessarily the *real* good. However, if we remember that Reason is understood as perfect Reason, or, as one might say, Reason perfected, then we can add that it is the real good, or the best, that informs Reason's arrangements. By identifying the good we can then determine what it is that directs the organization of the cosmos.[5] We can put the condition like this:

G x is the cause of y if and only if x is what is best for y.

---

4 *Nous* is often translated "mind," but it is important to highlight that the term refers not just to the capacity for reason but to the achievement or virtue of reason (see S. Menn, "Aristotle and Plato on God as *Nous* and as the Good," *Review of Metaphysics* 45 [1992], 554–555). If *nous* meant the mere capacity, Socrates would be less justified in expecting that *nous* had successfully organized the world for the best.

5 The lack of a distinction here between reason and causes has allowed scholars to draw opposite conclusions as to which has priority for Plato. For a classic argument that for Plato causes are reasons, see G. Vlastos, "Reasons and Causes in the *Phaedo*," *Philosophical Review* 78 (1969): 291–325. For an argument that we should continue to see *aitia* primarily as causes, see Sedley, "Platonic Causes." Agreeing with Sedley, one might say that at least in teleological contexts for Plato, reasons are causes. The standard modern reference for this sort of view in accounting for human agency is D. Davidson, "Actions, Reasons, and Causes," *Journal of Philosophy* 60 (1963): 685–700.

Socrates adds that the good should be a sufficient cause: if the good is given, no other cause is needed to explain the arrangement in question. We can add then a sufficiency requirement:

R2 if x is the cause of y, no other cause is required for y. (98a)

Socrates also thinks that the true cause is exclusive of other causes:

R3 if x is the cause of y, there is no other cause of y. (98a)

Socrates was in the end disappointed with Anaxagoras. When it came to giving actual cosmological accounts, Anaxagoras did not mention the good, but rather material stuffs, like air and earth (98c). Socrates compares Anaxagoras with somebody explaining why Socrates is sitting in prison by referring to his bones and sinews instead of Socrates's thought that it is best to stay and face his punishment rather than to run away. Clearly Socrates wouldn't be sitting in prison if he didn't have bones and sinews, but that is a mere necessary condition. The same body parts could just as well be on their way now to Megara, for all they are concerned. The explanation then confuses what is a mere necessary condition with the cause.

We could infer simply from the exclusivity claim in **R3** that if the good is the cause, then the bones and sinews are not also the cause. But Socrates's joke about the bones departing for Megara shows another reason why they could not be the cause.

R4 For x to be the cause of y, x should not also be a cause of the opposite of y.

R4 complements **R1** in stating that one thing cannot be the cause of opposite outcomes, where **R1** said that opposite things cannot be the cause of the same outcome.

Now **R1**–**R4** may seem to bear no particular connection with **G**, give no reason to suppose that the good is always the cause. Indeed, the theory of forms developed by Socrates after this discussion, the so-called method of hypothesis (100b ff.), does not single out the good as a cause. Here, for example, the form of beauty is said to be the cause, and the only cause, whereby beautiful things are beautiful. The form of beauty would satisfy, it seems, **R1–R4**. And the form of heat would do the same job for hot things, and so on. We can of course run the same explanation for good things: good things are good by the good itself. But the good itself is still just one instance of a cause, one among many forms, not the one and only proper cause, as insisted by **G**. Now the hypothesis of the forms is described as "safe"—rather too safe perhaps in offering such etiolated information as "beautiful things are beautiful by the beautiful"[6]—and Socrates tries a more sophisticated account when he allows for things that always instantiate a certain form also to be causes in virtue of possessing that form. So, for example, we may safely say not just that hot things are hot because of heat, but also that hot things are hot because of fire, since fire always brings heat with it. But the more we develop such "sophisticated" answers, the more we may wonder about the need for the good, and why we should insist on teleology rather than fitting material explanations to the more sophisticated account.

1.2. Teleology and Causal Holism

Now notice that Socrates says that he expected a cause to show not just the good for each thing but also for the whole:

> **T2** So I thought when he assigned the cause of each thing and of all things in common he would go on and explain what is best for each and *what is good for all in common*. (98b, my italics)

---

[6] Plato, *Phaedo* 100e.

What is required, then, is a holistic account: to show how the good works for the individual and for the whole. It may seem that "what is best for each and what is good for all in common" refers to two different goods, one that is good for the earth, say, and another that is good for the whole cosmos. So perhaps the good for the earth need not mention the good for the cosmos. Although the earth is part of the cosmos, and so would in a sense be included in the account of the good of the cosmos, the two goods could still be distinct as goods of distinct entities. Moreover, we might think that there is no guarantee that what is best for the cosmos is also best for the earth or vice versa. These could be different instances of goodness. In that case, the earth would be explained by what is good for it as one instance of goodness, the cosmos by what is good for *it* as another instance.

However, this is to misunderstand the force of the cosmological example. The questions why it is best for the earth to be round or flat, or in the center, or for the stars to move around with their characteristic orbits and relative speeds cannot be answered in isolation from each other. In order to explain the earth's position one needs to say something about the position of the other planets and its relation to the sun. We need to approach the good of the earth as part of the *kosmos*, recalling that the Greek word means "ordered whole." Of course, this is not to reduce the good of the earth to that of the cosmos; we can take it that the earth and the moon will be given explanations that are specific to each, but both will articulate the goodness of each in relation to that of the cosmos as a whole.

The *Phaedo*'s suggestion is then that a proper causal account is holistic. This could be why we need teleological causation. Only the good can give us the overall causal perspective that draws in a particular natural phenomenon under one cause. We may recall also the *Republic*'s insistence that the Form of the Good is the cause and ultimate object of all knowledge. Here the Good seems to work exactly as a principle which allows us to bring together different explananda, including the forms themselves, in a comprehensive—"synoptic" is Plato's word

(*Republic* 537c)—understanding. One way in which scholars have articulated this central role is in terms of teleology.[7] If you want to know something, you need to know what it does, its function. To know its function you must know what it is good for. But what something is good for depends on further ends. We see this typically in artifacts: to know what a hammer is you need to know its function, but this requires knowing the end of hammering, housebuilding, and such, which further requires knowing the ends of houses, how they are good for humans, and so on, until you reach some final end. The highest good would be the terminus of a series of such teleological explanations.[8] Plato's thought in the *Republic* would then be that natural things too have functions and are amenable to this sort of explanatory hierarchy where all paths lead ultimately to that single idea of goodness, which we know as "the Form of the Good." Whether or not this interpretation holds for the *Republic*, we shall see that the *Timaeus* backs up the idea that teleological accounts for Plato are inherently holistic.

1.3. Teleology in the *Timaeus*

In the *Phaedo* Socrates dismissed his teleological inquiries as too demanding, but the *Timaeus* takes up the challenge again. Here the main speaker, Timaeus (Socrates is in attendance but again deems himself unqualified), sets out to explain the generation of the cosmos down to and including the creation of man (27a). Timaeus starts out by arguing that the cosmos, beautiful as it is,[9] must have been caused by a divine craftsman (*dēmiourgos*).[10] The craftsman is said to be "responsible"

---

7 See, e.g., N. Denyer, "Sun and Line: The Role of the Good," in the *Cambridge Companion to Plato's "Republic"*, ed. G. R. F. Ferrari (Cambridge: Cambridge University Press, 2007), 284–309.
8 See Aristotle, *Nicomachean Ethics* I.1 for a clear statement of the hierarchy of ends within the arts.
9 As shown, for example, by the *Symposium*, the notions of beauty and goodness are inextricably linked for Plato.
10 See T. K. Johansen, "Why the Cosmos Needs a Craftsman: Plato's *Timaeus* 27d5–29b," *Phronesis* 59 (2014): 297–320.

(*aitios*) for the cosmos. However, this is not yet to say what the cause (*aitia*) of the cosmos is, that is, *why* the craftsman made it.[11] The cause rather was God's wish to make everything as like himself as possible. Since God is all good, becoming maximally like God means becoming as good as possible.

The good that Socrates sought in the *Phaedo* reappears here as the object of God's desire. This is less of a change than it may at first appear, if we remember the role played by Reason (*nous*) in Anaxagoras. The demiurge in the *Timaeus* is the counterpart to Anaxagoras's Reason. Since this Reason was understood as reason perfected, we could take it that the true good directed its actions. The demiurge similarly is essentially rational.[12] He is also referred to as the "intelligent cause," and the entire cosmos is an expression of his reasoning about how to make the world as good as possible. Even his desires may be seen as expressions of reason, as reason in Plato's psychology has its own desires.[13] Socrates in the *Phaedo* thought that *nous*, being perfectly rational, would do only what is good. Similarly, Timaeus not only portrays God as pure reason but also insists that he wants only what is good, himself being good, indeed, as he puts it, the best of all intelligible beings (37a). We may rest assured, then, that when he implements the good as he desires it, he really does make the world as good as possible, assuming of course that nothing else impedes his efforts.

Yet a cosmic explanation in terms of the actions of a crafting god is not just an explanation in terms of the good. It is an explanation of how the good is implemented by a *reasoning* agent. What sort of

---

11 "Now, let us state the reason (*aitia*) why becoming and this universe were framed by him who framed it. He was good, and what is good never has any particle of envy in it whatsoever; and being without envy he wished all things to be as like himself as possible. This indeed is the most proper principle of becoming and [30a] the cosmos and as it comes from wise men one would be absolutely right to accept it." On the distinction between *aitios* and *aitia*, see M. Frede, "The Original Notion of Cause," in *Essays in Ancient Philosophy* (Minneapolis: University of Minnesota Press, 1987), 125–150.

12 See Menn, "Aristotle and Plato," 554–555.

13 See Plato, *Republic* IX 580d–81e.

reasoning is involved is not obvious. Neoplatonists took the creation to be the result of the intellect's theoretical thoughts being reflected in matter.[14] In this case the creation would not be the result of specific deliberation about how to bring this world about but rather a byproduct of a sort of theoretical reasoning about eternal matters that Reason engages in anyway. However, there are clear signs in our text that Plato's demiurge is involved in a form of practical reasoning about how to craft the world. The demiurge's task itself calls for practical reasoning: how to make a world that is the greatest possible likeness of an eternal model. This is not simply a matter of copying the model, but of finding out which features best represent the eternal forms in a different ontological medium, that of change or coming-into-being. So when God wants to make the world like the eternal forms, he makes time as a *moving* image of eternity (37d–e). Or he makes the world complete in the image of the model by making it spherical, where the model has no geometrical shape at all (33b). Such likenesses in a quite different medium can only be found through a sort of analogical reasoning. There is no demonstrative reasoning from the characteristics of the model to those of its likeness, no certainty that this is the right way to make the likeness. The status of cosmological reasoning contrasts sharply, then, with the certainty expected of accounts about the eternal forms themselves. When discussing eternal and changeless matters, precise and certain accounts are appropriate. But we can at best achieve a likely account, Timaeus says (*Timaeus* 29c–d), when discussing a created and changing likeness of the eternal forms. The language Timaeus uses to describe God's reasoning matches the practical, nondemonstrative nature of this reasoning: "reckoning," "weighing up," "planning," and, of course, the verb "crafting" itself.[15]

---

14 See, e.g., E. Emilsson, *Plotinus* (London: Routledge, 2017).
15 Respectively, *logizomai*, 30b, 34b, *analogizomai* 75c; *dianoeomai*, 32c; *demiourgoumai*, 31a.

This is the job description of a craftsman. The demiurge is no doubt also theoretically wise, but that is not the concern of the *Timaeus*.[16] Cosmology is something we do when we set aside just thinking about the forms,[17] and so is cosmogony.[18] To be sure, the craftsman draws on information about the forms, for these are after all the model of his creation. But his creative thinking does not concern the forms as such but selects those features of the forms that are relevant to his creative project. While theoretical information may feature in the craftsman's reasoning, it is essentially directed at how to bring about a product, and so counts as in a broad sense practical.[19]

The implications for Plato's brand of teleology are significant, as a comparison with Aristotle will show. Aristotle in *Physics* II.5 distinguishes between two kinds of teleology or final causation: one whereby the end is brought about through reasoning (*dianoia*), another where the agent is nature (*phusis*). Now nature is for Aristotle studied by theoretical reason: in natural philosophy we contemplate eternal essences of the sort that are realized in matter and subject to change.[20] Craft, on Aristotle's own account, has a different object, the contingent, what may or may not be, and specifically contingent objects of the sort that we can bring about.[21] Craftsmen reason about how best to bring about this kind of product. Now inevitably in some circumstances this involves making up particular solutions to particular problems, while

---

16 See further, T. K. Johansen, "*Timaeus* and the Principles of Cosmology," in *The Oxford Handbook of Plato*, ed. G. Fine (Oxford: Oxford University Press, 2011), 463–483.
17 See Plato, *Timaeus* 59d–e.
18 As we may infer from the fact that cosmology is a recreation in words of what the god did in deed (Plato, *Critias* 106a).
19 I say "in a broad sense" since we may with Aristotle want to distinguish between practical and productive reasoning. But as *Statesman* 258d–e shows, Plato does not conceive of the practical in contrast to the productive.
20 Aristotle, *Metaphysics* VI.1 1025b25.
21 See Aristotle, *Nicomachean Ethics* VI.3–4.

in nature, Aristotle says, the causal sequence "is invariable, if there is no impediment" (*Physics* 199b25–26).[22]

Now from the point of view of teleology what matters here may be that teleological processes viewed from a theoretical science must focus on the invariable and eternal. An acorn grows in order to become an oak tree. We may say that each acorn grows in a somewhat different way in different conditions, but none of this is of interest to us as theoretical biologists. For craftsmen the situation is different. A craftsman's thinking is directed toward a particular product. As Aristotle says, the doctor heals the individual, not man in general.[23] A doctor's reasoning must take into account differing circumstances, the condition of the patient, the available medicines, other patients' demands on her time, and so on. Generally, a craftsperson must apply her general skill in varying conditions, constrained by the available time and materials. Sometimes this is plain sailing and no deliberation is required, sometimes not. The cosmic demiurge is similarly constrained: his reasoning needs to be flexible to particular circumstances. And this may seem an advantage of Plato's craft model over Aristotle's natural teleology: the sensitivity to individual circumstances allows the craftsman to track the best *actual* ways of bringing about the end.[24] Natural teleology may seem inflexible and "blind" in comparison, insensitive to how a general

---

[22] In *Physics* II.8, however, Aristotle is running craft and nature closely together, wanting to use the analogy with craft to show that final causes operate in nature. He is therefore led to claim that even "craft does not deliberate," in apparent contraction with his own use of craft as an analogy for ethical deliberation in his ethical works. Sarah Broadie, in "Nature, Craft and *Phronesis* in Aristotle," *Philosophical Topics* 15 (1987): 35–50 has rightly worried whether Aristotle doesn't end up misrepresenting craft, shoehorning it to serve as an analogue for nature.

[23] Aristotle, *Metaphysics* I.1 981a18–20.

[24] See Broadie's acute comment ("Nature, Craft and *Phronesis*," 48), "One such end that concerns us here is the transmission of forms of activity that are saved from dying with the individual only by being taught. Reflective rationality, according to this approach, is the means by which human nature compensates for its own failure to provide genetically all that it needs in order to flourish and continue. Non-human natures, on the other hand, are genetically adequate for their own needs, including the need to reproduce in kind. In comparing such natures to craft, Aristotle must prescind from just the feature of craft that so impressed Socrates and Plato: the craftsman's command of reasons for doing as he does."

good is best realized in a particular situation and unable to negotiate the particular impediments which a craftsman can cleverly work his way around. In a world like Aristotle's, without mutation and natural selection, the same species will forever operate in the same way to achieve the same ends.[25] Of course the eternity of the species is a sign that this generally works well; otherwise members of the species would not survive to generate the next generation. But is it necessarily always the way it would work *best*?

This contrast may seem less obvious in the case of a craftsman who builds up the whole cosmos from the bottom. While the created cosmos is a particular, it makes little sense, perhaps, to talk of particular circumstances to which the demiurge needs to be sensitive if all the circumstances lie within his remit, so to speak.[26] However, this is to ignore the extent to which the demiurge has to negotiate the consequences of his own creative actions. While the demiurge is free to create the basic materials as he sees fit, and his way of doing so will of course objectively be the best, the consequences of creating them in one way rather than another constrain his further actions. Let us look a little more closely at this point.

God's creation is not ex nihilo.[27] Like all craftsmen, he works with materials. Unlike a normal craftsman whose materials have certain fixed properties, a carpenter's wood is such and such, a blacksmith's metal thus and so, the cosmic demiurge picks up a world characterized by chaos and fluidity. The pre-cosmos contained traces (*ikhnē*) of the four elements, which moved around in a receptacle, but with no stability or purpose. The demiurge put a stop to this by structuring

---

25 For this kind of point see D. Charles, "Teleological Causation in the *Physics*," in *Aristotle's Physics: A Collection of Essays*, ed. L. Judson (Oxford: Oxford University Press, 1991), 101–128.
26 And unlike Zeus of the *Statesman* myth, there doesn't seem to be a particular moment when the world has degenerated to the point where the demiurge must step in. For the world seemed constantly uniformly disordered before the creation.
27 On the contrast on this point with the God of Abrahamic religions, see S. Broadie, *Nature and Divinity in Plato's "Timaeus"* (Cambridge: Cambridge University Press, 2012), 7–26.

the "elements"[28] mathematically, each receiving a proper geometrical shape which would determine its interactions with other elements and their compounds. Now once the demiurge had ordered the elements, they moved as they do by "necessity." Fire, for example, is made of sharp triangles which necessarily move fast and cut through other materials. "Necessity" stands for the processes and attributes that occur necessarily, given the elements' geometrical natures.[29] There is nothing the demiurge can do about that. So when the demiurge subsequently wants to make something using fire, he is constrained by the necessary properties of fire and has to work with them. Necessity is also called the "wandering cause" (48a7), since necessary processes are not as such goal-directed.

The cosmos is not just a product of divine intentions, but also of Necessity. Timaeus says that Reason (*nous*) had to *persuade* Necessity to work for good ends (47e–48a). Such "persuasion" may itself be taken as a kind of practical reasoning: it is a matter of reasoning out the best way of using the given properties of the materials available to bring about a certain end. When constructing the human body, for example, the demiurge will use the hardness of earth and the heat of fire to make bone (*Timaeus* 73e). However, this decision has consequences down the line: the hardness of bone when used for the cranium is not compatible with the sensitivity desirable in a human being. So God has to make the cranium thinner and more fragile than he would have wanted (75b–c). The compromise shows exactly how the craftsman's reasoning is constrained by the necessary properties of the available matter, even where it is the craftsman himself who has made it.[30]

---

28 I use "elements" for convenience. Timaeus is clear (48b–c) that he does not consider earth, water, fire, and air to be elements since they are themselves composed of geometrical bodies, which in turn have constituents.

29 For a defense of this reading, see T. K. Johansen, *Plato's Natural Philosophy* (Cambridge: Cambridge University Press, 2004), 92–116.

30 For ease of exposition, I ignore here the difference between the demiurge and the lesser gods, who are in charge of the creation of the human body (cf. 41a–d). The lesser gods imitate the demiurge

Teleology is limited by necessity. Ends need to be negotiated in light of what the material processes allow for. Material processes are constraining: it is because wood has its properties that you cannot make a balloon out of it. But they are by the same token enabling: it is because wood has these properties (and not those of butter, say) that you can make a house. When material processes are used by reason for a good end (*aitia*), Timaeus refers to them in this capacity as "co-causes" or "contributory causes" (*sunaitia*). Here is the key passage where Timaeus is commenting on the role of mechanisms of vision:

> **T3** All these are among the contributory causes which god uses as servants in shaping things in the best way possible. But they are thought of by most people not as contributory causes but as causes of everything, achieving their effects by heat and cold, solidification and liquefaction, and the like. Yet they are completely incapable of having reason or intelligence; for the only existing thing which properly possesses intelligence we must call soul, and soul is invisible, whereas fire, water, earth and air have all come into being as all visible bodies. So the lover of intelligence and knowledge is bound to investigate, first, causes of a rational nature, and, second, those causes that occur when things that are moved by some things of necessity move other things. Our procedure must be the same. We must deal with causes of both sorts, distinguishing those that with intelligence are craftsmen of what is beautiful and good from those which when deprived of wisdom on each occasion bring about a random disordered result. (*Timaeus* 46c–e)

Like Socrates in the *Phaedo*, Timaeus criticizes those people who confuse material processes such as heating and cooling with real causes. The material processes in themselves, "deprived of wisdom," bring about

---

in his providence, and from the point of view of teleology, the difference between the two is not significant here.

results lacking in good order. The material processes are governed by necessity, such that when one thing is moved it necessarily moves another with no regard for the goodness of the outcome. In contrast, the intelligent cause is rational and works for the good. The intelligent cause may use the necessary processes for the good, and then we refer to them as "contributory" causes. Indeed, Timaeus is willing in this case to call the material processes one kind of *aitia*, in apparent contravention of Socrates's statement in the *Phaedo* (99a) that it is "totally absurd" to call them so.

How do we explain this apparent upgrade in the causal status of the material processes? Consider the notion of a mere necessary condition in the case of Socrates's sitting in prison. There are countless conditions that are general conditions for any physical behavior, the law of gravity, the existence of matter, and so on. There are also more specific necessary conditions such as Socrates's having a body with sinews and bones, as Socrates says. But these again are not conditions specific to his sitting in prison. As Socrates said, these body parts might as well be on their way to Megara now for all that they are concerned: the material conditions failed to meet **R4**, the requirement that if X is the cause of Y, then X should not also equally be able to bring about the opposite of Y.

We can now see how the material conditions when brought in under the intelligent cause can be seen to satisfy **R4**. Consider Timaeus's own example of vision (*Timaeus* 45c–46c). God chooses to make the seeing part of the eye out of an especially fine kind of fire. Its fineness allows the fire to exit the eye, where it joins with the external light, a kindred form of fire. The union allows impressions to travel along the body of fire to the inside of the eye and of the body, where they get registered by the soul. Now this mechanism employs fire and relies on the necessary properties of fire (e.g., linear motion, great mobility, ability to merge with other fire). But in vision these properties are described with a view to the end of vision: vision works in this way because it allows us to see, to register differences in color and light, all of which, as Timaeus says, contributes to our obtaining an idea of day and night and number. The necessary mechanisms of vision are carefully selected to show their contribution to the specific function of vision. The mechanisms do not appear random in relation to a good end, as did Socrates's bones and sinews in relation to his staying in prison, but specifically geared to the functioning of vision.[31]

1.4. Craft and Teleology

This advance in Plato's teleological thinking is connected with the adoption of the craft model in the *Timaeus*. In the *Phaedo* there was no suggestion that Reason would work specifically as a craftsman. Nor, relatedly, was there any indication of how certain necessary conditions could be understood as instrumental in specifically bringing about certain good outcomes. Socrates's complaint that Anaxagoras did not make use of Reason can be read, from the point of view of the *Timaeus*, as a complaint not about employing material processes but about not integrating them in an account that showed how they worked for the good. This is exactly the viewpoint that the craft model provides. The craftsman chooses material processes insofar as they are instrumental in delivering this particular product. A blacksmith uses heat to soften the iron so that he can form it into a horseshoe: he directs the heat to burn in this way and to this degree, and not in some other way, because this is what is required to produce the horseshoe. Similarly, the demiurge chooses fire for vision, making it exit the eyes, merge with the external light, etc. Necessary processes are integrated into a larger causal story determined by a good end. With the craft model comes then a structure of explanation whereby causes are ordered as either directive ends or as instrumental causes specifically contributing to such ends.[32]

---

[31] For details, see Johansen, *Plato's Natural Philosophy*, Ch. 5.
[32] To see how calling mechanisms *sunaitia* is no small concession to their contribution to a causal explanation, see Plato, *Politicus* 281c–d, where the Eleatic Stranger says that while weaving is the

In relation to the *Phaedo*, this is not just a corrective to Anaxagoras's use of material processes, but also shows how one can develop a full teleological account that takes into account both the good and the necessary conditions for that good.

For good order, we can check off also the three other conditions **R1–R3** in the *Phaedo*. **R1**, the condition that if X is the cause of Y, then the opposite of X should not also bring about Y, is met. Expansion might be caused both by cooling and by heating: so water expands in a freezer, and air expands in a hot-air balloon. However, where the material processes are directed by an intelligent cause, one process will have been chosen rather than the other as the best one to bring about the particular result desired: if you want to go on a journey in a balloon you do not choose to fill it with freezing water: only the heating of air will serve that purpose. The process then is nonrandom given the specific end. As for **R2**, the sufficiency requirement applies not in the sense that the good brings about the result on its own. Contributory causes are after all required: there is no vision without the movement of fire. But the good is sufficient for these processes, and together they ensure the good result. Finally, **R3**, the exclusivity requirement, holds as long as we specify, as does Timaeus in **T3**, that the intelligent cause is the *primary* cause.

1.5. Craft and Hypothetical Necessity

In **T3**, Timaeus talks of one sort of necessity when "those causes that occur when things that are moved by some things of *necessity* move other things." This is the notion of Necessity that had to be persuaded by reason to bring about good ends. Once we conceive of material processes as contributing causes, however, it is possible also to link them with a new notion of necessity, the sort of necessity which in

---

cause (*aitia*) of woolly clothing, those arts which produce the instruments of weaving all have a claim to being the *sunaitia*.

connection with Aristotle will be known as "hypothetical" or "from a hypothesis."[33] The hypothesis is that if a certain end is to be achieved, then certain material processes have to occur. Where the first sort of necessity is backward looking, the result being necessary given the antecedent, hypothetical necessity is forward looking: if a certain result is to come about, then such and such has to happen. The contributory causes are necessary in this way if the good is to be brought about.

There are several places where Timaeus uses the notion of "necessary for an end." So at 41c the demiurge bids the assistant gods create "every kind of living creature which [the cosmos] must have *if it is* to be sufficiently complete" (my italics). The human souls meanwhile are embodied "by necessity" (42a), meaning necessary given God's intentions for the cosmos. The processes of vision as we saw involved the necessity of material processes, but they were also dictated by the end of vision: "For I reckon that sight has become the cause of the greatest benefit to us in that not a word of all that is being said now about the universe would ever have been said *if we had not seen* stars and sun and heaven" (47a, my italics). Pleasure and pain are a necessary consequence of the soul's embodiment (69c–d), but we also need to feed the appetites "*if mortals were to exist* at all" (70e5, my italics). There are, then, bodily processes which are in one sense necessary in the manner of material processes, but which can also be considered hypothetically necessary as required for realizing certain ends.[34]

Elsewhere in Plato we see a similar connection between contributory causes and hypothetical necessity. So the *Statesman* articulates what it is to be a contributory cause in terms of hypothetical necessity:

> T4 VISITOR: Well then, let's look at two sorts of expertise that are in relation to all the things that people do.

---

33 See M. Leunissen's article in this volume on what she calls "conditional necessity."
34 Cf. also 68e–69a, where Timaeus says that the divine cause cannot be understood or grasped without the necessary cause.

YOUNG SOCRATES: Which are they?
VISITOR: One which is a contributory cause of production, one which is itself a cause.
YOUNG SOCRATES: How so?
VISITOR: Those which do not make the thing itself, but which provide tools for those that do—tools which, if they were not present, what has been assigned to each expertise would never be accomplished. (281d–e; trans. C. J. Rowe)

The distinction between cause and contributing cause is a constant in these dialogues. The contributory cause is explicitly a necessary condition, a tool without which the end would not be accomplished.[35] A craftsman needs the right tool for the right job. As Socrates says at *Cratylus* 389b–c, there is a tool that is naturally suited to each kind of function, e.g., a shuttle that is suited to each kind of weaving, and each tool must be made to suit each function. Once we think of the contributing cause as an *instrument*, it becomes obvious that such causes are selected and configured in relation to a specific end, that is, that they are not a mere necessary condition but an integral part of the story of how a certain end is brought about. The craft model is the key to Plato's understanding of the means-end relationship in teleology.

1.6. HOLISM AGAIN

T3 distinguished "those that with intelligence are craftsmen of what is beautiful and good from those which when deprived of wisdom on each occasion bring about a random *disordered result*." Goodness contrasts with disorder. At the very outset of his creation the demiurge, finding "the visible universe in a state not of rest but of inharmonious

---

35 As Socrates says at *Cratylus* 389b–c, there is a tool that is naturally suited to each kind of function, e.g., a shuttle that is suited to each kind of weaving, and each tool must be made to suit each function. So we should understand contributing causes as necessary for the realization of a *specific* end.

and disorderly motion, brought it to order from disorder, as he judged that order was in every way better" (30a). By ordering the world, God makes the world as good as possible. We might think that order in itself is value neutral. There are countless ways one can order numbers, for example. However, for Plato order implies a proportionate, rationally understandable, beautiful structure, paradigmatically illustrated by musical harmony. It was such an order that made the ideal city of the *Republic* good,[36] and again it is this kind of order which determines the physical world in the *Timaeus*. More specifically, geometrical proportion is applied from the bottom to the top of the creation. The four basic bodies are each structured according to geometrical figures, their combinations and interactions are geometrically determined, as is the shaping of them into a spherical world body. The world soul is structured and divided according to similar mathematical proportions, and world body and soul are fitted together to form a sphere.[37]

Recall now the suggestion in the *Phaedo* that teleological explanation should be holistic. The account of the earth's position should show how it is good both for the earth and for the whole. There are two ways we can see this requirement satisfied by Timaeus's accounts. One is that each explanandum is explained as a certain structure of parts: an earth molecule, for example, is a cube composed of twenty-four rectangular isosceles triangles (55b), blood is a structure of water, earth, and fire (82c), and so on. That is to say, each explanandum is explained holistically as a certain good order of its constituents. One might call this an "internal holism." The other way in which the account is holistic, however, is that each structure is explained in such a way that it is combinable with other structures in a larger whole. So fire is structured so as to interact in an ordered way with the other basic bodies, to combine with or separate from other shapes according to

---

36 Cf. Plato, *Republic* 430e–432b.
37 Cornford, *Plato's Cosmology*, is still a useful guide to the details of the geometrical ordering of both the cosmic body and soul.

geometrical principles (56e–57d). The head is spherical to accommodate the circular motions of the human soul, just as the world body is to fit with the circular motions of its soul (44d). We might call this external holism, in the sense that individual structures are selected to fit the larger whole. The *Timaeus* operates with both sorts of holism. It is in a sense a stronger sort of holism than that demanded by Socrates in the *Phaedo* in that it is a feature of the theory that it is the same order that internally structures the explanandum that also makes it suitable as a part in the larger whole. It is, for example, the fact that fire is made of these triangles that also allows them to interact appropriately with other geometrical bodies. As with Lego bricks, we might admire the geometrical shape individually of each brick, but it is in their combinations with other bricks that we fully see their structure displayed.

Such holism is all of a piece with craftsmanship. Craft is not concerned with just a part of its product but seeks to make the totality an ordered whole.[38] To use the image of the statue in *Republic* IV (420c1–d5), a sculptor will try to make the whole statue as beautiful as possible, and so will not paint the eyes purple, for example, even if this color on its own might be considered more beautiful, but blue, say, because this is the color that fits a human being. Similarly, Timaeus's account (30a–b) highlights from the start the holistic character of the demiurge's reasoning: "As a result of reasoning, [the demiurge] found that among all things that are by nature visible, no work without intelligence will ever be more beautiful than one with intelligence, *if we compare them whole for whole*" (my italics). The concern for the whole is overriding: even if one might theoretically consider a part of a visible work which has no intelligence more beautiful than some part of a visible whole with intelligence, the whole with intelligence will be more beautiful than the other whole.

---

38 Cf. Plato, *Laws* X 900c–905d.

Craft, then, is not just teleological, it is teleological in a holistic manner. Craft does not just seek to realize the individual good, but where that individual is part of a whole, as in a cosmos, it prioritizes the good of the whole. Again, the answers available in the *Timaeus* to the *Phaedo*'s puzzles in large part stem from the adoption of the craft model.

1.7. Teleology and Anthropocentrism

It is customary in interpretations of Aristotle's teleology to distinguish at least three kinds of teleology: (a) species teleology, where the species (and its members as such) is the sole carrier of the good to be realized; (b) cosmic teleology, where the cosmos as a whole realizes the good also of the individual species; (c) anthropocentric teleology (which may be considered a particular sort of cosmic teleology), where the good of the whole is realized in the good for man.[39] So far, we have seen good reason to take Plato's teleology to be a form of (b) rather than (a). But there are passages also in the *Timaeus* which would suggest (c). Prima facie, anthropocentricism would be a surprising position for Timaeus to adopt given his emphasis on the good of the whole cosmos, of which man is just part. However, it is possible to see the cosmos as being structured in such a way that, in contributing to the human good, directly or indirectly, the cosmos realizes its own good. That is, a hierarchical conception of the goods, with the human good at the top, might establish a cosmic order. If, for example, one considered man as being in the position of a user of the entire creation, possibly also with man's good being planned for by God, then realizing an anthropocentric good would vouchsafe also the cosmic good. The strongest evidence for anthropocentrism in the *Timaeus*, however, falls

---

39 See M. R. Johnson, *Aristotle on Teleology* (Oxford: Oxford University Press, 2005), for a helpful overview of the different interpretations.

short of establishing this view. So when Timaeus accounts for the creation of the sun he says,

> **T5** And in the second of the orbits from the Earth god lit a light, which we now call "the Sun," to provide a clear measure of the relative speeds of the eight revolutions, to shine throughout the whole heaven, and *to enable the appropriate living creatures to gain a knowledge of number from the uniform movements of the same*. In this way and for this reason there came into being night and day, the period of the single and most intelligent revolution; the month, complete when the Moon has been round her orbit and caught up the Sun again; the year, complete when the Sun has been round his orbit. (*Timaeus* 39b–c, my italics)

The demiurge has a created the sun at least in part to help creatures like ourselves to discern the motions and periods of the planets. Observing the planets is of particular importance to human beings since it is in this way that we become more rational, calmer, and better people (*Timaeus* 44b, 47b–c). It seems then that the sun fulfills its function when we fulfill our purpose. Nonetheless, this falls short of cosmic anthropocentrism. First, while the sun clearly accommodates man's interests, this is after all only one feature of the cosmos; there are many others, for example, the spherical shape of the cosmos, that are not explained with reference to the good of man. That the demiurge takes a special interest in man is partly due to the fact that man has a unique ability to *acquire* or *lose* virtue. The other animals descend from men who have lost their virtue by failing to observe the planets in the proper way. Timaeus's reference to "the appropriate living creatures" is sufficiently vague to anticipate the soul's presence in other animals. But while the significance of the sun in this way connects with man's special role in the whole animal creation, this is still only a part of the creation. Second, there is no reason to think that the purpose of the sun is exhausted by helping man (or possibly other animals) do astronomy. The notion of being a clear measure is important in its own right by providing a unit of time for the motions of the other planets, and thereby increasing the likeness of the creation to its immortal model (37d–e). Plato's cosmic teleology in other words shows a concern for man that falls short of (c), cosmic anthropocentrism.

1.8. Plato's Legacy to Aristotle

Plato's teleology is sometimes compared negatively with Aristotle's natural teleology. One may gain the impression that Plato's cosmology is a rather unfortunate first stab at teleology through a too-literal application of the craft model, whereas Aristotle rightly saw its shortcomings, as an analogy of limited usefulness.[40] I think this impression is mistaken. Aristotle himself relies heavily on the craft analogy when he argues for natural teleology. In *Physics* Book II, his argument repeatedly takes the following form: craft displays feature F, craft is like nature, therefore nature has F, with the second premise presented as obvious to the reader. A possible explanation for the assumption of this premise is that Aristotle takes it that Plato has already shown the amenability of nature to craft explanation and thereby to a form of teleological explanation.[41] Aristotle's job in *Physics* II is to highlight those features of craft that display teleological explanation, as Aristotle understands this. Put differently, Aristotle is concerned not so much with showing that nature is like craft in displaying end-directedness but in showing how. This is why in the context of *Physics* II he only has to bring out a certain teleological feature of craft to demonstrate that nature displays end-directedness in this way. These are the features that in his view are basic to craft explanation qua teleological explanation

---

40 See, e.g., J. Cooper, "Aristotle on Natural Teleology," in *Language and Logos*, ed. M. Schofield and M. Nussbaum (Cambridge: Cambridge University Press), 187–188.
41 I argue for this interpretation in T. K. Johansen, "The Origins of Teleology," in *The Cambridge Companion to Ancient Greek and Roman Science*, ed. L. Taub (Cambridge: Cambridge University Press, forthcoming).

and so are features which will carry over to his own natural teleology. Saying this is of course compatible with there being other features which are specific to craft production, and different from natural causation, prominently the role of thinking (*dianoia*), as we saw earlier, and the externality of the craftsman to the product. For the same reason, in the expression "natural teleology" we should not see a rejection of Plato's basic notion of teleology, but rather a qualification of it through the addition of "natural." There is a general shared conception of teleology which applies to both craft and nature, as well as specific differences. Rather than seeing Aristotle's argument for natural teleology as a rejection of Plato's, we may see it as relying on and refining it.

This is not to say that the specific differences are not worth attending to. Let me in closing take just one. The difference that in craft the cause is external to the product, in nature internal, is revealing of a difference between how Plato and Aristotle view the natural world. For Aristotle the natural world has enough stability and integrity to sustain eternal forms as internal, or perhaps better, the natural world because it contains eternal forms has a high degree of stability and integrity. The motto "Man generates man"[42] reflects Aristotle's belief that the natural world is always (at least at the heights of the *scala naturae* occupied by human beings) sufficiently structured to ensure the perpetuation of the same eternal forms. Plato's starting point in the *Timaeus*, in contrast, is a world that is inherently unstable and chaotic and which only acquires a degree of stability by an external agent likening it to the formal paradigm. The world requires an external intervention (and possibly, according to at least one interpretation, continued external support) to sustain stable structures. The craft model, taken *au pied de lettre*, is therefore metaphysically appropriate for Plato in a way it could not be for Aristotle.

---

42 Aristotle, *Physics* II.2 194b14.

CHAPTER TWO

Teleology in Aristotle

Mariska Leunissen

2.1. ARISTOTLE ON THE BEAUTY AND GOODNESS OF NATURE

In the first book of the *Parts of Animals*—which offers a methodological introduction to the study of animals—Aristotle offers an elaborate exhortation to the study of sublunary nature.[1] For even though

---

1 "Since we have completed stating the way things appear to us about those [divine] things, it remains to speak about animal nature, omitting nothing in our power, whether of lesser or greater esteem.
   For even in the study of the ones [i.e., animals] disagreeable to perception, the nature that crafted (*hē dēmiourgēsasa phusis*) them likewise provides extraordinary pleasures to those who are able to know their causes and are by nature philosophers. Surely it would be unreasonable and absurd for us to enjoy studying their representations—on the grounds that we are at the same time studying the art that made them, such as painting or sculpture—while not prizing even more the study of things constituted by nature, at least when we can observe their causes.
   For this reason, we should not childishly be disgusted at examination of the less valuable animals. For in all natural things there is something wonderful (*ti thaumaston*). Just as Heraclitus

---

Mariska Leunissen, *Teleology in Aristotle* In: *Teleology*. Edited by: Jeffrey K. McDonough, Oxford University Press (2020). © Oxford University Press.
DOI: 10.1093/oso/9780190845711.003.0003

the heavenly bodies are the most divine and the most honorable, and even though knowledge about the heavenly realm yields the greatest pleasure,[2] thereby making cosmology one of the most respectable studies, Aristotle argues that the study of animals living in the sublunary world in fact takes the prize in terms of the expanse and thoroughness of our understanding, and that their study too offers extraordinary pleasure and wonder. The heart of this exhortation, however, is formed by Aristotle's appeal to natural teleology: it would be absurd, he claims, for us to enjoy the beauty of human depictions of animals and praise the art that went into their production if we did not also at the same time and even more praise the art and goodness that went into nature's production of those animals themselves. And, as the true philosopher will recognize, the sublunary realm is *full* of goodness and natural teleology: "that for the sake of which" pervades the natural world, thereby making it a worthy and wonderful domain for study.

As the analogy with representations of animals produced by human crafts makes clear, for Aristotle, animals—just like other natural things and the processes that bring them into being—are the result of a kind of craftsmanship and goodness that is *in their case* internal to and inherent in their own natures, that is, intrinsic in the goal-directed actions of their own internal, natural "principles of motion and rest." Natural teleology for Aristotle thus means that everything that exists or comes to be "by nature" comes to be or changes, unless prevented, for the sake of an end (*telos*) or function (*ergon*) that constitutes that

---

is said to have spoken to those strangers who wished to meet him, but who stopped as they were approaching when they saw him warming himself by the oven—he bade them to enter without fear, "for there are gods here too"—in the same way should one approach the investigation about each of the animals without disgust, since in all of them there is something natural and good (*kalou*). For what is not by chance but rather for the sake of something is in fact present most of all in the works of nature" (*Parts of Animals* I.5, 645a4–25). Aristotle's works are referred to by title and standard Bekker page numbers. They can be found in Aristotle's *Opera Omnia*, in *Thesaurus Lingua Graecae Canon of Greek Authors and Works*, 3rd ed., ed. Luci Berkowitz and Karl A. Squitier (Oxford: Oxford University Press, 1990). All translations in this chapter are my own.

2 *Parts of Animals* I.5, 644b22–645a4.

thing's final cause, and it has the capacities, structure, and parts that it does for the sake of that final cause.

For Aristotle, the beauty, functionality, and goodness of the sublunary natural world is as manifest as the beauty and orderliness of the heavenly realm, and these awe-inspiring features of the universe can *only* be explained by reference to teleology,[3] and specifically, in the sublunary realm, they can only be explained as the products of the "crafting" actions of goal-directed natures.

2.2. Aristotle's Conception of "Crafting Natures" and Immanent, Natural Teleology

As in the earlier exhortation, when speaking about the natural generation of animals, Aristotle often personifies the internal natural principles that produce them as "craftsmen" that act for the sake of something while following a certain *logos* or "guideline" for building. These "crafting natures"—also referred to as "formal natures" by Aristotle, and which incorporate the efficient, final, and formal causes of animals and which are to be identified with their soul[4]—are *not* to be mistaken for some kind of overarching Father Nature who providentially and

---

[3] In fact, Aristotle repeatedly offers the a fortiori argument that if one agrees that animals and plants neither come to be nor exist by spontaneity but for the sake of something, then the claim that spontaneity is the cause of the heavens—which is most divine and exhibits the greatest order—must be absurd, and that one has to conclude based on this that final causality pertains to the heavenly realm as well. See *Physics* II.4, 196a24–b5; *Physics* II.6, 198a1–13; and especially *Parts of Animals* I.1, 641b10–23: "In addition, natural science can pertain to nothing abstract, because nature makes everything for the sake of something. For it seems, just as in artifacts art is present, so too in things themselves there is some other principle and such cause, which like the hot and the cold we have from the universe. This is why it is more likely that the heavens have been brought into being by such a cause—if it has come to be—and is due to such a cause, than that the mortal animals have been. Certainly the ordered and definite are far more apparent in the heavens than around us, while the fluctuating and random are more apparent in the mortal sphere. Yet some people say that each of the animals is and comes to be by nature, while the heavens, in which there is not the slightest appearance of chance and disorder, were constituted in that way by chance and the spontaneous."

[4] See especially *Parts of Animals* I.1, 641a23–28; *De Anima* II.1, 412a19–21; and *Generation of Animals* IV.4, 770b17. On formal natures, see also James G. Lennox, *Aristotle's Philosophy of Biology: Studies in the Origins of Life Science* (Cambridge: Cambridge University Press, 2001),

out of his own goodness created everything for the sake of something, forcing recalcitrant matter to take on the best and most functional shapes possible.

In fact, Aristotle rejects the external, divine, and providential model of teleology as presented, for instance, in Plato's *Timaeus*. According to "the likely account" provided in this Platonic treatise, the goodness and functionality of the world and its natural components are due to the goal-directed actions of an intelligent and divine craftsman—the "demiurge"—who organized and created everything in the best and most beautiful way possible, while imitating the perfect and eternal models constituted by the Platonic Forms. On this account, the world exists and is the best it can possibly be because it is the creation of one intelligent and good God who did his very best in creating it.[5]

For Aristotle, by contrast, the teleology of nature resides *in* the individual natural beings themselves: the crafting natures are *immanent in* the individual animals they produce and maintain, and their operating power is not one of intentionality or deliberation, but rather one of a complex and dynamic "realization of pre-existing potentials for form."[6] That is, at the physiological level, when we translate Aristotle's talk of crafting natures or of natures acting or doing something for the sake of something into the processes that he thinks actually take place, physically speaking, natural teleology involves the realization of preexisting, internal potentials for form, as specified by the definition of the substantial being of the animal, and through stages shaped by what he calls "conditional necessity." In other words, the form of each animal

---

182–194. These "formal natures" are to be contrasted with animals' "material nature"—that is, their elemental constitution and the kinds of food they process.

5 On teleology in the *Timaeus*, see the chapter by Johansen in this volume. On the contrast between Plato's and Aristotle's conception of teleology, see Lennox, *Aristotle's Philosophy of Biology*, 182–204.

6 See Allan Gotthelf, "Aristotle's Conception of Final Causality," *Review of Metaphysics* 30 (1976–77): 226–254 and Mariska Leunissen and Allan Gotthelf, "What's Teleology Got to Do with It? A Reinterpretation of Aristotle's *Generation of Animals* V," *Phronesis* 55, no. 4 (2010): 342 for suggestions on how to cash out Aristotle's use of craft-language with respect to the goal-directed actions of nature in nonintentional, physiological terms.

specifies the functional features that need to be realized (e.g., the substantial being of birds defines these animals as flyers), and given that the animal has to realize its form, it has to have such and such parts (e.g., wings are required for flying) and such and such differentiations of parts (e.g., broad versus narrow wings), made of such and such constitutive materials, put in such and such a structure or configuration. Aristotle explains this conditional type of necessity that acts in the service of natural teleology as follows (*Parts of Animals* I.1, 642a7–12):

> For we say nourishment is something necessary according to neither of those two modes of necessity, but because it is not possible to be without it. And this is as in the conditional type (*ex hypotheseōs*). For just as—since the axe must split—it is a necessity that it be hard, and if hard, then made of bronze or iron, so too since the body is an instrument (for each of the parts is for the sake of something, and likewise also the whole), it is therefore a necessity that it be of such a character and constituted from such things, if that is to be.[7]

On this account, the fully realized form (e.g., the mature, fully developed bird with wings that allow it to fly in the way that is required for its particular way of life) constitutes the individual final cause of the process, while the good of the whole emerges from individual natures doing what is best for them. The supreme divine being of Aristotle's metaphysical system, namely the "Unmoved Mover," who is the ultimate final cause of all natural motion in the world,[8] exhibits no concerns for the world—which is eternal and uncreated—and has as its only activity the thinking of its own thoughts.

---

[7] See also *Physics* II.9, 200a10–15; *Parts of Animals* I.1, 640a33–35; *Parts of Animals* I.1, 642a7–12; *Parts of Animals* IV.10, 689a20–21; and *Generation of Animals* V.1, 778b15–19.

[8] According to Aristotle, the whole universe is teleologically organized toward this one perfect being that everything else desires to emulate: see *Metaphysics* XII.10, 1075a11–25; cf. *On the Heavens* II.12, 292b20–25.

In addition, and importantly, on this account, generation should be understood as being for the sake of being, and not the other way around, as some of Aristotle's predecessors thought (at least according to Aristotle). Empedocles, for instance, got this priority relation wrong, and is criticized by Aristotle for explaining the "being" of animals in terms of what happened to happen to them during generation (*Parts of Animals* I.1, 640a17–26):

> For generation is for the sake of being, but being is not for the sake of generation. This is why Empedocles did not speak well when he said that many things belong to animals because they turned out that way during generation—for example, that the backbone is such because it happened to get broken when it was being twisted; he failed to see, first, that the seed previously constituted must already possess this sort of potentiality, and, next, that the producer was prior not only in definition but also in time; for it is a human being who generates a human being, such that it is because the one *is* such, that the other's coming to be happens in that way.[9]

Aristotle's reference here is to Empedocles's model of zoogony that occurs under the influence of Love. According to this, first, the coincidental interactions among the four Empedoclean elements water, air, fire, and earth produce animal tissues such as blood, flesh, and bone. Next, similar coincidental interactions between these tissues produce separate animal parts, such as foreheads and arms, but also backbones constituted from several previously disjointed bones stacked together in a random way. Once Love's influence is strong enough, these parts will randomly stick together, thereby forming all kinds of animals, including hybrids. For Empedocles, the resulting animal species and their bodily features are thus the way they are because of what happened to

---

9 Cf. *Generation of Animals* II.1, 735a3–4.

them during the process of generation, which itself is entirely governed by what Aristotle calls material necessity (i.e., materials acting in accordance with their own material natures, such as water necessarily freezing when the temperature drops below zero) and chance. And while Aristotle does not deny the causal influence of material necessity and chance on the generation of animals (more on that in section 2.3), what Empedocles gets crucially wrong according to Aristotle is that one cannot explain the regular occurrence of good outcomes of natural processes (such as "humans giving birth to humans") by appealing to such causes alone, as simply being the coincidental outcomes of spontaneous combinations of material elements.

As Aristotle explains here, the core of his theory of teleology in natural generation is the fact that whatever organism comes to be already possesses its corresponding form in potentiality (where the process of generation is for the sake of realizing that form or the being of that animal), and that it receives that potentiality for form from something that already possesses that form in actuality. The process of natural generation involves the eternal replication of form (I will return to this in section 2.4), and this can only be explained through the assumption of nature—always or for the most part—operating as an internal efficient cause that acts for the sake of realizing those forms.

2.3. Aristotle's Defense of Natural Teleology

Aristotle argues for nature as an internal efficient cause being "among the causes that are for the sake of something" (*Physics* II.8, 198b10–12)—that is, for nature acting goal-directedly in natural productions—most explicitly in the following passage:

> There is a difficulty: what prevents nature not to act for the sake of something or because it is better, but in the way Zeus rains, not in order to make the crops grow, but of necessity (for it is necessary that that which has gone up cools down, and what cools down

becomes water and falls down: when this has happened, it turns out that crops grow), and in the same way also that if someone's crops are ruined on the threshing floor, it does not rain for the sake of this, in order that they be spoiled, but that it happened to come about. So what prevents also parts in nature from being this way, for example, that teeth shoot up of necessity, the ones in the front sharp, with a fitness for tearing, the molars broad and useful for grinding down food—not because they came to be for the sake of this, but because they turned out that way. And similarly about the other parts, in as many as "that for the sake of something" seems to be present. Wherever then all [the parts] turned out in a way they would also [have done] if they had come to be for the sake of something, those survived, having been organized in a fitting way by spontaneity. As many as did not [turn out] in such a way perished and continue to perish, as Empedocles says about the man-faced ox progeny. This then is the argument about which one might be puzzled, and there may be others just like it. (*Physics* II.8, 198b16–34)

In this so-called "rainfall passage,"[10] Aristotle raises a puzzle concerning the causal relation between natural processes and the goodness or badness of their outcomes, put in the mouth of a hypothetical materialist predecessor. That is, Aristotle's imaginary materialist objector conceptualizes the relationship between natural processes—such as the growth of crops, the coming to be of teeth in a way that is fitting for their function, or even the coming to be of complete, functional living beings—and their outcomes—such as their goodness or fittingness or functionality as an *accidental* one: natural things come to be due to

---

10 On this famous passage, see especially Lindsay Judson, "Aristotelian Teleology," *Oxford Studies in Ancient Philosophy* 29 (2005): 341–366; Diana Quarantotto, *Causa finale, sostanza, essenza in Aristotele: Saggio sulla struttura dei processi teleologici naturali e sulla funzione dei telos* (Naples: Bibliopolis, 2005); Margaret Scharle, "Elemental Teleology in Aristotle's *Physics* II.8," *Oxford Studies in Ancient Philosophy* 34 (2008): 147–183; and David Sedley, "Is Aristotle's Teleology Anthropocentric?," *Phronesis* 36 (1991): 179–197.

material necessity and by chance they have outcomes that happen to be "good" (or "bad"). Aristotle, however, thinks that it is impossible that the outcomes of natural processes mentioned by the materialist are due to chance:

> It is impossible that things are that way. For those things, and all things that are by nature, come to be that way either always or for the most part, and none of them belongs to things that are due to luck or spontaneity. For it does not seem to be due to luck or spontaneity that it rains often in wintertime, but [it does] when [it rains] during the dog days. Nor do heatwaves [seem that way] during the dog days, but [they do] when they occur in winter. If, then, it seems that [these things] are either by accident or for the sake of something, [and] if it is not possible that these things are by accident or by spontaneity, they are for the sake of something. But *that* such things are by nature, even the people who make this argument would claim this. There is thus that for the sake of something among the things that come to be and are by nature. (*Physics* II.8, 198b34–199a8)

For Aristotle, if natural processes produce certain outcomes either always or for the most part, that excludes the possibility of their being due to chance: instead, they must be for the sake of something.[11] The issue is not that material necessity cannot be responsible for the coming to be of regular or good outcomes. For instance, Aristotle too believes that the evaporation cycle that produces rain is a regular, materially necessary process,[12] and that the materials from which teeth are formed come to be of material necessity:

---

11 That is, of course, based on Aristotle's *own* definition of chance, which he provides in *Physics* II.4–6.
12 See *On Generation and Corruption* II.11, 338a14–b19; *Posterior Analytics* II.12, 96a2–7; and *Metaphysics* VI.2, 1026b27–35.

> We must say what the character of the necessary nature is, and how nature according to the account *has made use* of things present of necessity for the sake of something. ... For the residual surplus of this sort of [earthen] body, being present in the larger of the animals, is *used* by nature *for* protection and advantage, and [the surplus, which] flows of necessity to the upper region, in some animals it *distributes* to *teeth* and tusks, in others to horns. (*Parts of Animals* III.2, 663b22–35)[13]

Rather, the issue for Aristotle is that the regular *presence* of good outcomes requires the regular activity or intervention of goal-directed efficient causes. The rainfall passage illustrates exactly this: in the case of rain and crops, it is the intervention of humans—in particular of farmers who possess the art of agriculture and who play the role of goal-directed agents in agricultural processes such as these—that ensures that the regular occurrence of winter rain that happens of material necessity results in the good outcome that is the growth of crops.[14] For Aristotle, art is ontologically secondary to nature: it imitates or completes natural goals, which it achieves through means congenial to nature, and given that artistic processes are (visibly and ostensibly) for the sake of something, based on nature's ontological priority to art, so too Aristotle argues must natural processes.[15]

The natural case is more complicated, but essentially similar: the regular presence of good and functional features in nature is the result

---

[13] Cf. *Generation of Animals* II.6, 745a18–745b9 and *Generation of Animals* V.8; on the role of teleology and material necessity in the generation of teeth, see Leunissen and Gotthelf, "What's Teleology Got to Do with It?"

[14] Aristotle's claim that winter rain is for the sake of growing crops is thus an illustration of artificial teleology (the goals of which are necessarily human-centered), and not of a natural teleology that is allegedly anthropocentric; for this latter view, see Sedley, "Is Aristotle's Teleology Anthropocentric?"

[15] This is Aristotle's second argument in defense of natural teleology: on this, see *Physics* II.8, 199a8–20 and Sarah Broadie, "Nature and Craft in Aristotelian Teleology," in *Biologie, logique et métaphysique chez Aristote*, ed. Daniel Devereux and Pierre Pellegrin (Paris: Editions du Centre National de la Recherche Scientifique, 1990), 389–403.

of formal natures producing materials, through conditional necessity, and organizing them for the sake of realizing preexisting potentials for form, *or* the result of formal natures (actively) adapting or (passively) co-opting features that come to be of material necessity for the sake of promoting the well-being and overall functionality of living beings.

These are both cases of natural teleology (both are natural processes "governed" by the goal-directed actions of immanent natures), but the first is a case of "standard" or of what I call "primary" teleology, while the second is a case of what I call "secondary" teleology.[16] The primary type of teleology involves the realization of preexisting, internal potentials for form through stages shaped by conditional necessity. This type of teleology is responsible for the coming to be and presence of parts and features that are necessary for the performance of the vital and essential functions of each living being, as specified by the definition of its substantial being. The secondary type of teleology involves formal natures *using* materials that happen to be available (usually residues that have come to be of material necessity and that are not conditionally necessitated) for the production of parts that serve the animal's well-being. The presence of these parts is not a necessary prerequisite for the realization of the animal's form; instead, their presence is said to be "for the better." For instance, as in the passage from the *Parts of Animals* quoted earlier, Aristotle believes that large land animals often have a surplus of earthen material, which, because of its hard potential, nature then uses for the production of teeth and tusks in some males, and horns in other males, which all serve the (nonnecessary though useful) function of defense. In these cases, functional features emerge as it were from the potentials of the materials that happen to

---

16 See Mariska Leunissen, *Explanation and Teleology in Aristotle's Science of Nature* (Cambridge: Cambridge University Press, 2010). On alternative distinctions between Aristotle's conception of teleology, see Thomas K. Johansen, "The Two Kinds of End in Aristotle: The View from the *De Anima*," in *Theory and Practice in Aristotle's Natural Science*, ed. David Ebrey (Cambridge: Cambridge University Press, 2015), 119–136, and Monte R. Johnson, *Aristotle on Teleology* (Oxford: Oxford University Press, 2005).

be available, and the operation of the formal nature is secondary to the operation of material necessity that produced the materials.

In sum, what Aristotle does, then, in his defense of natural teleology through the rainfall passage, is to have his materialist opponent come up with cases that in Aristotle's own view represent increasingly stronger cases of teleology: moving from artificial teleology in which human artists are the external goal-directed agents, to secondary, natural teleology, in which natures are the internal, immanent goal-directed "agents" that are responsible for using materials that come to be of material necessity for something good, to primary natural teleology, in which the goal-directed actions of the internal natures are responsible for the coming to be and presence of complete functional living beings.

2.4. Teleology in Aristotle's Account of Animal Generation

Animal generation, according to Aristotle, is a natural teleological process that involves the transmission of the species-form from parent to offspring and that has as its end the (eternal) replication of the species, and thereby, ultimately, the participation in the eternal and the divine in the only way possible for mortal beings:[17]

> For the most natural among the functions for living beings—for as many as are perfect and not deformed or whose generation is spontaneous—is to produce another one like oneself, an animal [producing] an animal, a plant a plant, such that they can participate in the eternal and the divine to the extent that is possible. For

---

[17] On the role of teleology in Aristotle's account of reproduction, see especially Devin Henry, "How Sexist Is Aristotle's Developmental Biology?," *Phronesis* 52 (2007): 251–269; Devin Henry, "The Cosmological Significance of Animal Generation," in Ebrey, *Theory and Practice*, 100–118; and also Karen Nielsen, "The Private Parts of Animals: Aristotle on the Teleology of Sexual Difference," *Phronesis* 53 (2008): 373–405.

everything desires this and does whatever it does in accordance with nature for the sake of this.... Since then it cannot take part in the eternal and the divine with an uninterrupted continuation, for the reason that nothing among the perishables can remain the same and one in number, each—to the extent that it can take part in it—participates in it, some more and some less, and it remains not as oneself but as something like oneself, and as not one in number, but as one in form. (*De Anima* II.4, 415a27–b7)

In other words, the process of generation consists in the production of another one like oneself by living beings who are biologically speaking only capable of participating in the divine through this process of "eternal replication of form" and not through living for eternity themselves as individuals.

Physiologically speaking, Aristotle often speaks of embryogenesis as a form of matter being concocted and thereby being "refined" and "informed"—and thereby perfected—to an appropriate degree. In most animals, this process of "concoction" takes place through sexually differentiated parents, where each parent supplies its own principle(s) of reproduction: the male supplies the form and the source of movement, usually via his semen, while the female supplies the matter in the form of her menses, which already possess the species-form in potentiality. Now, even though in sexually differentiated animals the end of reproduction similarly lies in the production of viable offspring of the same species (or, more specifically, in the replication of their form in another living being that also has the capacity to successfully engage in reproduction and subsequently replicate its form), and hence not in the production of *male* offspring per se (forms are not sexually differentiated), Aristotle holds that reproduction is "most natural" when the motions of the father and male go together and those of the female and mother go together,[18] and is best when the male principle is able to "dominate"

---

18 *Generation of Animals* IV.3, 768a21–25.

and is able to transmit the species-form into the matter *in exactly the same way* as it is realized in him.[19]

As a consequence of this, reproduction in sexually differentiated animals is deemed to be the least disturbed and the least departed from the form when reproduction results in *male* offspring resembling its father in all of his formal aspects, because in that case only the male principle will have succeeded in transmitting its own particular and distinctive form.[20] The offspring that results when the process remains undisturbed is thus a perfect formal replica of that which already has that very same form in actuality and which "happens to be" the father—i.e., a *male* individual of the same species. In this way, Aristotle characterizes the birth of a male offspring that is identical to its male parent as a kind of success—i.e., as a natural teleological process running its course. In contrast, Aristotle characterizes the birth and existence of female offspring (or even of male offspring resembling its female parent) as forms of imperfections, as deviations or departures from the replication of form, and as resulting in deficiencies. Aristotle believes that with regard to whatever extent the male principle does not succeed in leading the female menses to its own proper form (that is, to the species-form *in the way that it is realized in him*), the developing embryo ends up with a deficiency, the most important of which is the incapacity to concoct seed. It is as a result of this latter incapacity that the embryo

---

19 See especially *Generation of Animals* IV.3, 767b5–23: "For even the one who does not resemble his parents is already in a way a monster: for in those cases nature has in a way departed from the form [that is being replicated]. The first [departure] is that a female is born and not a male—but this is necessary in accordance with nature: for the kind that has been separated into female and male needs to be preserved.... And when the spermatic residue in the menses has been properly concocted, the motion of the male produces a form in his own likeness.... Therefore when it [i.e., the motion of the male] dominates, it will produce a male and not a female, and it will resemble its father but not its mother; and when it is dominated, with regard to whichever capacity it does not dominate, it produces the corresponding deficiency."

20 For Aristotle, the causal factors involved in sexual differentiation are the same as the ones involved in familial resemblances.

develops female reproductive organs and hence becomes anatomically speaking female.[21]

For Aristotle, the existence of the female is conditionally necessary for the preservation of the species,[22] and he certainly thinks that females are functional, capable beings. However, he also believes that their coming to be and existence is a product of the nonstandard, secondary type of teleology sketched earlier:[23]

> That the male and female are principles of generation has been said earlier, and also what their capacity is and the definition of their substantial being.
>
> The cause on account of which there come to be and exist the female and the male, that it is, on the one hand, *of necessity* and *because of the first mover and the quality of the matter*, is necessary to try to show in the following account, but, that it is, on the other hand, *on account of the better* and *because of the for the sake of something*, takes its principle from further away. . . .
>
> Now it is impossible for the animal to be eternal as an individual—for the substantial being of the things that are is in the particular; and if it were such it would be eternal—but it is possible for it [to be eternal] as a species. That is why there is always a continuous

---

21 *Generation of Animals* IV.1, 766a22–28; *Generation of Animals* IV.3, 767b22–23 and 768a2–11. It is also in these contexts that Aristotle infamously characterizes female offspring as being somehow "like a disabled male" (*Generation of Animals* II.3, 737a27–28) or "like a natural deformation" (*Generation of Animals* IV.6, 775a15–16).

22 See *Generation of Animals* IV.3, 767b8–10 and *Politics* I.2, 1252a26–28.

23 Similarly, Aristotle believes that female menses come to be "of necessity" and are then used by nature "for the better" and are thus a product of secondary teleology (*Generation of Animals* II.4, 738a33–b5): "Thus the coming to be of this residue [i.e., the menses] among females is the result of necessity, because of the causes mentioned. Because her nature is not capable of concoction, it is necessary that residue must come to be, not only from the useless nourishment, but also in the blood vessels, and that they must overflow, when there is a full complement of it in those very fine blood vessels. And nature uses it for the sake of the better and the end for this place, for generation, in order that it may become another creature of the same kind as it would have become. For, even as it is, it is in potentiality the same in character as the body of which it is the secretion. In all females, then, residue necessarily comes to be."

generation of humans, animals, and plants. And since the principles of these are male and female, male and female will be present for the sake of generation in each of the things that possess them. But the primary moving cause is better and more divine in its nature than the matter, insofar as the definition and the form belong to it, *and it is better that the superior cause be kept separate from the inferior one. It is on account of this that (in those species where this is possible) the male is separated from the female.* ... However, the male comes together and combines with the female in order to perform the function of reproduction, for this is something common to both. (*Generation of Animals* II.1, 731b18–732a11)

In specifying the final cause of the coming to be and existence of the male and the female, Aristotle takes for granted as facts that sublunary beings are mortal and can only participate in the divine by engaging in a continuous cycle of reproduction and that the principles of reproduction are two—one formal-efficient principle called male, one material called female. The reason why these two principles are separated, when this is possible, is because it is a general teleological principle of nature that it is better to keep the superior separated from the inferior.[24] Sexually differentiated species thus exist for the better: for it is better, *when possible*, for nature to separate the superior cause of reproduction from its inferior one and put them in separate beings. One part of the explanation Aristotle provides for sexual differentiation is thus explicitly teleological.

However, this separation is in fact possible because the process of reproduction is complex, and achieving the "perfect concoction," so to speak, of the female menses by the male principle is difficult.[25] So this is where the "of necessity" and "the first mover and the quality of the matter" figure into the explanation: for when the female menses

---

[24] Cf. *On the Heavens* II.8, 290a29–b11.
[25] *Generation of Animals* II.6, 743a26–32.

are too copious or too cold (that is, when the quality of the matter is suboptimal), or when the male principle is not hot enough or too hot (that is, when the first mover is not strong enough or produces "excessive concoction"), the male principle will fail to dominate the female menses and will produce "defects" in the offspring.[26] And the same problems can occur due to any kind of material-efficient disturbance that happens, of material necessity, during the process of embryogenesis, such as due to changes in climate or due to the particulars of the mother's diet. Due to these possible influences of material necessity on the process of reproduction, the process of concoction—and hence the offspring—achieves varying degrees of perfection. Some offspring are mostly perfect, possess the relevant species-form, and are capable of concocting blood into semen; some offspring are less perfect, and while they possess the relevant species-form, they are incapable of concocting blood into semen due to a lack of heat; and, finally, some offspring constitute monstrosities that lack the relevant species-form and the ability to reproduce (and they are therefore "not usable by nature" as a container for a principle of reproduction). However, given the availability of two usable types of "vehicles for reproduction" and the fact that in animals who possess both perception and the capacity for locomotion the two principles of reproduction *can* be separated without there being any practical problems for them to reunite, nature matches, as it were, the superior principle with the superior body (males carry the male principle) and the inferior principle with the inferior body (females carry the female principle).

In sum, since perfect concoction is difficult and since therefore, of material necessity, materially less perfect beings will come to be with some regularity, nature, as a good craftsman, uses these beings for something good, namely for the containment of the inferior principle

---

[26] Cf. Aristotle's explanation of the dysfunctional eyes of moles in terms of a deformity that happens during generation in *History of Animals* I.9, 491b27–34 and IV.8, 533a11–12 and their characterization as "imperfect" in *History of Animals* I.9, 491b27 and *De Anima* III.1, 425a9–11.

of reproduction. In this way, nature achieves a general teleological good, for in these beings the superior and inferior principles of reproduction are separated.

2.5. Teleology in Aristotle's Explanation of the Parts and Features of Animals

The process of embryogenesis and the coming to be of the parts and features of animals is thoroughly teleological, and Aristotle likes to conceptualize it as involving the goal-directed actions of crafting natures who use the hot and the cold as the tools of their craft.[27] For instance, Aristotle describes the actions of nature in producing the body of the developing embryo as being analogous to those of painters:

> The upper half of the body, then, is first marked out in the order of development; as time goes on the lower also reaches its full size in the blooded animals. All the parts are first marked out in their outlines and acquire later on their color and softness or hardness, exactly as if nature were a painter producing a work of art, for painters, too, first sketch in the animal with lines and only after that put in the colors. (*Generation of Animals* II.6, 743b18–25)[28]

Later on in the same chapter, Aristotle sketches a hierarchy of parts in which he links the ontological status of a part (i.e., whether it is necessary for the sake of vital or essential functions or whether it is "merely" instrumentally necessary for other parts) to the quality of its constitutive material and its place in the sequence of coming into being. He

---

[27] See, e.g., *Generation of Animals* II.6, 743a36–b1.
[28] Cf. *Generation of Animals* II.4, 740a28–9; *Parts of Animals* II.8, 654a24–6; *Parts of Animals* II.14, 658a21–3; *Parts of Animals* II.14, 658a31–5. For the male principle or the animal's soul being depicted as a craftsman, see, e.g., *Generation of Animals* I.22, 730a32–b32, *Generation of Animals* II.1, 734b20–735a29; *Generation of Animals* II.4, 740b25–741a4; and *Generation of Animals* II.6, 743a36–b5.

then fleshes out this picture by comparing nature to a good housekeeper: according to the image drawn, nature uses the best materials to make the most important parts of the body, and makes those first, just as in a household, the housekeeper gives the best food to the most important members of the household, who are fed first. The other parts, namely those that are subsidiary to the first category of parts, are made out of inferior nutriments, and only come to be if and when nature has enough left over to spare.[29]

Aristotle provides similar descriptive comments about the teleological actions of natures involved in the production of parts in his *Parts of Animals*, which provides an impressive collection of mostly teleological explanations for why animals have (or lack) the parts and features they have. In many cases, especially when explaining the presence of parts that are necessary for one of the vital or essential functions a given animal has, Aristotle simply identifies that function. The larynx, for instance "is naturally present for the sake of breath; for through this part animals draw in and expel breath when they inhale and exhale."[30] In other cases, Aristotle points out how a part is necessary given the need for the performance of a certain function that is specified in the definition of the substantial being of that animal. For instance, "it is on account of being swimmers" that fish "have fins": "being swimmers" technically constitutes the formal cause of the presence of fins, but it includes the specification of its final cause, namely "swimming." Fish thus have fins for the sake of swimming.[31]

Most of these features are due to what I have called primary teleology, and there is no need for Aristotle to specify that in these cases nature acted for the sake of something or that the necessity involved in their production is conditional necessity rather than material: the fact

---

29 See *Generation of Animals* II.6, 744b11–27 and my discussion of this image in Leunissen, *Explanation and Teleology*.
30 *Parts of Animals* III.3, 664a17–20.
31 *Parts of Animals* IV.13, 695b17–26. Cf. *Parts of Animals* IV.8, 684a14–15; IV.9, 683b16–23; and IV.12, 694b10–12.

that a part is necessary for the sake of an essential or vital function is presumed to imply that its constitutive materials have been produced by conditional necessity and that nature produced and organized these parts in the way they are for the sake of realizing those essential or vital functions.

However, the situation is different and more complicated for parts and features that are due to secondary teleology: in those cases, Aristotle often identifies material necessity as the cause for the coming to be of the part and characterizes nature as having used that material for some function that makes the animal somehow better off. Take, for instance, Aristotle's explanation for why animals have an omentum:[32]

> The generation of this part [i.e., the omentum] occurs of necessity in the following way; when a mixture of dry and moist is heated, the surface always becomes skin-like and membranous, and this location is full of such nutrient.... The generation of the omentum, then, occurs according to this account, and nature makes use of it for a good concoction of the nutrient, in order that the animals may concoct their nutrient easier and faster; for what is hot is able to concoct, and what is fat is hot, and the omentum is fat. (*Parts of Animals* IV.3, 677b22–32)

There does not appear to be a function for the sake of which the omentum is conditionally necessary; rather, the presence of dry and moist materials that make up the stomach and intestines—combined with the presence of heat—results of material necessity in the solidification of the materials on the outside of the stomach, and nature then uses this fatty "sheet" or membrane to make the process of food concoction more efficient (for what is fat is hot, and what is hot aids in concoction).

---

[32] The omentum is an apron-like, membranous double layer of fatty tissue that hangs down from the stomach and that covers the intestines and organs in the lower abdominal area.

Sometimes Aristotle's descriptions of nature as using features for something good pick out even more subtle forms of teleology, as in the case of nature's *reusing* entire parts that are said to be already present for the sake of some necessary function. A nice example of such a reused part is the elephant's trunk.[33] In a long passage (*Parts of Animals* II.16, 658b32–659a36), Aristotle first explains why elephants have the specific nose they have. Elephants have *a* nose in virtue of being a breather of air (that is, noses are a necessary prerequisite for the performance of the necessary function of cooling, which happens according to Aristotle through the circulation of air), but they have the *specific, long* nose they have because they need an organ for breathing air while being in the water looking for nourishment: long noses function for elephants like snorkels do for human divers. However, in order for trunks to be so long, they have to be—of conditional necessity—soft and flexible, and Aristotle goes on to explain how nature makes use of these material potentials of the trunk in order to *make up* for the uselessness of their feet for grasping food:

> Since [the trunk] is such [i.e., soft and flexible], *nature, as it is used to, uses [parakatachrētai] the same parts for several things*, [here using] it in place of the use of front feet. For four-footed animals with many toes have front feet in place of hands, not merely for the sake of supporting their weight. And the elephants are members of this group; that is, they have feet that are neither cloven nor solid-hoofed. But since the size and weight of their body are great, their feet are only for the sake of support, and because of their slowness and their natural unsuitability for bending, they are useless for anything else.... And the use of its feet having been taken away, nature,

---

33 See Allan Gotthelf, "The Elephant's Nose: Further Reflections on the Axiomatic Structure of Biological Explanations in Aristotle," in *Aristotelische Biologie: Intentionen, Methoden, Ergebnisse*, ed. Wolfgang Kullmann and Sabine Föllinger (Stuttgart: Franz Steiner, 1997), 85–95.

as we said, also makes use of this part *for the service that would have been provided by the feet.* (*Parts of Animals* II.16, 659a20–36)

Typically, four-footed animals with many toes have feet that are capable of providing both support for their bodies and means to transport food to their mouths: the form "many-toed four-footer" is "normally" realized by giving these animals four supporting, but bendable, feet. However, in elephants, this use of feet is taken away, and so their natures have to assign a second function to the elephant's trunk, but without having to change any of its features. Although physically, the "design" of elephants thus does not undergo any changes, Aristotle claims that their nature had to move the function of grasping food—which was "supposed to be" performed by its feet—to the trunk.[34]

Even more complicated are cases where the functions for the sake of which a part (or its differentiation) is present is not immediately discernable, either because the operation of a part is hidden from view (dissection can be helpful, but does not offer observations of the part while active), or because multiple parts can be observed to be associated with a given function and it is unclear what role is played by the part in question, or because what is needed is an explanation not of why a part is present but instead of why a part that one could reasonably expect to be present in a given animal is in fact absent. In these cases, Aristotle often appeals to teleological principles such as "Nature does nothing in vain, but always, given the possibilities, does what is best for the substantial being of each kind of animal," or "Nature does everything either because it is necessary or because it is better," or "Nature always places the more valuable parts in the more valuable locations, where nothing greater prevents it." These principles are empirical hypotheses, belonging properly to the science of nature,[35] and

---

34 See also *Parts of Animals* II.16, 659a34–660a2; III.9, 671a35–b2; IV.10, 688a19–25; IV.10, 689a5–7; IV.10, 689b34–690a4; and *On Respiration* 7, 473a23–25.

35 See *Progression of Animals* 2, 704b12–705a2 and *Generation of Animals* V.8, 788b20–5.

they posit certain "rules of action" formal natures "always" or "never" follow when producing animals.[36] Aristotle uses them as heuristic devices:[37] by conceptualizing nature as an intelligent, creative designer, Aristotle is able to engage in a kind of thought experiment that reveals "for the sake of what" such an intelligent designer would have made that particular design choice and therefore made the animal the way it is. Take, for instance, Aristotle's appeal to a teleological principle in the following text:

> Now if nature does everything either because it is necessary, or because it is better, this part [i.e., testes], too, must be because of one or the other. That it is not necessary for generation is evident: for it would be present in all that generate, but as it is, neither the snake nor the fish has testes (for they have been seen coupling and with the channels full of semen). It remains then that they are for the better in some way.... Those who need to be more temperate have in the one case [of nutriment] intestines that are not straight, and in the other case [of sexual reproduction] their ducts twisted to prevent their desire being too violent and hasty. The testes are contrived for this; for they make the movement of the spermatic secretion steadier. (*Generation of Animals* I-4, 717a11–31)

In this passage, Aristotle seeks to explain why it is that some males who reproduce sexually possess ducts for semen, testes, and a penis, whereas others only possess ducts. All parts are associated with the function of reproduction, and observation does not straightforwardly reveal their specific functional differentiation. However, assuming that nature only produces parts if they are either necessary for the performance of a certain function or if they are for the better, one can derive from the

---

[36] On the scientific status and use of teleological principles, see Lennox, *Aristotle's Philosophy of Biology*, 182–194, and Leunissen, *Explanation and Teleology*.

[37] Aristotle discusses the importance of the heuristic use of teleology in *On Respiration* 3, 471b24–29.

fact that ducts are the only reproductive parts present in *all* sexually reproductive males that these must be necessary, while having testes and a penis must "merely" be for the better. And whatever their *specific subsidiary* function is, it must be related to the specific nature of the male animals in which these parts are found. As it turns out, these latter parts are present only in the most passionate and intemperate of males, and their function, then, must be to *slow down* reproduction in these animals.

Let me conclude with my favorite example:

> In snakes the cause of why they are footless is, both that nature does nothing in vain, but always from among the possibilities, [does] what is best for each thing, preserving the proper substantial being of each and its essence; and, in addition, that which we stated before, namely that no blooded animal can move itself at more than four points. For from these [two principles] it is evident that of the blooded animals whose length is out of proportion to the rest of the nature of their body, like snakes, none of them possibly can have limbs. For they cannot have more than four feet (since in that case they would be bloodless), and *if they had two feet or four they would be almost completely immobile*: so slow and useless would their movement necessarily be. (*Progression of Animals* 8, 708a9–20)

Observation shows that all blooded animals that live on land have four feet: they share to a certain extent the same form, and their design can therefore be expected to share certain coextensive features like the possession of a maximum of four feet. The snake, however, possesses all the typical properties that belong to blooded land-dwellers, except for feet. Aristotle explains this absence by pointing out that the presence of four feet in snakes *would have been* in vain, on account of the snake's disproportionate dimensions (and giving more than four feet is impossible, as this would violate the substantial being of blooded animals). A quick thought experiment reveals that no blooded animal whose length is out of proportion to the rest of their body would be able to move swiftly with either two or four feet, and in order to remedy that design problem, nature "decided" not to produce feet in such animals.[38]

What these examples show, then, is that for Aristotle, the theory of natural teleology is not an a priori assumption, but a scientific hypothesis that he uses to make as much sense of the natural world around him as he possibly can and thereby to locate the good and show that "there are gods here too."

---

[38] See also *Parts of Animals* II.13, 658a6–10; IV.11, 690b14–18; IV.12, 694a16–18; IV.13, 696a10–15; *Progression of Animals* 2, 704b12–18 and 4, 705b25–29; *On Respiration* 10, 476a11–15; and *Generation of Animals* V.1, 781b22–28.

Reflection I

TELEOLOGY AND FUNCTION IN GALENIC ANATOMY

Patricia Marechal

Galen of Pergamum (AD 130–210) was the most celebrated physician of antiquity, one of the founding fathers of experimental medicine, and a great anatomist. He is famous for his spectacular, and often public, animal dissections and vivisections—aside from many Barbary apes, he dissected a giraffe, a snake, an ostrich, a dolphin, and at least one, perhaps even two, elephants. He is remembered for systematizing the now defunct, but once popular, humoral theory, for his extensive use of "venesection," or bloodletting, and for advocating a combination of experience and reason in medical investigation.[1]

Perhaps less known is that Galen was also one of the great teleologists of antiquity. In the seventeen books of *De usu partium corporis humani*, Galen amassed a wealth of anatomical findings in support of the view that bodily parts are perfectly designed to perform activities that contribute to the organism as a whole:

---

[1] Arguing that the best doctor is also a philosopher, Galen championed the use of deductive proofs to establish empirical conclusions. See V. Nutton, "Logic, Learning, and Experimental Medicine," *Science* 295 (2002): 800–801, for a brief summary of Galen's use of logic in medical research.

All the parts of the body are in harmony with one another, that is, all cooperate in producing one function (*ergon*). The large parts, the main divisions of the whole animal, such as the hands, feet, eyes, and tongue, came to be for the sake of the activities of the animal as a whole, and all cooperate in performing these activities. But the smaller parts, which are the components of the parts I have mentioned, refer to the function of the entire organ. For example, the eye is the instrument of sight, composed of many parts, all of which cooperate for one function: vision.[2] (*UP* I.8, I 13.7–14 H = III 18.9–19 K)

Galen is not charting new terrain here. Plato's *Timaeus* and Aristotle's *De partibus animalium* argued that bodily parts can be properly understood in light of their ends. In Plato's "likely account" our bodies are living artifacts whose every part has been optimally designed by a divine craftsman, the *dēmiourgos*, in order to perform goal-directed activities that contribute to the beauty and harmony of the entire creation.[3] Aristotle, in turn, went so far as to declare the priority of explanations that appeal to ends over accounts that describe the organism's material composition and its efficient mechanism. On Aristotle's view, knowing what, say, an eye essentially *is* necessarily involves identifying what an eye is *for*. Only then will we be in a position to understand why an eye is the way it is, and why it works the way it does. A bodily part exists "for the sake of" the end or function (*ergon*)—i.e., the final cause—essential

---

[2] For *De usu partium corporis humani* (*UP*), I refer to the volume, page, and line of the Greek text of G. Helmreich (H), *Galeni De usu partium Libri XVII*, 2 vols. (Leipzig: Teubner, 1907–9), followed by the reference to volume and page in the edition of C. G. Kühn (K), *Claudii Galeni Opera Omnia*, 20 vols. in 22 (Leipzig: Knobloch, 1821–33; repr. Hildesheim, 1965). I consulted the translation by May: Galen, *Galen on the Usefulness of the Parts of the Body. Peri chreias moriōn. De usu partium*, trans. Margaret Tallmadge May (Ithaca, NY: Cornell University Press, 1968). For other works by Galen, I refer to the volume and page in the edition of C. G. Kühn.

[3] Plato, *Timaeus*, in Desmond Lee, trans., *Timaeus and Critias*, revised by Thomas K. Johansen (New York: Penguin, 2008), 29c2–3. On teleology in the *Timaeus*, see Johansen's chapter in this volume.

to its nature.[4] Disagreeing with Plato, Aristotle argued that the goal-directed activities that define these bodily parts are internal potentials for development, instead of the result of providential design.

Always eager to agree with "the best philosophers," Galen synthesized Aristotle's and Plato's teleological views.[5] With Aristotle, he claimed the priority of explanations that appeal to final causes over all other accounts,[6] and he characterized the structure and workings of bodily parts in light of their ends, showing how their presence furthers the survival, well-being, and reproduction of the whole animal.[7] Nature, Galen repeatedly claims, does nothing in vain.[8] But, following Plato, Galen dedicated his anatomical descriptions to the *dēmiourgos*. *De usu partium* is presented as a "hymn" of praise to the divine craftsman,[9] and as proof—even if only in the form of an argument to the best explanation—of its existence.[10] According to Galen, his dissections offered new and powerful evidence for the providential design of the world of living creatures. Anatomical evidence, says Galen, shows us that the *dēmiourgos* is perfectly artful. The divine craftsman fashioned the universe in the most beautiful and

---

4 *Parts of Animals* 640a33–35, 642a7–12. On teleology in Aristotle, see Leunissen's chapter in this volume.
5 *UP* I.8, I 14 H = III 20.12 K.
6 *De causis procatarticis* VI 67 = 92, 17–21; *UP* III 465 H = I 339, 12–18 K.
7 *UP* VI.7, I 318.8–11 H = III 435.15–17 K. Galen is following Aristotle: *De anima*. 435b17–25, 435b20–21, *Parts of Animals* 640a33–b1 and 670b23–7.
8 *UP* I.18, I 47.6–7 H = III 64.14 K; II.12, I.100.22 H = III 137.9 K; III.6, I 141.24–25 H = III 193.18 K. Galen borrows the expression ἡ φύσις οὐδὲν ποιεῖ μάτην from Aristotle; *De incessu animalium* II 704b15. See Part III of chapter 14 in J. Jouanna, P. Van der Eijk, and N. Allies, vol. 40 of *Greek Medicine from Hippocrates to Galen: Selected Papers* (Leiden: Brill, 2012) for a discussion of this phrase in Galen's works. Galen occasionally acknowledges the existence of structural byproducts. The hair in the armpits, for example, is not due to providential design, but to organic fluids in that area of the body (*UP* XI.14, II 160.20–161.1 H = III 908–9 K).
9 *UP* XVII.3, II 451 H = IV 366 K.
10 *De placitis Hippocratis et Platonis* IX.8, II.590–6 De Lacy = V.782–91 K. For Galen's debts to Plato and Aristotle on teleology, see M. J. Schiefsky, "Galen's Teleology and Functional Explanation," *Oxford Studies in Ancient Philosophy* 3 (2007): 369–400.

economical way possible, given the constraints imposed by the materials at its disposal. Skeptics who like to point out seeming imperfections in our bodies as evidence against design make a mistake. For, as Galen tells us, unlike the "God of Moses," but much like Plato's *dēmiourgos*, the divine craftsman did not create ex nihilo; rather, the universe was fashioned from preexisting matter.[11] And, "just as you would never demand an ivory statue of Phidias if you had given him clay, so, when blood is the material you give, you would never obtain the bright and beautiful body of the sun or moon."[12]

But even if the philosophy in *De usu partium* is not new, the adoption of a teleological framework in medicine had consequences that went far beyond theoretical speculation. The combination of teleological thinking with experimental anatomy contributed to important discoveries concerning the human body. For Galen, teleology is as much a method for anatomical inquiry as it is a metaphysical commitment. In particular, teleology guides the chief tool of anatomical investigation: dissection. But what is this method? Thinking about bodily parts as fulfilling functions that contribute to an organism as a whole makes the questions "What is this part *for*?" and "Why is this part *here*?" central to anatomy. Using ends as heuristics, inner structures that appear at first sight as undifferentiated masses of muscles, sinews, and fluids—in Galen's own words "a slime of fleshes and juices"[13]—are revealed to be distinct structures individuated by, and understood in light of, their specific functional contributions. Purpose and function help us uncover the nature of anatomical parts, their number, "position, size, shape, and all other qualities."[14]

---

11 *UP* XI.14, II 4 H = III 905–6 K.
12 *UP* III.10, I 176 H = III 240.1–5 K.
13 *UP* XVII.1, 2.447.16–448.3 H = IV 360–1 K.
14 *UP* III.10, I 177 H = III 242.6–7 K.

Galen describes his teleological approach using one of his favorite examples, the hand, to which he devotes the entirety of the first book of *De usu partium*. The hand's overall structure—its divisions into four fingers and an opposable thumb, each composed of both soft flesh and hard nails—is optimal to achieve its purpose: grasping objects of different sizes and shapes. Using the hand as paradigm, Galen's goal is to "devise some universal method which will enable us to find the usefulness of *each* part and its attributes."[15] We should "start with those parts whose activities we know with certainty, since then we should be able to move on to the other parts also."[16] For, even though "everyone knows what the work of the hands is—it is very clear that they are for grasping," Galen argues, "not everyone yet perceives that *every subpart of the hand* is of such a nature and size that it cooperates in the one function (*ergon*) performed by the whole instrument."[17] With the function of the hand in mind, Galen proceeds to describe its muscles, which we can individuate and number only when we reflect on how they contribute to the hand's overall grasping motion. It is precisely attention to function that leads Galen to classify muscles, which look alike to the naive observer, into flexors and extensors.[18]

As Galen remarks, knowing the teleological arrangement of the body is not only useful for the person of science who loves knowledge for its own sake. If they want to be successful practitioners, doctors must know the functions of bodily structures. In *De anatomicis administrationibus*, he tells us that only attention to function reveals, for example, that muscles are best cut along the fibers, since transverse incisions paralyze them.

---

15 *UP* I.8, I 12 K = III 17.13–16 K; emphasis added.
16 *UP* I.8, I 13 K = III 18.1–4 K.
17 *UP* I.8, I 13 K = III 19.4–8 K; emphasis added.
18 For example, *De anatomicis administrationibus* II 438.3–4 K; II 244.11–245.33 K; *De motu musculorum* III 369.7–8 K.

As Galen says, "surgical precision demands knowledge of the actions of the muscles, for the action is so important that, if they become inactive, the whole part becomes useless." Physicians who ignore the function of bodily parts tend to "make grave mistakes in venesection" by impairing vital functions.[19] Similarly, knowing anatomical functions is useful for the physician who "has to remove splinters and missiles efficiently, to excise parts properly, or to treat ulcers, fistulae, and abscesses."[20] Knowing the function of inner organs is also "important for diagnosing diseases," since it allows a doctor to identify the affected parts by noting what functions have been impaired.[21] Conversely, "by knowledge of the action of the severed [part] you might predict which function is destroyed."[22]

Using functional considerations as guides for anatomical research proved fruitful. In fact, Galenic anatomy would not be superseded until the European Renaissance. The resurgence of experimental anatomy at that time did not occur by chance. Galen's texts, including *De usu partium*, were lost to the western European world and preserved by Arab scholars. Their reintroduction to the European continent would soon rekindle experimental anatomy and lead physicians to perform, once again, the functionally guided dissections that had been central to Galen's method. It is true, however, that the new physicians were often harshly critical of Galen's statements. As Andreas Vesalius, the founder of modern anatomy, puts it, Galen's descriptions often "disgrace rather than honor Nature."[23] Yet these criticisms pertain to Galen's mistaken

---

19 *De anatomicis administrationibus* I.3, 229 5–10 K. I consulted the translation by Singer: C. Singer, *Galen: On Anatomical Procedures. De anatomicis administrationibus* (New York: Oxford University Press, 1956).
20 *De anatomicis administrationibus* II.2, 286 8–12 K.
21 *De anatomicis administrationibus* II.2, 286 15–16 K.
22 *De anatomicis administrationibus* I.3, 229 1–2 K.
23 A. Vesalius, *De humani corporis fabrica* II.15 (Basel: Ex officina Joannis Oporini, 1543), 248. Criticizing Galen's conclusions earned Vesalius considerable trouble. He and his followers were

observations and conclusions—many of them, according to Vesalius, the result of relying on the dissection of apes instead of human corpses—and not to his functional approach.[24] For the new doctors, as for Galen, a functional framework would turn out to be key for understanding the human body.[25]

---

accused of being the "Lutherans of Physic" by those who followed Galen's conclusions to the letter, but not his anatomical method and his emphasis on empirical investigation.

24 See N. G. Siraisi, "Vesalius and the Reading of Galen's Teleology," *Renaissance Quarterly* 50 (1997): 1–34, for the influence of Galen's functional approach in the works of Vesalius.

25 See McDonough's chapter in this volume for the importance of a functional approach in early modern science.

CHAPTER THREE

Avicenna on Teleology

FINAL CAUSATION AND GOODNESS

Kara Richardson

3.1. Introduction

Avicenna (Ibn Sīnā) was the most eminent of the Arabic philosophers who flourished in Islamic lands in the ninth to twelfth centuries. Though he saw himself as an Aristotelian, his extant philosophical works are not commentaries on Aristotle, but independent treatises in which he departs from or, in his own words, "corrects," the First Teacher as he sees fit. And while Aristotle is his chief source, his writings also reflect later developments of ancient Greek thought.

Throughout his corpus, Avicenna defends Aristotle's claim that the end or "that for the sake of which" is one of four types of causes. The meaning of this claim is unclear in certain respects. One ambiguity is the relationship between final causation and goodness. According to some interpreters, Aristotle's claim that the end is a cause primarily conveys that some things are caused to occur by goodness.[1] On this view, the concept of an end or goal, for Aristotle, is the concept of something good (from some perspective), and the concept of final causation is that of causation by goodness.[2] I will refer to this as the "good-centered" view of the final cause. According to others, Aristotle's basic theory of the final cause says that it is the goal of the efficient cause, or the object of a power, i.e., what the power is for.[3] On this view, Aristotle's fundamental account of what it is for something to be an end need not and should not refer to the goodness of that end.[4] I will refer to this as the "agent-centered" view of the final cause.

This chapter aims to clarify Avicenna's theory of the final cause in light of the good-centered and agent-centered views of Aristotle's final cause. This theory is most fully developed in the *Physics* and *Metaphysics* of his masterwork, *The Book of Healing*.[5] These treatises circulated widely in the Middle Ages in their original Arabic, as well as in Hebrew transliteration and Latin translation. Though Avicenna's philosophical legacy is insufficiently studied, it is already clear that his discussions of the final cause in these treatises were broadly influential.[6]

---

[1] See David Charles, "Teleological Causation," in *The Oxford Handbook of Aristotle*, ed. Christopher Shields (Oxford: Oxford University Press, 2012), 226–266, and J. M. Cooper, "Aristotle on Natural Teleology," in *Language and Logos*, ed. M. Schofield and M. Nussbaum (Cambridge: Cambridge University Press, 1986), 187–222.

[2] Cooper, "Aristotle on Natural Teleology," 197.

[3] This view is developed in most detail by Allan Gotthelf, "Aristotle's Conception of Final Causality," *Review of Metaphysics* 30 (1976): 226–254 and Allan Gotthelf, "The Place of the Good in Aristotle's Teleology," *Proceedings of the Boston Colloquium in Ancient Philosophy* 4 (1988): 13–39.

[4] Gotthelf says, "Now, I of course agree that for Aristotle a natural goal or end is always something good and is a (final) cause in virtue of that about it which makes it good, but I do not believe that the fundamental account of what it is for something to be an end for Aristotle must—or indeed should—refer to the goodness of that end" (Gotthelf, "Place of the Good," 115).

[5] Analyses of a broader range of Avicenna's writings on the final cause can be found in Robert Wisnovsky, "Avicenna on Final Causality" (Ph.D. diss., Yale University, 1994); and Robert Wisnovsky, *Avicenna's Metaphysics in Context* (London: Duckworth, 2003).

[6] See Pasnau in this volume. See also Anneliese Maier, *Metaphysische Hintergründe der spätscholastischen Naturphilosophie* (Rome: Edizioni di Storia e Letteratura, 1955), 273–299. See also Jon McGinnis and Anthony Ruffus, "Willful Understanding: Avicenna's Philosophy of Action and Theory of the Will," *Archiv für Geschichte der Philosophie* 97, no. 2 (2015): 160–195. See also Kara

As we will see, two features of Avicenna's account of the final cause show that he adopts an agent-centered view: his portrayal of the final cause as the "cause of causes" (section 3.3) and his response to the question of whether every end is a good (section 3.4). While he also holds that every essential agent acts for the sake of something that is good, or apparently good, for the recipient of action (section 3.5), his explanation for this claim is compatible with his fundamentally value-neutral account of what it is to be a final cause (sections 3.6–3.7). Before turning to these various aspects of his view, we will survey his preliminary claims about the final cause as one of four causes.

3.2. THE FINAL CAUSE AS ONE OF FOUR TYPES OF CAUSES

Following Aristotle, Avicenna introduces the final cause (*al-ʿillah al-ghāʾiyyah*) as one of the four types of causes: efficient, material, formal, and final. In his *Physics*, Avicenna describes these four in relation to change. At *Physics* I.2 §7, he says that the agent (*al-fāʿil*) of the change impresses the form of a body into its matter, while the end (*al-ghāyah*) is that for the sake of which the form of a body is impressed into its matter.[7] At *Physics* I.10 §10, he adds that the end of every *essential* efficient cause is some good, or apparent good.[8] (See section 3.5.)

In his *Metaphysics*, Avicenna describes the four types of causes in relation to existence. He regards the formal and material causes as intrinsic to the effect: each is a "cause that is part of the subsistence of the thing [caused]."[9] The formal cause is that "through which the thing is

---

Richardson, "Two Arguments for Natural Teleology from Avicenna's Shifāʾ," *History of Philosophy Quarterly* 32 (2015): 123–140.

7 Avicenna, *Physics*, I.2 §7 [15]. Unless otherwise noted, quotations of the *Physics* are taken from Avicenna, *The Physics of the Healing*, trans. Jon McGinnis (Provo, Utah: Brigham Young University Press, 2009). In my references to them, the number of book and chapter is followed by the paragraph number of this translation and, between square brackets, the page number of the Arabic text as given in the Cairo edition.

8 Avicenna, *Physics*, I.10 §10 [52].

9 Avicenna, *Metaphysics*, VI.1 §2 [257]. Unless otherwise noted, quotations of the *Metaphysics* are taken from Avicenna, *Metaphysics of the Healing*, trans. Michael Marmura (Provo, Utah: Brigham

what it is in actuality," while the material cause is that "through which the thing is what it is in potency and in which the potentiality of its existence resides."[10] He regards the efficient and final causes as extrinsic to the effect. The agent is "the cause which bestows an existence that is distinct from itself," and the end is "the cause for whose sake the existence of something distinct from itself is realized."[11]

As these passages indicate, Avicenna tends to describe the final cause with reference to the efficient cause (*al-ʿillah al-fāʿilah*) or agent. He divides the efficient cause into two broad types. One is the voluntary agent, i.e., the agent that acts via an appetitive principle (desire or will). Avicenna does not trouble over the general point that voluntary actions are for the sake of something: in one passage, he suggests that their being for an end is obvious, since their principles include appetite, and appetite is for something.[12] However, he is concerned to show that the final causation of divine voluntary action is quite different from that of human voluntary action. Our actions typically aim at things that will enhance our existence, or so we hope. God, an absolutely perfect being, cannot act for any self-enhancing purposes. (See section 3.6.)

The second broad type of efficient cause is the natural agent, which acts via its nature. According to Avicenna, natures are posited in order to explain certain bodily motions that proceed from the moved bodies themselves, rather than from external causes. For example, a stone's rising proceeds from an external cause, but "when we raise the stone and then leave it alone, it falls through its nature."[13] Following

---

Young University Press, 2005). In my references to them, the number of book and chapter is followed by the paragraph number of this translation and, between square brackets, the page number of the Arabic text as given in the Cairo edition.

10 Avicenna, *Metaphysics*, VI.1 §2 [257].

11 Avicenna, *Metaphysics*, VI.1 §2 [257–258].

12 Avicenna, *Metaphysics* VI.5 §7 [285].

13 He continues as follows: "This belief is also fairly close to our belief that there are plants because of the alteration of seeds and animals because of the generation of semen. Similarly, we find that animals, through their own volition, have a freedom of action in their [various] kinds of movements, [since] we do not see some external agent forcibly directing them to those actions. So, there is impressed upon our souls an image that those [movements], and, on the whole, the actions and passivities that proceed from bodies, are sometime caused by a foreign, external agent and

late ancient commentators on Aristotle, especially John Philoponus, Avicenna defines nature as an efficient causal principle.[14] On this view, the way in which the nature of the stone moves its body downward is akin to the way in which the soul of the animal moves its body toward food or away from predators, even though only the latter involves volition. One similarity is that natures are end-directed active principles: being at the center of the world is the end of the stone's natural motion, just as securing food or safety is the end of the animal's voluntary motion.

As we will see, for Avicenna, the claim that nature is an efficient causal principle implies that nature acts for the sake of something: in his view, efficient causation requires final causation. But Avicenna also argues for natural teleology on other grounds. In his *Physics*, he attacks the ancient Greek materialists, especially Empedocles and his followers, who are said to describe all kinds of natural phenomena as the result of chancy contact and the combination of a few basic types of bodies. In his most extended argument against them, Avicenna maintains that their principles are insufficient to account for generation from seed; but the phenomena can be explained if we posit in the seed an active principle that directs matter toward the form of a living organism. And this, he says, is just what we mean in saying that nature acts for an end: that natural bodies possess active principles by which they cause matter "to move toward some definite terminus according to a natural intention belonging to [the nature]."[15] This line of reasoning involves no appeal to the goodness of natural ends. But at

---

sometimes are a result of the things themselves without an external agent" (Avicenna, *Physics* I.5 §1).

14 In discussing Aristotle's definition of "nature" as a principle of motion and rest that belongs to its bearer essentially, Avicenna adds that by "principle of motion" is meant "an efficient cause from which proceeds the production of motion in another, namely, the moved body." Avicenna, *Physics*, I.5 §6 [31]. On the late ancient background to this view, see Andreas Lammer, "Defining Nature: From Aristotle to Philoponus to Avicenna," in *Aristotle and the Arabic Tradition*, ed. Ahmed Alwishah and Josh Hayes (Cambridge: Cambridge University Press, 2015), 121–142.

15 Avicenna, *Physics* I.14 §8 [70].

the close of his discussion of natural teleology, he mentions, almost in passing, that "whoever closely considers the usefulness of the animal's limbs and the parts of plants will have no doubt that natural things are for the sake of some end."[16] As we will see in section 3.6, Avicenna ultimately explains the utility of the parts of plants and animals for their survival and well-being in terms of divine providence.

3.3. The Final Cause as the "Cause of Causes"

One striking (and influential) feature of Avicenna's theory of the final cause is his portrayal of the end as the "cause of causes," i.e., the cause of the rest of the four causes being causes.[17] As he explains, the end is a cause of the agent being a cause. And the agent, by putting some form into some matter, is a cause of form and matter being causes. So, the end is a cause of the form and matter being causes by means of its causing the agent to be a cause.[18] For example, the end of health is the cause of my exercising, and my exercising is the cause of my body acquiring the form of health.

The linchpin of Avicenna's account of the end as the "cause of causes" is the assertion that the end is a cause of the agent's being a cause.[19] In his *Physics*, he supports this point on the ground that "the agent acts

---

16 Avicenna, *Physics*, I.14 §17.

17 See Pasnau in this volume. In what follows, I discuss this doctrine as it appears in Avicenna's *Physics*. It also appears in *Metaphysics* VI.5, where Avicenna uses it to defend final causation against the objection that it violates the principle that causes are prior to their effects. As the "cause for the rest of the causes being causes in actuality," explains Avicenna, the final cause is prior to the efficient cause and thus to the effect (Avicenna, *Metaphysics*, VI.5 §28 [292]). According to Anneliese Maier, Avicenna's response to this objection led some of his Latin readers to restrict final causation to intentional action, on the ground that the claim that the end is prior to motion holds only in cases where the end exists in the soul of the agent prior to motion. Although this is not Avicenna's own view, he can be said to inspire it: for he twice mentions the essence of the end existing in the soul of the agent prior to action to support his claim that the final cause is prior to the other causes. See Maier, *Metaphysische Hintergründe*, 273–299.

18 "The end is a cause of the agent as an agent, and a cause of the form and matter by means of its moving the agent of compound" (Avicenna, *Physics*, I.11 §3 [53], trans. slightly modified).

19 Avicenna acknowledges that the agent is also a cause of the end in the sense that the agent brings about a state of affairs specified by the end (in cases where the agent's activity fulfills its end). For example, if I exercise for the sake of my health, and I achieve my end, my action is a cause of my end in the sense that my action brings about a state of affairs specified by my end. But he emphasizes

only for the sake of [the end] and otherwise does not act."[20] He gives the example of exercising for the sake of health, a voluntary motion. But the context of the claim shows that it also applies to natural motion, such as the stone's action of moving itself toward the center (of the world).

Avicenna's claim that the agent acts only for the sake of the end, and otherwise does not act, makes one thing clear: in his view, final causation is required for efficient causation, whether voluntary or natural. But he provides little explanation of this key claim. Applied to the example of exercise, the claim is that, in the absence of the end of health, the one who exercises would not act. The latter phrase might mean that this person would not perform the act he does in fact perform, i.e., the act of exercising; or, it might mean that he would not do anything at all. Both of these claims follow from Avicenna's account of voluntary motion, where the end serves as the object of the animal's appetite. As such, the end determines, or partly determines, the character of the action the agent performs; in the case of rational agents, practical deliberation about the best means to some end is also needed. And the end determines that the voluntary agent does something, rather than remains at rest: no body moves voluntarily in the absence of an end that serves as the object of appetite.

Applied to the example of the stone, the claim is that, in the absence of the end of being at the center, the stone would not act. Again, the latter phrase might mean that the stone would not perform the act it does in fact perform, i.e., the act of moving itself toward the center; or it might mean that the stone would not do anything at all. Do these claims follow Avicenna's account of natural motion? As we have seen, Avicenna defines "nature" as an efficient causal principle of bodily

---

that the causal relationship between the end and the agent is asymmetrical in this respect: "the end is a cause of the agent's being an agent and so is a cause of its being a cause, whereas the agent is not a cause of the end with respect to its being a cause" (Avicenna, *Physics* I.11 §2 [53]).

20 Avicenna, *Physics* I.11 §1 [53].

motion. Roughly speaking, it serves as an active power: given suitable conditions, it actualizes the body's potential for being in some state with respect to quality, quantity, or place. The end is the object of this active power, i.e., what the power is for. As such, it sets the course of natural motion: it determines that the stone moves toward, rather than away from, the center (whenever it is away from the center and is unimpeded). So, we may infer from Avicenna's account of natural motion that, in the absence of the end of being at the center, the stone would not perform the act it does in fact perform, i.e., the act of moving itself toward the center. Can we also infer that, in the absence of the end of being at the center, the stone would not move itself at all? Certainly, if the stone moves in place, it must move in some direction. By hypothesis, its course cannot be set by an external cause (for we are considering only the stone's natural motion, i.e., the motion that proceeds from the stone itself). And Avicenna's commitment to the principle of sufficient reason rules out random action.[21] So, in the absence of the end of being at the center, the stone would not move itself at all because a condition for its moving itself is that it move itself in some direction.

Notably, Avicenna's portrayal of the end as the cause of causes and his claim that, in the absence of the end, the agent would not act, offers an account of what it is to be a final cause that involves no explicit reference to the goodness of the end; rather, on this view, the role of the final cause is described solely in terms of its causing the efficient cause to act.

3.4. Is Every End a Good?

Avicenna directly addresses the relationship between final causation and goodness in *Metaphysics* VI.5, a text devoted to difficulties

---

[21] See Kara Richardson, "Avicenna and the Principle of Sufficient Reason," *Review of Metaphysics* 67 (2014): 743–768.

surrounding the final cause. Here he treats the question whether every end is a good, a question to which he gives a somewhat frustrating response: "considered in one way, every end is an end; and considered in another way, every end is a good or an apparent good."[22] In the discussion that precedes this conclusion, Avicenna offers an account of the relationship between final causation and goodness via two examples: human generation and housebuilding.

According to Avicenna, the form of humanity is the end of human generation and its good. He explains this point as follows. The form of humanity is an end in relation to the agent of human generation: it is that toward which the agent of generation (i.e., the sperm) is directed.[23] And the form of humanity is a good in relation to the patient of human generation, namely, human matter: for the patient's reception of this form perfects the patient.[24] Roughly speaking, for Avicenna, a perfecting form is one by which matter is a complete, fully functioning member of a species, while a perfecting accident is one that promotes the survival or well-being of a species-member.[25]

Avicenna holds that shelter is the end of housebuilding and its good. But this example is less straightforward. Shelter is an end in relation to the agent of housebuilding, i.e., the builder, but it is not a good in relation to the patient of housebuilding, namely, stones and wood. For the patient's reception of a house-wise arrangement does not perfect it: the

---

22 This is how he phrases the question when he gives his answer to it at *Metaphysics* VI.5 §38. In the introduction to *Metaphysics* VI.5, he puts the question as "whether the end (*al-ghāyah*) and the good (*al-khair*) are one thing (*shay'*) or different?" (Avicenna, *Metaphysics* VI.5 §2 [284]).

23 This form "is an end for the power enacting formation in the human matter, and [it is] toward it that [the agent's] action and its moving [another] are directed" (Avicenna, *Metaphysics* VI.5 §34 [294]).

24 More precisely, he holds that the form of humanity is a good "in relation to the recipient when the latter is in potency" (Avicenna, *Metaphysics* VI.5 §37 [295]). To explain this point, he says: "because evil is the nonexistence of its perfection [or completion]. The good that is the opposite of [this evil] is existence and realization in actuality" (Avicenna, *Metaphysics* VI.5 §37 [295]).

25 He discusses evil as the absence of perfection in more detail in *Metaphysics* IX.6. See Carlos Steel, "Avicenna and Thomas Aquinas on Evil," in *Avicenna and His Heritage: Acts of the International Colloquium, Leuven, September 8–11, 1999*, ed. Jules Janssens and Daniel De Smet (Leuven: Leuven University Press, 2002), 171–196.

stones and wood are not made better by being in this arrangement, though a blinkered person may say of a "piece of wood that is split, and whose one half is used for a mosque while its other half is used for a public lavatory, that its one half is fortunate, while its other half is unfortunate."[26] While shelter is not a good in relation to the stones and wood, it is a good in relation to the recipient of the house: whoever acquires the house comes to possess shelter for herself and her belongings, which helps her survive and thrive.[27] We may gloss his point as follows: shelter, the end of housebuilding, is not a good in relation to the proximate recipient of the builder's activity (the stones and wood), but rather in relation to the ultimate recipient of the builder's activity, the person who acquires the house.

Avicenna adds that the end of motion is not in every case a good that perfects the ultimate recipient of motion. Where motion is natural or voluntary and rational, it is such a good. But where motion is produced by a voluntary agent, who grasps its end via imagination (a nonrational apprehensive faculty common to all animals), the end may be merely an apparent good. This is because the imagination impels appetite by its perception of an object as pleasant; imagination cannot discern its objects as (true) goods.[28]

As this discussion shows, Avicenna holds that in many cases the end of motion is its good, but he also maintains that being the end of motion is different from being its good. To be the end of motion

---

26 Avicenna, *Physics* I.13 §14.

27 Avicenna, *Metaphysics* VI.5 §35; §38 [294; 295–296]. He also notes that, in the housebuilding case and others like it, the action has (at least) two ends: a proximate end that is a form or an accident in the patient receptive of the action, and a remote end that is a form or an accident in the agent whose quest instigates the action. In the case of housebuilding, the proximate end is the form of house in stones and wood, and the ultimate end is the accident of shelter in the agent who seeks shelter (Avicenna, *Metaphysics* VI.5 §36 [294–295]).

28 He says that the end would be a good if the recipient's change from potency to actuality "pertained to a meaning beneficial in existence or [for] the permanence of existence, and if the movement was either natural or [a] voluntary, rational [movement]. But, if [the end is] imaginary [i.e., apprehended by the imagination], it does not follow necessarily that it would be a true good, but it could be [only] an opined good" (Avicenna, *Metaphysics* VI.5 §38 [296]).

is to stand in a relation to the agent of motion. And to be the good of motion is to stand in a relation to the patient or ultimate recipient of motion. In drawing this distinction, Avicenna appears to raise an objection to the claim that every end is a good: this claim is misleading insofar as it conflates the end of motion and the good of motion. This objection underlies his cryptic answer to the question whether every end is a good. When he says, "considered in one way, every end is an end," he refers to his point that being the end of motion is different from being its good. When he says, "considered in another way, every end is a good or an apparent good," he refers to his point that the end of natural or voluntary action is something that really perfects the patient or ultimate recipient of motion, or seems to do so. Given that every agent is either a natural or a voluntary agent, this point yields the conclusion that every end is a good or an apparent good.

Avicenna's claim that to be an end is to stand in a relation to an agent, together with his distinction between being an end of motion and being a good of motion, supports an agent-centered view of the final cause: the account of what it is to be an end need not and should not refer to the goodness of that end. Furthermore, his distinction between the end of motion and its good suggests that, in order to function as an end, a thing need not be good or apparently good. In other words, it suggests that the relationship between final causation and goodness, or apparent goodness, is merely contingent.

On the other hand, Avicenna also claims that every end is something that really perfects the patient or ultimate recipient of motion, or seems to do so. This claim suggests that goodness, or apparent goodness, is a necessary feature of the end. Call this "the problem of the ubiquity of good ends." In brief, the problem is that Avicenna seems to endorse a fundamentally value-neutral view of the end, i.e., his basic account of what it is to be a final cause does not involve the idea that ends are goods or apparent goods. Yet he also appears to hold that all ends are goods or apparent goods. Sections 3.6 and 3.7 attempt to resolve this problem on Avicenna's behalf. The next section clarifies Avicenna's claim that every end is something that really perfects the patient or ultimate recipient of motion, or seems to do so.

3.5. Essential Agents and Their Good Ends

As we saw in section 3.1, when Avicenna describes the final cause as one of four types of causes in his *Physics*, he says that "any production of motion that proceeds—not accidentally, but essentially—from an agent is one whereby it seeks some good in relation to it. Sometimes it is truly good, and at other times it is [only] apparently good, for it either is such or appears to be such."[29] In this passage, he appeals to a distinction between essential and accidental agents. Through this distinction, he clarifies his claim that every end is something that really perfects the patient or ultimate recipient of motion, or seems to do so, by separating it from the implausible view that whatever happens is good from some perspective.

Avicenna uses a variety of examples to explain the distinction between the essential and the accidental efficient cause. Fire burning a flammable body is an essential efficient cause, while fire burning the poor man's cloak is an accidental efficient cause.[30] The stone falling is an essential efficient cause, while the stone fracturing the head of a passerby is an accidental efficient cause.[31] The hunter shooting a pheasant is an essential efficient cause, while the hunter shooting a man is an accidental efficient cause.[32] These examples give us a rough idea of what is meant by the term "essential efficient cause." A natural agent is

---

29 Avicenna, *Physics*, I.10 §10 [52], trans. slightly modified. The wording of the passage deserves comment. What does Avicenna mean by "seeks" (*yarūmu*), a verb that brings to mind action involving apprehension of the goal? Given that the passage occurs in Avicenna's *Physics*, i.e., in the context of a discussion of natural philosophy, we should assume that he means it to apply to natural agents. And since the things he sees as natural agents (elemental bodies and plants) do not have the apprehensive powers of animal or rational souls, we must conclude that he uses "seeks" in a metaphorical way (or, perhaps, that he considers this verb to have a broader meaning, one not restricted to action involving apprehension of a goal).

30 Avicenna, *Physics*, I.12 §2 [55]; *Physics* I.14 §16 [74].

31 Avicenna, *Physics* I.12 §2 [55–56].

32 Avicenna, *Physics* I.12 §6 [58]. Though he uses the example of the hunter to illustrate the accidental end, it also illustrates the accidental agent.

an essential efficient cause of motion insofar as that motion proceeds toward the end to which its nature directs it. And a voluntary agent is an essential efficient cause of motion insofar as that motion proceeds toward the end to which the agent's appetite directs it.

As the distinction between essential and accidental efficient causes shows, Avicenna does not hold the implausible view that whatever happens is good or apparently good. Rather, he maintains that bad events are unintended byproducts of actions directed toward things that are real or apparent goods. However, it appears that, on this view, events that are neither good nor apparently good are nonbasic: for example, when Avicenna explains the stone's fracturing the head of a passerby in terms of the action of the stone and the action of the passerby, he suggests that the former is, in some sense, reducible to the latter. Furthermore, it appears that, on this view, every basic action is directed toward things that are real or apparent goods. And this view may also seem implausible (albeit less so than the view that whatever happens is good or apparently good). We can see the rationale for this view in the following sections, which address the problem of the ubiquity of good ends.

3.6. The Goodness of Voluntary Ends

As we have seen, Avicenna holds that voluntary action proceeds from an appetitive principle (desire or will) and that the end of voluntary action is the object of appetite. Furthermore, he distinguishes two types of voluntary actions, rational and nonrational. In cases of rational action, the agent apprehends its end via intellect and reason.[33] In cases of nonrational, voluntary action, the agent apprehends its end via the "lower" cognitive powers of estimation and imagination.[34] As we have

---

33 Avicenna, *Psychology* V.1, in Avicenna, *Kitāb al-Nafs*, ed. Fazlur Rahman (London: Oxford University Press, 1959), 206–208; Avicenna, *Metaphysics* VI.5 §3-17 [284–288].

34 Avicenna, *Psychology* IV.4, in Avicenna, *Kitāb al-Nafs*, 194–196; Avicenna, *Metaphysics* VI.5 §3-17 [284–288].

also seen, Avicenna holds that the end of rational action is something genuinely good, i.e., something that really perfects the patient or ultimate recipient of action. This view follows from the claim that the end of rational action is apprehended by intellect, and the further claim that the object of intellectual knowledge is true. So, by definition, the rational agent takes as her end something truly good for the patient or ultimate recipient of action, and if she attains her end, the patient or ultimate recipient of her action is perfected. Likewise, Avicenna holds that the end of voluntary, nonrational action is something that seems good to the agent, i.e., something that may not really perfect the patient or ultimate recipient of action, but that the agent believes will do so. This view follows from the claim that the end of voluntary, nonrational action is apprehended by the "lower" cognitive powers of estimation and imagination. Through these powers, the voluntary agent apprehends an object as pleasant or painful, or as friend or foe, and she directs her action accordingly; but this sort of apprehension is not truth-tracking. So, by definition, the voluntary, nonrational agent takes as her end something that seems to her to be good, in some sense, for the patient or ultimate recipient of her action. And as she may be mistaken about the goodness of her end, the patient or ultimate recipient of her action may or may not be perfected. But in cases where the patient or ultimate recipient is not perfected, it undergoes a change that the agent mistakenly believes to be a perfection.

In brief, Avicenna's claim that voluntary action is directed toward things that perfect the patient or ultimate recipient of action, or seem to do so, follows from his view of the sorts of things that trigger appetite and thus serve as the ends of voluntary action. In this way, he can explain the ubiquity of good, or apparently good, ends in the realm of voluntary action, even though he maintains a fundamentally value-neutral account of what it is to be a final cause. But how does he explain the ubiquity of good ends in the realm of natural action?

Avicenna defends the claim that natural action is directed toward things that perfect the patient or ultimate recipient of action by appeal to empirical evidence. Following Aristotle, he frequently uses examples of living organisms, whose activities are directed toward ends whose attainment promotes the survival of the individual plant or animal, or of its species.[35] He suggests that the empirical evidence for the claim that natural active principles are directed toward ends that promote the survival of the bearers of those principles is overwhelming.

However, to establish the truth of this claim is not to explain the ubiquity of good ends in nature. The next section presents a solution to the problem of the ubiquity of good ends in nature found in Avicenna's account of divine providence.

3.7. Divine Providence and the Goodness of Natural Ends

To appeal to divine providence to explain the goodness of the world order is not unusual; ancient Greek philosophers did so, as did many Christian philosophers in medieval and early modern Europe.[36] But Avicenna's use of this strategy is a bit unusual, because his account of God rules out some of the standard elements of divine providence. To explain this point, it will be helpful to introduce Avicenna's account of God.

Avicenna identifies God as the Necessary of Existence by itself and as the principle of the existence of everything. He is perfect, or even "above perfection," and he is one in number and in essence. From God's perfection, Avicenna infers that he is pure intellect entirely dissociated from matter, and that his knowledge is purely intellectual.[37] So his knowledge is of universals, not particulars. And he seeks nothing in

---

35 See Avicenna, *Physics* I.14 §17 etc. for the general point. Behind this account of goodness is the idea that permanent existence is better than fleeting existence. From this point of view, the survival of a plant or an animal is good. And the survival of the species is even better, since species persist through eternity.

36 See McDonough and Melamed in this volume.

37 Avicenna, *Metaphysics* VIII.6 §6 [356–357].

such a way that would involve his being deficient in some respect: everything good that is not incompatible with the order of the good "is willed [by God] but not in the way in which something is willed by us."[38]

Avicenna begins his defence of divine providence by acknowledging that his account of God seems to preclude his being providential: for we have shown, he says, that God "cannot act for our sake," and indeed that he cannot act from "any motive or preference."[39] The first constraint follows from his view that God knows universals, not particulars. (Of course, the universal character of God's knowledge entails that he does not know and cannot act for the sake of *any* particulars, not just human particulars. Presumably, Avicenna mentions that God cannot act for *our* benefit because he thinks that his reader may assume that God has a plan for each individual human life.) The second constraint—that he cannot act from any motive or preference—follows from his view that God seeks nothing in such a way that would involve his being deficient in some respect.[40]

So, Avicenna admits that his account of God seems to tell against his being providential. But he maintains other evidence tells in favor of divine providence: "there is no way for you to deny the wondrous manifestations in the formation of the world, the parts of the heavens, and the parts of animals and plants—[all of] which do not proceed by coincidence but require some [kind of] governance."[41] As the evident goodness of the world cannot arise by coincidence, and as the world

---

38 Avicenna, *Metaphysics* VIII.7 §10 [366].

39 Avicenna, *Metaphysics* IX.6 §1 [414–415]. He applies this point not only to God, but to the "exalted causes" more generally. By these he means God and the lower intellects that produce the created world in a stepwise fashion.

40 As these constraints show, Avicenna severely limits the scope of divine providence. While this approach is unusual in the medieval period, it is in keeping with the views of other Islamic *falāsifah*, such as al-Fārābī and Averroës. And a similarly austere account of divine providence is found in Plotinus. On Plotinus's account, see Chris Noble and Nathan M. Powers, "Creation and Divine Providence in Plotinus," in *Causation and Creation in Late Antiquity*, ed. A. Marmodoro and B. Prince (Cambridge: Cambridge University Press, 2015), 51–70.

41 Avicenna, *Metaphysics* IX.6 §1 [415].

has God as its ultimate efficient cause, Avicenna concludes that this goodness is a result of the world's being a product of God's intellectual knowledge of "the order (*niẓām*) of the good."[42]

Though Avicenna's view of the extent of divine providence is still unclear, some aspects of its role in the natural realm are evident. As we have seen, he mentions the parts of plants and animals as examples of the wondrous manifestations that imply a providential world order.[43] In referring to their "parts," he almost certainly means not just their physical organization, but their functional structure, i.e., the array of powers that promotes the survival of a plant or animal and of its species. Additional examples are found in his *Psychology*, where he discusses the infant's ability to breastfeed, or to put out its arms when it is about to fall, and the sheep's fear of and resulting flight from the wolf, which occurs even when the sheep has had no prior acquaintance with the wolf.[44] Avicenna locates these powers in the estimative faculty of the animal soul. But he also says that they "emanate" from "divine mercy," presumably because they appear to be innate.[45] These passages suggest that, even though he limits the scope of divine providence as described earlier, he sees it as extensive enough to explain manifestations of good order in nature.[46] Thus, he could appeal to divine providence to solve

---

[42] Avicenna says that God knows "the order (*niẓām*) of the good in the highest possible manner, whereby what He intellectually apprehends in the highest possible way as an order and a good would overflow from Him in the manner, within the realm of possibility, that is most complete in being conducive to order" (Avicenna, *Metaphysics* IX.6 §1 [415]).

[43] He also argues for the existence of a religious prophet on the grounds that such a person would be provided by divine providence since he is needed for social cooperation, and social cooperation is needed for human survival: "Thus, with respect to the survival and actual existence of the human species, the need of [a prophet] is greater than the need for such benefits as the growing of hair on the eyebrows, the concave shaping of the arches of the feet, and many others that are not necessary for survival but are, at best, useful for it. [Now,] the existence of the righteous man to legislate and to dispense justice is possible, as we have previously remarked. It becomes impossible, therefore, that divine providence should ordain the existence of those [former] benefits [i.e., eyebrows and arched feet] and not these [latter], which are their bases" (Avicenna, *Metaphysics* X.2 §3 [442]).

[44] Avicenna, *Psychology* IV.3, in Avicenna, *Kitāb al-Nafs*, 183–184.

[45] Avicenna, *Psychology* IV.3, in Avicenna, *Kitāb al-Nafs*, 183.

[46] These examples suggest that the goodness of the created world consists in its being populated by substances whose powers promote their survival and well-being. But Avicenna may also see

the problem of the ubiquity of good ends in nature, while maintaining his agent-centered view of what it is to be a final cause. On this view, the fundamental role of the final cause is to direct the efficient cause, for efficient causation requires final causation. The reason that every natural agent acts for the sake of something that perfects the patient or ultimate recipient of action is that natures (i.e., the end-directed active principles by which natural agents act) are, ultimately, products of God's intellectual knowledge of the order of the good.

3.8. Conclusion

Some of Aristotle's interpreters suggest that the key idea underlying his doctrine of the final cause is that some things are caused to occur by goodness, and that he sees a conceptual link between acting for a goal and acting for a good. On this good-centered view of Aristotelian final causation, to act for an end is to act for the sake of something good (from some perspective). In his discussions of the final cause, Avicenna diverges from the good-centered view in two main ways. First, he portrays the end as the cause of the agent being a cause, and he supports this view on the ground that, in the absence of the end, the agent would not act. This suggests that the key idea underlying Avicenna's doctrine of the final cause is that final causation is required for efficient causation. Second, he suggests that it is a mistake to conflate the role of the end of motion and the role of the good of motion: to be an end of motion is to stand in a relation to the agent of motion, but to be a good of motion is to stand in a relation to the patient or ultimate recipient of motion. In sum, Avicenna's account of the end as the cause of the agent being a cause shows that the goodness of the end *need* not feature in

---

the created world as good in another way. Using the example of fire, whose nature is to burn and consume what it touches, he says, while fire's burning the good man's cloak is bad for that individual man, still, fire's burning and consuming what it touches is generally beneficial (Avicenna, *Metaphysics* IX.6 §9 [418]). This suggests that, in Avicenna's view, the goodness of the world involves a relational order among substances that is, on balance, good for all.

our basic account of what it is to be a final cause, and his distinction between the role of the end of motion and the role of the good of motion shows that the goodness of the end *should* not feature in our basic account of what it is to be a final cause.

Avicenna's claim that both natural and rational action is directed toward things that perfect the patient or ultimate recipient of action continues an ancient Greek tradition of attributing the beauty and goodness of the world to final causes. In this way, Avicenna's account of the final cause is in keeping with a good-centered view. But as we have seen, his explanations for the ubiquity of good ends are compatible with an agent-centered view of what it is to be a final cause.

CHAPTER FOUR

Teleology in the Later Middle Ages

Robert Pasnau

A history of teleology might be expected to register an upward spike of enthusiasm through its middle chapters, as the heightened religious commitments of European philosophy inspired a soaring interest in finding ultimate reasons for why the world is the way it is. In fact, however, teleological explanation is one of the legacies of antiquity that received a surprisingly muted response in the Middle Ages. As we will see, there was little enthusiasm for Aristotle's naturalized approach to teleology, and grave doubts over whether final causes are a legitimate kind of cause at all. The one place where reflection on ends did play a robust role in medieval philosophy was in ethics. Even here, however, the consensus of antiquity—that human beings are and ought to be ultimately motivated by their own happiness—met with growing resistance and eventually outright rejection.

4.1. Final Causes in Nature

Although the character of teleological explanation shifted in the Middle Ages, there was never any doubt over the fundamental assumption that nature, in some sense, acts for a purpose. Averroës, for instance, in the series of commentaries that lies at the foundation of the European revival of Aristotelianism, insisted that the principle that nature acts for a purpose is "maximal and fundamental" in both physics and theology.[1] This is to say that, for anyone working in one of these two sciences, it should be accepted as a self-evident first principle that there is a goal at which the natural world aims. If this is denied, Averroës argues, then the rest of the Aristotelian causal framework goes with it: matter would not be for the sake of form, and there could be no agents or movers, since nothing acts or moves except for the sake of something. Likewise, without this sort of teleological framework, divine science "could not prove that God has concern for the things that are here."[2]

Thomas Aquinas similarly introduces into the foundation of his theology the idea that nature, somehow, exhibits teleological directedness. Just as the *Summa theologiae* begins its discussion of the divine nature by establishing that God exists, so the second part of the *Summa*, devoted to the acts of human beings, begins by establishing that all human actions are for an end, and more generally that "it is necessary that all agents act for the sake of an end."[3] Like Averroës (and Avicenna before him), Aquinas insists that "the final cause is the first among all causes." This view—that every natural event has a final cause or, to use

---

1 *Long Commentary on the Physics* Bk. II sec. 75, in *Aristotelis opera cum Averrois commentariis* (Venice: apud Junctas, 1562; reprint, Frankfurt am Main: Minerva, 1962). I follow the Latin version because the original Arabic is lost.

2 *Long Commentary on the Physics* Bk. II sec. 75.

3 *Summa theologiae* 1a2ae 1.2c. All translations of Aquinas are my own, and refer by title and the standard enumeration of articles as found in his *Opera omnia*, ed. Leonine Commission (Rome: Commissio Leonina, 1882–). On Aquinas's teleology more generally, see Stephan Schmid, "Teleology and the Dispositional Theory of Causation in Thomas Aquinas," *Logical Analysis and History of Philosophy* 14 (2011): 21–39.

the common slogan, that nothing in nature is pointless (*vanum*)—was almost unanimously accepted during the Middle Ages.[4] As a start toward cataloging the various commitments of the standard theory, let us say that medieval teleology is **universal**.

The Aristotelian theory of the four causes—formal, material, efficient, final—goes hand in hand with an account of the epistemic ideal that the sciences ought to pursue. Averroës explains that the enumeration of causes in *Physics* Book II "is necessary, because the goal of this study of the science of natural things is a science made certain and perfect, and we do not believe that we know (*scire*) something perfectly unless we know it with its first causes, up until we reach its proximate causes."[5] This sort of ideal understanding of the natural world requires grasping all four of the causes. To know in this way is to have knowledge of the best sort, knowledge of the reason why (in Latin: *scientia propter quid*). As Aristotle had put it, "study of the reason why (*to dioti*) is what reigns supreme in knowledge."[6] Any of the four causes might be particularly salient to an explanation of the reason why, but inasmuch as knowledge ideally requires an explanation in full, it requires a grasp of the final cause.

To pursue this fourfold explanatory project in natural philosophy, the Aristotelian seeks to understand the nature of a thing. This nature will be the proximate intrinsic explanation for why natural entities behave as they do. At this point, however, a deep disconnect emerges between Aristotle and standard medieval views. Aristotle seems to have thought of natures as possessed of their teleological orientation in a

---

[4] For some unusual examples of dissent, see Yitzhak Melamed's contribution to this volume. It should be noted as well that it is doubtful whether universality extends beyond the natural domain. Aristotle himself, for instance, suggests that mathematical truths do not have an end (*Physics* II.9, 200a15–19). All references to Aristotle are by title and standard Bekker page and line numbers, as published in the *Complete Works of Aristotle: The Revised Oxford Translation*, ed. J. Barnes (Princeton, NJ: Princeton University Press, 1984).

[5] *Long Commentary on the Physics* II.27. Averroës is commenting on the start of *Physics* II.3. This conception of *scientia*—science or knowledge; *epistēmē* in Greek; *'ilm* in Arabic—gets its canonical statement at *Posterior Analytics* I.2, 71b9–12.

[6] *Posterior Analytics* I.14, 79a24.

way that removes the need for any appeal to some extrinsic supernatural plan. Considering the objection that nature cannot be thought to act for an end in the way that an artisan does, because nature does not deliberate, Aristotle responds that nature works not so differently from an art like shipbuilding. The shipbuilder does not need to deliberate; he just knows what he is aiming at. Nature works similarly:

> If the shipbuilding art were in the wood, it would produce the same results by nature. Thus, if the final cause is present in art, it is present also in nature. This is made quite clear by the case of a doctor's doctoring himself. Nature is like that.[7]

Aristotle seems, in this suggestive series of images, to ascribe teleology to nature in a way that does not require any external guidance.[8] Later medieval authors, however, generally decline to take this path. Aquinas's commentary on the passage is characteristic. The artist does not deliberate, Aquinas suggests, because the artist has *already* deliberated and no longer needs to. The art of shipbuilding might come to be in the wood, then, if the shipbuilder could somehow insert it there, just as God actually does in natural cases. What the passage shows, then, is that "nature is nothing other than the conception (*ratio*) of a certain art, namely, the divine, endowed to things, by which those things are moved to determinate ends."[9]

This perspective gets developed more fully in Aquinas's argument from *Summa theologiae* 1a2ae 1.2 for the thesis that all agents act for an end. The truth of this thesis, he thinks, can be shown from the fact that every agent has to be determined to some definite effect; otherwise, "it would no more do one thing than another." Aquinas characterizes this

---

7 *Physics* II.8, 199b28–31.
8 See Mariska Leunissen's contribution to this volume for further discussion of this intriguing thought.
9 Thomas Aquinas, *Commentary on the Physics* II.14.8.

determination as an "intention for the end," and then he proceeds to distinguish between two sorts of cases: the case of rational agents who move themselves toward an end by determining their own intentions; and the case of nonrational agents, who are moved by another. Here is how he characterizes the latter case:

> Those that lack reason tend toward an end on account of natural inclination, as if moved by another rather than by themselves. For they do not grasp the concept (*ratio*) of an end, and so they cannot *order* anything toward an end, but are only *ordered* toward an end, by something else. And so all of nonrational nature is compared to God like an instrument to a principal agent.[10]

Although teleology is universal throughout nature, the only way it can be present in a nonrational being (including animals and plants as well as inanimate objects) is if something else—a rational being that has the concept of an end—forms an intention with regard to some end and orders that being to it. We do this all the time with nonnatural motion, and as an illustration of this Aquinas offers the example of an arrow. In the case of natural motion, however, this kind of ordering requires that a being be endowed with a nature. The only being that could do that, Aquinas assumes, is God. Natural teleology thus takes on the twin features of being **intelligent** and, in nonrational cases, **extrinsic**.

It would be natural to suppose that medieval authors insist on intelligence and extrinsicality just because they like to put their gods at the center of everything. But the story is more complicated and interesting than that. As is well known, Aristotle's four causes (*aitiai*) are best viewed as *explanations* in a very broad sense of the word. Thus it contributes to an explanation of the natural order to understand the teleological orientation of a thing's nature. To think of this

---

10 *Summa theologiae* 1a2ae 1.2c.

sort of explanation as a *final cause*, in our modern sense, is liable to mislead. Even as far back as the later medieval period, however, there was already a tendency to think of efficient causation as the paradigm case for what it is to be a cause. In effect, the medieval conception of *causa*—the Latin word—is already very much like our conception. This is an important part of the story of why later medieval metaphysics became increasingly vulnerable to the reductive approach of early modern mechanism. After all, if each of the four causes essentially works like an efficient cause, then it is easy to suppose that all the natural philosopher really needs is efficient causes: bodies moving other bodies. Eventually, this mechanical philosophy would undermine later Aristotelian theories of form and matter, but in some ways its most striking impact occurs earlier, in the medievals' own quite un-Aristotelian conception of final causality.[11]

When final causes are conceived of on the model of efficient causes, it is natural to think of them not as intrinsic tendencies within a thing's nature, but rather as concrete objects in the world. The shipbuilder is working for the sake of a specific boat that is slowly coming into existence. God has an individual plan in mind for each and every thing that exists. The theory, then, is **particular** and **forward-looking**. On this sort of approach, there is no room for the sort of account—familiar from modern biology—that understands teleology in terms of generalized dispositions that can be given historical explanations. That oak trees evolved over millions of years to be genetically disposed to grow tall is no kind of teleological explanation, from this point of view, even

---

11 For the growing dominance of the efficient cause as the paradigm of causality, see Robert Pasnau, *Metaphysical Themes, 1274–1671* (Oxford: Clarendon Press, 2011), esp. 100–101, 198–199, 557–559. For the special case of final causality, see Stephan Schmid, "Finality without Final Causes? Suárez's Account of Natural Teleology," *Ergo* 2 (2015): 393–425, who focuses on the late (circa 1600) scholastic example of Francisco Suárez, where it becomes explicit that all causes are expected to work along the lines of efficient causes. Michael Frede has argued that the tendency to treat all causality along the lines of efficient causality first arises with the Stoics ("The Original Notion of Cause," in *Essays in Ancient Philosophy* [Minneapolis: University of Minnesota Press, 1987], 125–150), though I know of no reason to think that the Stoics shaped later medieval views in this specific area.

if we add that this happened so that oak trees would compete more successfully for sunlight. That might be a case of nature's acting *as if* it has an object in mind, but this oak tree is of course not looking ahead to a future day when it will reach above the neighboring trees and capture a greater share of the light that shines down on this particular forest. That sort of thing obviously requires cognition and desire. To be sure, the demands of explanation drive us toward generalizations on the basis of these particulars. Indeed, scientific demonstrations in the Aristotelian tradition require universal claims as their premises. At a *causal* level, however, teleology holds between particulars, just as much as in the case of efficient causation.

When final causes are understood in this way, the theory immediately becomes vulnerable to an obvious objection: how can something that does not yet exist, and perhaps never will exist, be a cause? Given the particular and forward-looking character of the theory, the difficulty is obvious enough. And it is equally obvious that it will not do to ascribe some sort of magical influence to this possibly future object. As Aristotle himself had remarked, ends are active only "metaphorically."[12] But that remark leaves considerable leeway in constructing a reply to the present objection. The most important reply, judging from how often it is cited, is Avicenna's, who puts the question this way: "Why have you made it a prior cause when in truth it is the effect of every cause?"[13] His answer turns on distinguishing between the final cause's reality as an existent object and its status as a "thing" (*shayʾ*) in the mind. When the object is taken in the first way, it is an effect, but in the second way it is a cause.[14]

---

12 *On Generation and Corruption* I.7, 324b14–15.

13 *The Metaphysics of "The Healing"*, ed. and trans. M. E. Marmura (Provo, UT: Brigham Young University Press, 2005), VI.5 §2. Translations of Avicenna are my own, from the Arabic, and cite by book, chapter, and section number.

14 Avicenna develops this view at *Metaphysics* VI.5 §§27–32. For an overview of his conception of final causes, see *The Physics of "The Healing"*, ed. and trans. J. McGinnis, 2 vols. (Provo, UT: Brigham Young University Press, 2009), I.2 §8 and I.11 §§1–2. For a detailed discussion, see Kara Richardson's contribution to this volume.

Avicenna describes this understanding of final causality as "one of the principles of the natural philosophers,"[15] which suggests that he does not regard this as his own innovation. Whatever its origins, the view permeates later medieval thought. Aquinas, for instance, as the very first objection to the second part of the *Summa theologiae*, considers this: "A cause is naturally prior. But an end has the character (*ratio*) of something ultimate, as the name itself suggests. Therefore an end does not have the character of a cause." To this he offers a terse reply: "An end, even if it comes last in execution, still comes first in the agent's intention. And in this way it has the character of a cause."[16] John Duns Scotus too defends this account at some length, describing it as how "the end is commonly spoken of, namely in intention and in reality (*in re*)."[17] According to the standard medieval account, then, teleology is understood to be **intentional**. The ship under construction exerts final causality inasmuch as it exists intentionally in the mind of the shipbuilder. The view remains particular and forward-looking, but achieves this by harnessing the view's intellectuality, which makes possible not just the conceptualization of an end as an end, in the way we saw Aquinas describe, but also the intentional directedness that gives rise to directedness in action.

Although this seems to have been the standard view, it met with some resistance, in particular from Averroës. He accepts the distinction between the final cause as it exists in the soul and as it exists outside the soul. But whereas Avicenna had characterized the first of these as the final cause, Averroës argues that this is instead an efficient cause (*fāʿil*) of motion, whereas the end outside the soul is the final cause. He illustrates the point as follows:

---

15 Avicenna, *Metaphysics* VI.5 §31.
16 Thomas Aquinas, *Summa theologiae* 1a2ae 1.1 ad 1.
17 *Questions on the Metaphysics of Aristotle*, trans. G. J. Etzkorn and A. B. Wolter (St. Bonaventure, NY: Franciscan Institute, 1997–98), Book V question 1, in codex K n. 51.

The hammam, for example, has two forms, a form in the soul and a form outside the soul. If the form that is in the soul arises in us, then we desire the hammam and move toward it—that is, toward the form that exists outside the soul—that is, toward entering the hammam. The form of the hammam, then, with respect to its being in the soul, becomes an agent (*fāʿila*) for the desire and the motion, whereas with respect to its being outside the soul it becomes an end for the motion and not an agent.[18] (*Long Commentary on the Metaphysics* XII.36)

Averroës does not here attack Avicenna by name, but when these texts entered into the Latin tradition they were regularly understood to offer competing accounts of how to identify the final cause. On both views the hammam is the final cause, but the Avicennian view avoids the seeming absurdity of making something that may exist only in the future (or may never exist) exert backward causality. The hammam *does* exist now, in the mind of the one who seeks a bath. Averroës does not dispute that we can understand the hammam to exist in the soul, but he thinks that we should focus on that mental hammam only if we seek to understand the efficient cause of the action. It is not the hammam in the soul that the bather seeks, but the physical hammam in the medina.

William Ockham takes Averroës's side in this debate, explicitly citing the hammam text: "The end causes through its proper reality so that its own proper reality is desired. That reality need not exist when the effect is caused."[19] In a way, the question here looks

---

18 *Tafsīr mā baʿd al-ṭabīʿa [Long Commentary on the Metaphysics]*, ed. M. Bouyges, 3rd ed., 3 vols. (Beirut: Dar el-Machreq, 1990), Bk. XII sec. 36, my translation.

19 *Quodlibetal Questions*, trans. A. Freddoso and F. Kelley (New Haven: Yale University Press, 1991), IV.1. The issue is discussed in more detail, with references to both Averroës and Avicenna, in Ockham's *Quaestiones variae* q. 4, in *Opera theologica* (St. Bonaventure, NY: Franciscan Institute, 1967–89), 8: 114–117. This text, however, is based on the *reportatio* of an unsympathetic and marginally competent student (8:13*), and so should be approached with some care. I discuss this dispute between the Avicennian and Averroistic view in more detail in "Intentionality and Final Causes," in *Ancient and Medieval Theories of Intentionality*, ed. D. Perler (Leiden: Brill, 2001), 301–323.

fundamental, inasmuch as it requires a choice between two very different candidates for the role of final cause: is it something in the mind or something in the world? Yet ultimately there is perhaps little more at stake than a squabble over labels. All parties to the debate agree that we can distinguish between the hammam as it exists in the world and as it exists intentionally in the mind. All parties agree that, of course, it is the real bath that is sought, and all parties agree that deliberate action occurs through some conception of, and desire for, the real thing. Which one we decide to refer to as the final cause will have various implications—for instance, it will influence whether we think something that does not exist can be a "cause." But ultimately these issues look to be mainly verbal. Either way, the view retains its distinctive features, being universal, intelligent, particular, forward-looking, intentional, and (in nonrational cases) extrinsic.

The real significance of Ockham's view is his strikingly skeptical attitude toward teleology. For most of the twentieth century, medieval scholarship labored under the misimpression that Ockham's overall philosophical outlook is corrosively skeptical. As we have learned more, it has become obvious just how wrong this is. Ockham makes bold and creative positive claims across all areas of philosophy, in areas like logic, ontology, ethics, and mind.[20] Yet when it comes to final causation Ockham really does take just the sort of skeptical position that his old reputation might lead one to expect. For although he accepts that cognitive beings can grasp and desire ends—and that we have good reason to believe that they do so—he does not think that we have good philosophical grounds for supposing that natural causes are aimed at any sort of end. He recognizes, to be sure, that the faith requires maintaining that God has a plan for *everything*, which entails

---

20 The work that makes this case in most detail is Marilyn McCord Adams's magisterial two-volume *William Ockham* (Notre Dame, IN: University of Notre Dame Press, 1987). Although she does not discuss final causality, she does consider these questions in some detail in "Ockham on Final Causality: Muddying the Waters," *Franciscan Studies* 56 (1998): 1–46.

that all natural causes are in fact aimed at an end. Yet he does not think that this is something reason can establish. Thus, to the question of why fire heats the wood rather than cools it, it is enough of an explanation to cite the thing's nature. Moreover, given Ockham's overarching commitment to parsimony, this is not just an epistemic possibility but is in fact what someone *ought* to say who is committed to following reason alone:

> Someone strictly following reason would say that the question "for the sake of what" has no place in natural actions, because he would say that there is no question to be asked about that for the sake of which fire is generated. This has a place only in voluntary actions.[21]

Lest there be any doubt just how far this takes Ockham from Aristotle's teleological orientation, he expressly considers "all the arguments of the Philosopher,"[22] and claims that they are conclusive only in the case of free agents whose actions lack the uniformity exhibited by the rest of nature. For everything else, the necessity of nature is a perfectly adequate explanation.[23]

---

21 Ockham, *Quodlibetal Questions* IV.1.
22 Ockham, *Quodlibetal Questions* IV.1.
23 Accordingly, at *Summula philosophiae naturalis* II.6.51–63 (in *Opera philosophica* [St. Bonaventure, NY: Franciscan Institute, 1967–89], 6:229–230), Ockham takes Aristotle to be committed, in nonvoluntary natural cases, only to a looser sense of final cause in which nature acts merely *as if* it had a known and desired object.
 It is worth noting that in one respect Ockham's theory allows more scope for teleology, in that he expressly enlarges the standard view to include nonrational animals, which he allows can act for an end in virtue of desiring it (see *Summula* II.6.12–24). Here, then, intentionality is sufficient for teleology without intelligence, suggesting that Ockham, unlike Aquinas, does not think genuine teleological action presupposes a *concept* of the end.
 John Buridan, a generation after Ockham, provides another example of medieval skepticism regarding natural teleology. For discussion see Henrik Lagerlund, "The Unity of Efficient and Final Causality: The Mind/Body Problem Reconsidered," *British Journal for the History of Philosophy* 19 (2011): 587–603; Pasnau, "Intentionality and Final Causes"; and James J. Walsh, "Teleology in the Ethics of Buridan," *Journal of the History of Philosophy* 18 (1980): 265–286.

4.2. Final Causes in Human Action

Ockham's skepticism regarding natural teleology is unusual for the era. Even so, his position points to the real center of gravity of later medieval discussions. Because all teleology was ultimately intellectual, it could be invoked universally in the natural world only as a claim about the divine plan. And although no one could doubt (at least not publicly) that there is a divine plan for everything, it was not considered the job of the natural philosopher to speculate regarding what that plan might be. Philosophers from this period accordingly have a great deal to say about material, formal, and efficient causes, but not so much to say about final causality. There is an exception to this rule, however, in the case where, as Ockham says, the role of final causes *is* clear—the case of voluntary actions. So if one wants to see final causes at work in later medieval philosophy, the place to look is not natural philosophy but rather ethics. Here teleological thinking plays a central role. Here again, moreover, ancient views are transformed in the most striking of ways.

According to the nearly unanimous verdict of antiquity, human beings act to promote their own happiness. This was thought to be true both as a descriptive fact about our psychology, and also as a normative claim about what we ought to do. Of course, much ingenuity was devoted to explaining how this kind of self-interest could serve as a basis for the other-regarding considerations of morality, but it seems that no one in the ancient world was even tempted to ground morality in something other than our ultimate self-interest. According to the standard history, this consensus remained in place until Scotus and Ockham came along in the fourteenth century and advanced a voluntaristic ethic unmoored from the inclination toward self-interest. Depending on one's perspective, this marks either the first great defense of genuine human freedom, or the start of a slow slide toward the irrationalism of modernity.

Something like this broad narrative may be correct, but the details are tremendously complex. To establish a baseline for later medieval developments, one might start with Cicero, whose ethical writings had considerable influence on the Middle Ages. His work *On Duties* (*De officiis*) begins by treating it as obvious that the good cannot be identified with one's own personal interest (*commodum*). This might suggest that, even here, the moral has been detached from self-interest, but as the treatise continues it becomes clear that this is not so. Cicero ultimately contends that we cannot help but pursue personal advantage:

> People overturn the fundamental principles established by nature when they divorce the advantageous (*utilitas*) from moral rectitude (*honestas*). For we all seek to obtain what is advantageous, we are irresistibly drawn toward it, and we cannot in any way do otherwise. For who is there who would turn away from what is advantageous? Indeed, who does not exert himself to the utmost to secure it? But because we cannot find it anywhere except in good report, propriety, and moral rectitude, we accordingly hold these to be the first and the highest of things, whereas what we term advantageous we consider not so much a shining distinction but instead a necessity.[24]

From Cicero's point of view, morality has its force only because, as it happens, it is generally to our advantage to act morally. If the world were to change in such a way that "propriety" and "rectitude" no longer worked to our advantage, then we would have neither reason nor ability to adhere to such principles. The first sentence makes clear that Cicero was familiar with the idea that morality and self-interest might be wholly separate domains. It is not as if he was unable even to conceive of such a thing. But, in keeping with the philosophical traditions

---

[24] Cicero, *De officiis*, trans. W. Miller (Cambridge, MA: Harvard University Press, 1913), III.28.101.

before him, he regarded ethical egoism as the only naturalistically plausible morality.

Moral theory, was, however, on the brink of change—indeed, the most radical change in its history so far—as a result of the teachings of Jesus of Nazareth. This is not to say that the Gospels provide an accurate historical record of those teachings, that the teachings were particularly original, that they amounted to a moral theory, or that they immediately transformed ethics. But the massive influence of Christianity on European philosophy exerted a steady pressure in various domains, and nowhere more so than in ethics. For it was, indisputably, the central message of the Gospels that we should let self-interest give way to a generalized concern for all people. Here is Matthew 22:34-40:

> Hearing that Jesus had silenced the Sadducees, the Pharisees got together. One of them, an expert in the law, tested him with this question: "Teacher, which is the greatest commandment in the Law?" Jesus replied: "'Love the Lord your God with all your heart and with all your soul and with all your mind.' This is the first and greatest commandment. And the second is like it: 'Love your neighbor as yourself.' All the Law and the Prophets hang on these two commandments."

Both of these commandments are taken directly from the Hebrew Bible,[25] and further historical parallels are not hard to find, not just for these familiar claims, but also for the golden rule and the injunction to love one's enemies.[26] Yet even if the Gospel message is scarcely

---

25 See Deuteronomy 6:5: "Love the Lord your God with all your heart and with all your soul and with all your strength"; Leviticus 19:18: "Do not seek revenge or bear a grudge against anyone among your people, but love your neighbor as yourself. I am the Lord."
26 For the golden rule in Confucianism as well as in western antiquity, see Jeffrey Wattles, *The Golden Rule* (New York: Oxford University Press, 1996). Stoicism also deserves mention here for its commitment to impartiality among all human beings (see, e.g., Julia Annas, *The Morality of Happiness* [New York: Oxford University Press, 1993], 265–276).

original, its focus on an other-regarding ethics poses a challenge to any Christian philosopher intent on staying within the sort of egoistic framework that Cicero inherits from the Greek tradition.

To be sure, the challenge need not be regarded as insurmountable. After all, ancient ethics itself sought to wield eudaimonism to account for other-directed values such as friendship, justice, and sacrifice for the common good. Naturally, then, this was the initial tendency of Christian ethics as well. Augustine, for instance, takes for granted that if we are to embrace a Christian life, this will be only because we perceive it to be in our self-interest:

> To desire a happy life (*beata vita*), to want a happy life, to yearn for, wish for, pursue a happy life—I hold this to belong to all human beings. So I see that I understated the claim that this desire for a happy life is common to philosophers and Christians; I ought to have said that this belongs to all human beings, absolutely all of them, good and bad. For those who are good are good in order to be happy, and those who are bad would not be bad unless they hoped they could thereby become happy.[27]

The trouble is that, in this fallen state, we have a great difficulty both with seeing what our ultimate good consists in and with steadfastly pursuing it.

The obvious question, then, is whether our natural teleological drive toward our own happiness is compatible with the ethics of the Gospel. According to one line of thought, we are incapable of living up to those ideals on our own, without the supernatural grace of God. This sort of

---

[27] Sermon 150 n. 4, in *The Works of Saint Augustine: A Translation for the 21st Century*, ed. J. E. Rotelle (New York: New City Press, 1990–), 3/5:32. There is some measure of disagreement regarding Augustine's commitment to eudaimonism, and it may be that his view changes over time. For accounts that emphasize his continuities with antiquity, see Terence Irwin, *The Development of Ethics: A Historical and Critical Study* (Oxford: Oxford University Press, 2007–9), vol. 1, §224 and Bonnie Kent, "Augustine's Ethics," in *The Cambridge Companion to Augustine*, ed. N. Kretzmann and E. Stump (Cambridge: Cambridge University Press, 2001), 205–233.

pessimism about human nature, however, in combination with the idealistic altruism of the Gospels, threatens to undermine the teleological underpinnings of the view. For if we suppose that our natural drives are ultimately a product of the divine plan, then the problem arises of why God would have created us with natures incapable of adhering to the moral standards he has revealed. The answer at this point turns on the doctrine of original sin. We were *not* created with such flawed natures, but rather given the knowledge and inclinations to pursue the good steadfastly. Still, we were also given free will, and when Adam and Eve freely chose evil, they and their descendants lost the inborn grace that would have allowed them to remain steadfast in the good. This idea runs through Augustine,[28] and appears in Anselm with the idea of the will's two affections, one for our own advantage, which is always with us, and another for justice, which we have lost due to original sin.[29] One finds it as well in Bernard of Clairvaux and in various scholastic sources, including this remarkable passage from Albert the Great:

> The love of concupiscence is due to nature, and is always curved into itself. Whatever it loves it twists back toward itself—that is, toward its own private good—and unless it is elevated above itself by sanctifying grace, everything that it loves it twists back toward its own good and loves on account of itself.[30]

---

28 For a concentrated statement of Augustine's views, see *The Punishment and Forgiveness of Sins and the Baptism of Little Ones* II.17.26, in *Works*, 1:23.

29 See *On the Fall of the Devil*, chaps. 12–14 and *De concordia* III.11–13, in *Basic Writings*, trans. T. Williams (Indianapolis: Hackett, 2007).

30 Albert the Great, *Summa theologiae* part II 4.14.4.2c, in *Opera omnia*, ed. P. Jammy (Lyon, 1651), 18:112b. See also Bernard of Clairvaux, *On Loving God*, trans. M. S. Burrows, in *Christian Spirituality: The Classics* (London: Routledge, 2009), chap. 9: "in the beginning man loves God, not for God's sake, but for his own." Bernard is cited at the end of the thirteenth century by James of Viterbo, *Quodlibet* II.20, who defends this sort of sharp demarcation between our natural inclinations and the inclinations we ought to have, which we can hope to attain only supernaturally, through God's grace. This view, in turn, is sharply criticized by James's contemporary, Godfrey of Fontaines, who seeks to hold together our natural teleology and our normative ends. Both sides of this exchange are translated in A. S. McGrade, John Kilcullen, and Matthew Kempshall, *The Cambridge Translations of Medieval Philosophical Texts*, vol. 2: *Ethics and Political Philosophy*

The difficulties that beset original sin and grace are obvious and notorious, but for now we need remark only on how such views pull ethics away from the teleological framework of antiquity. Our natural inclinations no longer provide a framework for establishing the good that we ought to seek. Indeed, the very question of what our true natures are becomes clouded over by the possibility of a punishment that infects our whole species.

Yet with the recovery of Aristotle's complete corpus in the thirteenth century, Christian philosophers in western Europe began to take seriously again the idea that we might be able to ground at least the fundamentals of ethical theory in eudaimonism. Aquinas is the leading example of this trend. Human beings have an ultimate end, their own happiness, that shapes all of our voluntary choices:

> The will naturally tends towards its ultimate end: for every human being naturally wills happiness (*beatitudo*). And this natural willing is the cause of all other willings, since whatever a human being wills, he wills for the sake of an end.[31]

For Aquinas, this thesis rests on more than simply the empirical observation of human self-interest. It rests instead on an intricate theory of rational choice that treats the will as essentially rational appetite, fixed by nature to desire the human good. The character of that good, in turn, is grasped by intellect, through reflection on the distinctive function of a human being, as a rational animal, in a world governed by divine providence. Human beings who correctly deliberate along these lines, and steadfastly choose in accord with those deliberations,

---

(Cambridge: Cambridge University Press, 2000). For a detailed discussion of these thirteenth-century debates, see Thomas Osborne, *Love of Self and Love of God in Thirteenth-Century Ethics* (Notre Dame, IN: University of Notre Dame Press, 2005).

[31] Thomas Aquinas, *Summa theologiae* 1a 60.2c.

will do both what is morally correct and what promotes their own self-interest.

Can a strictly eudaimonistic teleology along these lines account for the other-directed principles of the Gospels? An easy route to an affirmative answer begins by pointing out that our ultimate happiness in this context is the beatitude that comes from the reward of eternal life in heaven. If we have reason to think that following the teachings of the Gospel is the path that will earn this reward from God, then self-interest quite unproblematically yields a commitment to Christian ethics. This, however, by all accounts, is the wrong sort of commitment. God must be loved more than us, which precludes loving God (and God's commands) only as a means to our own happiness. Nor will it work to resolve, in light of this situation, that to get the result I need I must somehow habituate myself to love God more. That still puts one's love of God within the scope of a choice made for instrumental reasons. One's own flourishing, rather than God's, remains the ultimate end. And, indeed, how could it be otherwise, given the strictures of Aquinas's theory? For how could we truly, ultimately love God more than ourselves, if whatever we will, we will for the sake of our own happiness?

Aquinas's answer, which departs remarkably from the view of his teacher Albert the Great, is that we do so because we expand the boundaries of our self. Although it is an unshakeable principle that one's love, if it is to be the voluntary love of rational appetite, must be grounded in the pursuit of one's own happiness, this leaves room for an enlarged conception of the self. So Aquinas reasons as follows: "Angels and human beings naturally love themselves. But that which is one with something is that very thing. Hence anything loves that which is one with itself."[32] The task then becomes to identify the various forms of union that can serve as a ground of love, and Aquinas speaks of the

---

32 *Summa theologiae* 1a 60.4c.

union that arises through political community, friendship, family relations, and shared species membership. Sometimes he describes the cause of love in these sorts of cases as *similarity*,[33] which might give the unfortunate impression that we love others out of a kind of cognitive confusion: what we really love is ourselves, but others remind us of ourselves, and so our natural self-love accidentally spills over onto others. This is the sort of story that would later find a place in a theory, like David Hume's, that takes root in our nonrational passions. But Aquinas can hardly approve of will's rational appetite being grounded in our mistaking one thing for another. Rather, the point must be that in some very real way we *are* the same as other people.

Inasmuch as these forms of union obviously amount to less than full numerical unity, Aquinas allows that we love ourselves more than other people. In particular, he argues, the biblical injunction to love others "as ourselves" does not require that we love others as much as ourselves.[34] But what about cases—preeminently, the case of God—where we are required to love others *more* than ourselves? In explaining these sorts of cases Aquinas shifts over to a different sort of metaphysical relationship between ourselves and others, that of part to whole. Merely as a matter of self-interested prudence, one ought to be concerned about the whole community in which one lives, because "one's proper good cannot exist without the common good."[35] But this is of course the same sort of narrowly self-interested reasoning that Aquinas wants to transcend. So he needs a stronger claim, that putting the common good first is required by the same rational principles that ground the eudaimonistic framework. The hand naturally sacrifices itself to save the whole body; the citizen sacrifices himself for the republic; in general, "any part naturally loves the common good of the whole more

---

[33] See, e.g., *Summa theologiae* 1a2ae 27.3.
[34] See, e.g., *Summa theologiae* 1a 60.4 ad 2.
[35] *Summa theologiae* 2a2ae 47.10 ad 2.

than he loves his particular proper good."³⁶ And just as one cares about the republic as a whole, so one cares about the leader of that republic on whom its well-being relies. All the more, then, one will love God, and indeed will love God above all things: "because the universal good is God himself, and under this good is contained angels, human beings, and all creatures . . . , it follows that angels and human beings, even by their natural love, love God more and more principally than they love themselves."³⁷

In insisting that this love is *natural*, Aquinas means to reject explicitly those views that treat concern for others as grounded in a supernatural charity that transcends our natural moral inclinations. This would require treating our natural state as fundamentally flawed, whereas in fact "it is impossible for any natural inclination or love to be perverse."³⁸ But given the insistent rationalism of the theory, he can account for such apparent altruism only if he can square it with our overriding teleological commitments. He attempts to do so by insisting on the role played by the part-whole relationship. Where one stands to another as merely partially united, one's obligations are imperfect, as we have seen. But parts take their identity from the whole in a way that somehow makes their own good subservient to the good of the whole: "every part naturally loves the whole more than itself. And every individual naturally loves the good of its species more than the

---

36 *Summa theologiae* 2a2ae 26.3c. The idea that citizens will sacrifice themselves for the good of the commonwealth was an ethical commonplace of Aquinas's era, perhaps in part because of its prominent endorsement at John 15:13. See, for instance, Henry of Ghent's explanation for why this is morally right even for someone who has no hope of reward in the next life (*Quodlibetal Questions on Moral Problems*, trans. R. J. Teske [Milwaukee: Marquette University Press, 2005], XII.13). Aristotle had spoken approvingly of such a case at *Nicomachean Ethics* IX.8, 1169a25, though his rationale for such an action—one does it for a last great burst of glory—was so startlingly egoistic that even a devotee such as Aquinas seeks some other way to account for such cases. Compare Scotus, who denies that self-sacrifice for country can in any way be understood in terms of self-interest (*Ordinatio* III.27 nn. 48–50, in *Selected Writings on Ethics*, trans. T. Williams [Oxford: Oxford University Press, 2017], 171).

37 *Summa theologiae* 1a 60.5c.

38 *Quodlibet* I.4.3c.

good of itself as an individual."[39] This yields for Aquinas a startlingly strong form of altruism, but it has its limits. Although our concern for the human species should be greater than our concern for ourselves, we will have only an imperfect concern for the good of other species. And even in the case of God, quite remarkably, Aquinas makes clear that our self-transcending love for God comes not from some abstract fact about his goodness, but from God's relationship to us: "God will be, for any person, the whole rule of love (*ratio diligendi*) from the fact that God is the whole good for human beings. For if we suppose, *per impossibile*, that God were not the good for human beings, then he would not be the rule of love." [40] Aquinas thus gets the result that we should love God above all things, even above ourselves. But this holds only because of God's relationship to us.

Is this still eudaimonism? Aquinas is attempting to reconcile two doctrines that, perhaps, cannot be reconciled: the Aristotelian idea that our unique ultimate end is our own happiness, and the Christian ideal that we should love God above ourselves. Aquinas's strategy for reconciliation is to expand the self, but this finds little support in his metaphysics. Quite apart from what we might think of the idea that partial degrees of unity—e.g., sameness of species—can ground moral commitments, this claim faces the difficulty that Aquinas does not think members of the same species literally share any sort of universal form or property. Properties, for Aquinas, are particulars.[41] Nor does the shift from part to whole resonate with Aquinas's larger theory. We might expect the hand to look out for the whole animal, because the animal is the complete substance, and substances are what have the

---

39 *Summa theologiae* 1a 60.5 ad 1.

40 *Summa theologiae* 2a2ae 26.13 ad 3. For illuminating discussions of the relationship between self-interest and morality in Aquinas, see Scott MacDonald, "Egoistic Rationalism: Aquinas's Basis for Christian Morality," in *Christian Theism and the Problems of Philosophy*, ed. M. Beaty (Notre Dame, IN: University of Notre Dame Press, 1990), 327–354, and David Gallagher, "Thomas Aquinas on Self-Love as the Basis for Love of Others," *Acta Philosophica* 8 (1999): 23–44.

41 See, e.g., *De ente et essentia* 3.80–82: "no commonness is found in Socrates; rather, whatever is in him has been individuated."

most fundamental claim to existence within Aquinas's system. But a species has no such primacy, relative to individual members of the species, nor does the universe as a whole. It is appealing, from an intuitive moral point of view, to think that we might put the good of the universe ahead of our own good, and so love above all else the creator of that universe. But this does not seem to be a conclusion that can be credibly derived from Aquinas's form of eudaimonism.

It should be no surprise, then, that the major rivals to Thomism in later scholastic thought introduce dramatic changes to the Aristotelian framework. If we consider, first, Scotus, we find a kind of minimal intervention in eudaimonism that, by making a change at the teleological foundations, leads to a dramatically different kind of ethical theory. The change Scotus makes is to embrace Anselm's dual affections of the will, but with the affection for justice now understood as something innate within the will rather than as a contingent gift of grace. The result is that whereas Aquinas treats the will as necessarily aimed at the unique final end of happiness, Scotus sees the will as free to choose between unconstrained self-interest (arising from the will's "affection for advantage") and the moral law (arising from the will's "affection for justice"). It is natural here to understand Scotus as doubling the sort of teleological framework one finds in Aquinas, so that the will must choose between two ends, self-interest and justice. But this overstates the difference between their views. Scotus accepts that the will always chooses under the aspect of its own happiness—this remains, on his theory, our ultimate end, and so to that extent the view remains fundamentally eudaimonistic.[42] Accordingly, he does not describe the will's affection for justice as inclining the will toward a distinct end—as if

---

42 See John Duns Scotus, *Ordinatio* II.6.2 nn. 61–62 (*Selected Writings on Ethics*, 118), where "the good angels were neither able nor willing to nill happiness for themselves." For the picture of the two affections as offering us a choice between two teleological ends, see, e.g., Calvin G. Normore, "Picking and Choosing: Anselm and Ockham on Choice," *Vivarium* 36 (1998): 23–39. For Scotus's theory as starkly antieudaimonistic, see, among others, Thomas Williams, "From Metaethics to Action Theory," in *The Cambridge Companion to Duns Scotus*, ed. T. Williams, 332–351 (Cambridge: Cambridge University Press, 2003), and Irwin, *Development of Ethics*, vol. 1, §25.

one affection pulls the will toward the good even while another affection pulls it toward its own selfish pleasure. Rather, Scotus repeatedly describes the affection for justice as a power to "moderate" our desire for happiness.[43] Its function is not to allow us to choose something other than our own happiness—this is a choice we could not make—but to ensure that we pursue happiness in the right way. The inclination toward justice thus serves as a kind of side-constraint, a concern for the moral law that motivates us to put boundaries around our pursuit of self-interest.[44]

Such boundaries are necessary, Scotus thinks, because our will to happiness, left unchecked, wills immoderately to maximize every sort of self-advantage that it encounters: "its act could not be moderated so as not to be elicited to the maximal extent that it could be elicited."[45] This sort of unfettered teleological drive toward advantage is fine for other animals, but for us it leads to sin, because it causes us to will in ways that ignore the moral law. Here the difference with Aquinas is instructive. When Aquinas insists that we will everything for the sake of happiness, he counts on a rational agent's ability to weigh greater and lesser, proximate and remote, part and whole, and arrive in the end at the ultimate good that is God. From this perspective, Scotus's worry about unfettered maximization seems misplaced, because it ignores the very sort of ability to reason toward the correct ultimate end that lies at the core of a eudaimonistic ethics. But Scotus, like Albert the Great, does not think that even the most enlightened self-interest will

---

[43] See *Ordinatio* II.6.2 nn. 49–62, in *Selected Writings on Ethics*, 114–118.

[44] For a reading of Scotus that, like mine, stresses that the affection for justice is not simply a second countervailing impulse, see Peter King, "Scotus's Rejection of Anselm: The Two-Wills Theory," in *John Duns Scotus, 1308–2008: Investigations into His Philosophy*, ed. L. Honnefelder et al., 359–378 (Münster: Aschendorff, 2011). But King, it seems to me, goes too far in claiming that the affection for justice "has no motivational force whatsoever" (376). Although its role is only to moderate the desire for happiness, still it exercises that influence out of a love for something else, justice. (But justice, so understood, is not an end that competes with the end of happiness.) Hence Scotus argues that the perfection we receive from the infused virtue of charity is a perfection to *the affection for justice* (see *Ordinatio* III.27 n. 17, in *Selected Writings on Ethics*, 163).

[45] *Ordinatio* II.6.2 n. 56, in *Selected Writings on Ethics*, 116.

lead us to put God's end truly above our own. Hence there has to be some other motivation at work within the will. For Albert, as with most earlier medieval authors, that motivation is supplied by the grace of God. What is distinctive about Scotus is that he identifies it as a natural inclination.

In turning Anselm's affection for justice into one of the will's natural capacities, Scotus shares Aquinas's ethical naturalism. But because he does not accept Aquinas's strategies for expanding the scope of self-interest, he cannot ground this affection in any sort of connection to ourselves. Explicitly considering Aquinas's impossible counterfactual scenario involving a God who is disengaged from humanity, Scotus reaches a different conclusion: that the act of loving God above all else "is not desiring a good for the one loving insofar as it is advantageous for the one loving; instead, its act is tending toward the object for its own sake, even if *per impossibile* its advantageousness for the one loving were ruled out."[46] Where self-interest clashes with rules that dictate loving and obeying God, the will faces an open choice between two rival inclinations.

For a medieval view that, rather than constrain our teleological orientation, seeks to eliminate it entirely, one needs to look a generation later, to William Ockham. He denies the foundational Aristotelian doctrine that there must be a single ultimate end at which all actions are directed, and he further denies the Aquinian view that beings are aimed at the good of the universe more than their own good.[47] This is not to deny that we do have an ultimate end, and that ours is happiness. In this minimal sense, even Ockham subscribes to eudaimonism, but this is a thin sense indeed. As we saw earlier, Ockham allows that agents can set ends, and he thinks we should take it on faith that God has created us in order to be happy in heaven with him for all eternity.

---

46 *Ordinatio* III.27 n. 16, in *Selected Writings on Ethics*, 163.
47 For both claims, see Ockham, *Quodlibetal Questions* IV.2, in *Opera theologica*, vol. 9, lines 165–178 and 122–128.

But he does not think we can establish through natural reason that this has in fact been established as our end.[48] Moreover, even granted that this is the divinely established end of human life, it does not follow that the human will has any such natural inclination toward happiness. Because of the will's radical autonomy, he denies that it has any natural inclination at all, and so "the will is not naturally inclined to its ultimate end."[49] Accordingly, the will can make choices that go against its own happiness, even its own recognized happiness, which is to say that the will can choose contrary to the dictates of its own intellect.[50]

Do these conclusions mire Ockham's ethics in irrationality? On the contrary, the foundations of his ethics are, if anything, *more* rooted in reason than is the prior eudaimonistic tradition. After all, there is nothing especially *rational* about the pursuit of one's own happiness, as opposed to anyone else's happiness. In the eudaimonistic tradition, this is taken simply as an obvious fact about us as beings of nature. Moreover, Ockham adheres to the traditional characterization of morally good action as action in accord with right reason. But, like Scotus, he takes moral reasoning to be grounded not in enlightened self-interest, but rather in recognizing the existence of a perfectly good being whom we should love above all else, and whose commands we should follow. Reason, Ockham argues, can establish the rightness of all this.[51] Where Ockham's view diverges even from Scotus's is in refusing to postulate an innate volitional inclination to adhere to reason, or

---

48 *Reportatio* IV.16, in *Opera theologica*, 7:346.

49 *Ordinatio* I.1.6, in *Opera theologica*, 1:507.

50 In *Ordinatio* I.1.6, Ockham describes various limited scenarios under which the will can choose against its own happiness. The full radicalness of his view emerges only at *Reportatio* IV.16 (in *Opera theologica*, 7:350), where he maintains that "with the intellect's judging that this is the ultimate end, the will can nill that end"—not because of some special circumstance, but just because the will has the power to nill whatever it can will. More generally, "the will can be moved against the judgment of reason" (doubt 2 at *Opera theologica*, 7:354, with concessive response at 7:357–358), and can will something bad even without its having any appearance of being good (*Quaestiones variae* 8, in *Opera theologica*, 8:442–445).

51 On the rational foundations of Ockham's moral theory, see Marilyn McCord Adams, "The Structure of Ockham's Morality," *Franciscan Studies* 46 (1986): 23–24.

to justice, or to anything at all. The will is radically open in its choices. This means that there is no internal link between moral goodness and desirability. Perhaps for the first time in the history of ethics, the good becomes choice-worthy for purely external reasons: simply because it *is* good, independently of any benefit it might have for the agent, or any natural inclination the agent might have to prefer it. This is precisely the result Ockham is after: by abandoning teleology even here, Ockham makes morality *wholly* the responsibility of the free agent who chooses, or fails to choose, to be motivated by the good.

Acknowledgments

Thanks for their help to Fouad Ben Ahmed, Tomas Ekenberg, Mitzi Lee, and particularly to Jeff McDonough and the other participants in a Radcliffe teleology conference

Reflection II

TELEOLOGY IN CIMABUE'S APOCALYPSE MURALS AT ASSISI

Holly Flora

Christian theology views the life and death of Christ as the means by which the world will be purged from evil and Christians will receive salvation. This teleology is interpreted uniquely in a cycle of murals illustrating the Apocalypse in the Upper Basilica of San Francesco at Assisi, painted circa 1280 by the Florentine painter Cimabue (ca. 1240–1302). In this chapter, I argue that Cimabue and his Franciscan patrons offered an atypically hopeful view of the end of time in which humans, including Francis and his friars, play a key role in determining the outcome of the salvation process.

In the south transept of the Upper Basilica, Cimabue painted scenes from the Apocalypse (or Revelation), the final book of the Bible in which John the Evangelist recounts his vision of the end of the world. Interest in this eschatology was on the rise in Europe in the thirteenth century, in part because of the controversial prophecies of Joachim of Fiore. Joachim was a Cistercian monk whose twelfth-century commentaries on the book of Revelation declared that a "third age," predicted to begin in 1260, would render the church obsolete. Despite the condemnation of Joachim's prophecies as heretical in 1263, some continued to interpret the rise of the mendicant orders, including the Franciscans, as a sign of this third age.[1]

Exegetes had long explained the allegorical imagery of the Apocalypse in terms of Christ's Incarnation, stating that Christ would return at the end of time to redeem humankind. Building on some of these ideas, the Franciscans invoked the Apocalypse in their celebration of Francis, who was so piously identified with Christ that he received the stigmata, the wounds of Christ, imprinted in his flesh. Cimabue's mural cycle aims to tie Christ's death on the cross to the visionary events from John's text; the human Christ and, by association, Saint Francis, a human, become the efficient causes of the happy ending of the story of humankind.

Cimabue's apocalyptic murals begin with an image of John's first vision, the *Adoration of the Lamb* (Figure 1). John describes seeing "one seated" on a throne in heaven, holding a book with seven seals and surrounded by twenty-four elders and angels. Around the throne he sees four living creatures, the man, ox, lion, and eagle of Ezekiel's vision (Ez. 4:3–8). A lamb with "seven eyes and seven horns" opens the book's seals to set in motion the apocalyptic events. Two key details from the text are collapsed in Cimabue's painting: the lamb is on the throne, implying the incarnational unity of God, the "one," and Christ, the sacrificial lamb of God according to Christian exegetes. Stretched out on the throne with its head turned to the left toward the Crucifixion scene on the adjacent wall (Figure 2), the lamb visually connects apocalyptic glory with the human sacrifice and suffering of Christ. Such an association would be particularly appropriate because the friars celebrated Mass, a reenactment of Christ's sacrifice, in front of the murals.

---

[1] David Burr, "Franciscan Exegesis and Francis as Apocalyptic Figure," *Sewanee Medieval Studies* 4 (1989): 51–62.

FIGURE 1

In their emphasis on Christ's humanity, the Franciscans subscribed to a nuanced view of Christian teleology. They were leading proponents of the notion of the primacy of Christ—that is, the idea that God's taking human form was predestined from the beginning of time, not contingent on the Fall of mankind.[2]

---

2 Elia Delio, "Revisiting the Franciscan Doctrine of Christ," *Theological Studies* 64 (2003): 3–23.

FIGURE 2

The teleological outcome of Christ's Incarnation is therefore not just salvation from damnation, but the forging of a direct, sympathetic connection between humanity and God. The foremost Franciscan theologian of the period, Bonaventure, asserted that God had planned to take on the actual, physical form of humanity and experience humanity's suffering even before humankind's relationship to God was ruptured by the Fall.[3]

The Franciscan emphasis on Christ's suffering can therefore be further connected to apocalyptic interpretations of Francis's stigmata. Francis meditated on Christ's suffering and imitated Christ's piety so intently that he became marked with the wounds

---

3 Bonaventure, *Breviloquium*, trans. Dominic Monti (New York: Franciscan Institute, 2005), 160.

FIGURE 3

Christ received on the cross. Bonaventure's *Life of Saint Francis*, made the official biography of the saint in 1266, compares the stigmata, the physical signature of God, to the seals that are opened as the apocalyptic vision unfolds.[4] For a Christian, then, devotion

---

4 Bonaventure, "Legenda maior," in *Francis of Assisi: Early Documents*, ed. and trans. Regis J. Armstrong, William J. Short, and J. A. Wayne Hellman (New York: New City Press, 2000), 527.

FIGURE 4

to Francis, the highest model of the *imitatio Christi*, becomes a pathway to salvation.

To further illustrate this teleology, Cimabue includes an image of *Christ in Glory with Seven Angels* in which Franciscan friars help to set in motion the final conquest of evil during the Apocalypse (Figure 3). Here, Cimabue depicts Christ in a traditional almond-shaped aura of light (a mandorla) surrounded by seven angels. He hovers above an altar as an eighth angel swings a censer below it. An entirely novel addition on Cimabue's part, Franciscan friars are shown kneeling in the foreground. It is their prayers that lead to the destruction of evil and triumph of good. Again, humans become the efficient cause of the ordained outcome of the story.

This victory is depicted in the adjacent *Fall of Babylon* scene on the southwest wall (Figure 4). Here, a crenellated wall encloses tumbling towers and houses infested with snakes, demons, monkeys, apes, and an ostrich—signs of evil for medieval viewers. To the right, a group of devils enter the city while citizens flee on the left. Although the evil city is destroyed, the innocent citizens of Babylon escape. This ending to the Apocalypse cycle at Assisi is therefore extraordinarily hopeful in its approach.[5] The *Fall of Babylon* is the most violent episode represented; signs of the end of time from the text such as the moon turning to blood or the plagues, seen typically in Apocalypse imagery of this period, are not shown. Instead, the clear path to salvation—the human, crucified Christ, as promoted by Saint Francis and his friars, also humans—is emphasized. The unusual emphasis on humanity as a goal-directed efficient cause in the mural cycle can be explained in light of the Franciscan promotion of both Francis himself and the order as a whole. Francis's deeply spiritual humanity, combined with the prayers of the friars, is presented as the means to the Apocalypse's happy ending.

---

[5] For related discussion of this image, see Chiara Frugoni, *Quale Francesco? Il messagio nascosto negli affreschi della Basilica Superiore ad Assisi* (Turin: Einaudi, 2015), 126.

CHAPTER FIVE

Teleology in Jewish Philosophy

EARLY TALMUDISTS TO SPINOZA

Yitzhak Y. Melamed

Medieval and early modern Jewish philosophers developed their thinking in conversation with various bodies of literature. The influence of ancient Greek—primarily Aristotle (and pseudo-Aristotle)—and Arabic sources was fundamental to the very constitution of medieval Jewish philosophical discourse. Toward the late Middle Ages, Jewish philosophers also established a critical dialogue with Christian scholastics. In addition to these philosophical corpora, Jewish philosophers drew significantly upon rabbinic sources (Talmud and the numerous Midrashim) and the Hebrew Bible.

In order to clarify the unique as well as shared elements in the thought of medieval Jewish philosophers, I will begin this chapter with a brief study of some early rabbinic sources on the purpose of the world, i.e., why it came to be and why it is sustained in existence. In the second section of this chapter, I will study Maimonides's critique of the veracity and usefulness of the belief in (anthropocentric) teleology, and the critical reception of his views by later philosophers. The third section will address discussions of divine teleology in Kabbalistic literature. The exposition will concentrate mostly on a specific early eighteenth-century text that is one of the most lucid and rigorous presentations of Lurianic Kabbalah. The fourth and final section will elucidate Spinoza's critique of teleology, its precise target and scope, and its debt to earlier sources discussed in this chapter.

5.1. Early Rabbinic Sources on the Purpose of the World

Rabbinic Judaism never developed a definitive theology.[1] Consequently, it is quite common to find within this literature widely diverse and even opposed views on many theological issues. The question of the purpose of the universe (if it has any) is no exception. The following discussion is not meant to be a comprehensive presentation (and given the space limit of this chapter, cannot be), but merely an illustration of *some* tendencies within this literature.

The Babylonian Talmud, *Tractate Shabbath*, records the following saying in the name Reish Lakish (a leading third-century CE Palestinian Talmudist) and R. Yehuda, the Prince (~137–~220 CE), the compiler of the Mishnah:

---

[1] The most significant attempt to establish Jewish principles of faith was carried out by Maimonides in his "Preface to Chapter *Heleq*" and the thirteen principles delineated therein. The two most salient features of this attempt were its popular nature (i.e., it was meant to be propagated among the masses) and its colossal failure (these principles were accepted by some, explicitly rejected by many, and radically reinterpreted by others). With regard to the first feature I would only note that a common joke among Maimonides scholars is that the real question regarding these principles is whether Maimonides believed in seven or only six of his thirteen principles. Leon Roth once quipped that "dogmalessness [is] the only dogma in Judaism." I would doubt even that.

Reish Lakish said in the name of R. Yehuda, the Prince: "The world endures only for the sake of the breath [הבל פיהם] of school children."[2]

Upon hearing this saying cited, a later Talmudist objected to his colleague, "But what about mine and yours?" i.e., does not *our* study provide sufficient reason for the world's endurance? His colleague retorted: "Breath in which there is sin is not like breath in which there is not sin."[3] The later Talmudist stresses the absence of sin as the reason for singling out the study of *children* as the aim of the universe, though one may well suggest alternative explanations, such as the formative role of rudimentary schoolchildren's study. A world without top scholars may still generate such scholars in a generation or two, while a world without the basic foundations of intellectual endeavor (the "breath of school children") is likely to suffer an irrevocable loss.

An alternative explanation of the purpose of the world's endurance appears in another Talmudic passage:

Rav Yehuda said in the name of Rav: "Everyday a Heavenly Voice is heard declaring: 'The whole world draws its sustenance because [of the merit] of Hanina, my son, and Hanina my son suffices himself with a *kab* of carobs from one Sabbath eve to another.'"[4]

Hanina, the son of Dosa, was a destitute early Talmudist, known for his selfless care for others. For his weekly sustenance he needed no more than a *kab* (an ancient unit of volume, less than a third of gallon) of carobs. Thus, Rav Yehuda's statement amounts to a paradox: the

---

2 *Babylonian Talmud*, ed. I. Epstein (London: Soncino Press, 1952–), *Tractate Shabbath*, 119b. "Breath" (*Hevel*) here also means the *words* pronounced by schoolchildren.
3 Babylonian Talmud, *Tractate Shabbath*, 119b. Hasdai Crescas, *Or ha-Shem* [Heb.: *Light of the Lord*], ed. Shlomo Fisher (Jerusalem: Ramot, 1990, II 6 1 (p. 245 in this edition), for an interesting gloss on the last saying.
4 Babylonian Talmud, *Tractate Ta'anit* 24b. Cf. Babylonian Talmud, *Tractate Berakhot*, 33a.

entire universe endures for the sake of a person who needs virtually nothing. A reader who wonders about the disproportionality of the means (the sustenance of the entire universe) and the end (the sustenance of the meritorious Hanina) might expect to find partial relief in a third source, an apparent corrective of the unreasonable mismatch between means and end:

> Rav said: The world was created only for Ahab, the son of Omri, and for R. Hanina, the son of Dosa. For Ahab the son of Omri *this* world, and for R. Hanina, the son Dosa, *the future* world.[5]

Notice that this passage, just like the previous one, is cited in the name of Rav.[6] Whereas the previous passage wonders about the disproportionality of sustaining the entire world for the sake of the poor and righteous Hanina, the current passage severs any connection between our world ("this world") and Hanina. Rather than being sustained for the sake of the poor and righteous Hanina, the son of Dosa, it turns out that our world was created, *ab initio*, for the sake of the wicked and rich king Ahab, the son of Omri. Indeed, the needs of a rich and wicked king seem to be extensive, and thus provide a far better explanation for the existence of the world than the meager needs of Hanina. Still, the last passage exposes an urgent and disturbing question: if the best explanation for the purpose of the creation of this world is to benefit the wicked Ahab, then why create this world at all? The author of the saying leaves the question unanswered.

Early rabbinic sources questioned the aims of the universe and came up with a variety of answers (some of which may well appear to us surprising). Perhaps one reason for this open exploration was a common tendency among Talmudists to reject the identification of the *natural* with the *good* (an identification which they associated with Hellenistic

---

5 Babylonian Talmud, *Tractate Berakhot*, 61b. Italics added.
6 Rav was an early third-century CE Babylonian Talmudist.

thought).⁷ Thus, in one striking Midrash the Roman governor of Judea, Quintus Tineius Rufus, asks Rabbi Akiva whether the deeds of men are better than the deeds of God (i.e., nature). Rabbi Akiva, realizing that Tineius Rufus is really asking about the justification for circumcision, openly proclaims that the deeds of men *are* better insofar as they are able to correct and improve nature.⁸ For Rabbi Akiva, the fact that naturally men are created uncircumcised does not provide even the slightest justification for preferring that state: what is or is not natural has nothing to do with value.

5.2. Maimonides's Critique of Teleology

Demonstrating the cunning of divine wisdom in creation has been a common topos in medieval Jewish philosophy.⁹ Most medieval philosophers endorsed the claim that the final cause is the noblest of the four Aristotelean causes.¹⁰ Still, as we will shortly see, Maimonides—by far the most influential medieval Jewish philosopher—was reluctant to employ teleological reasoning in attempting to explain the world's existence.

Saadia Gaon, an early tenth-century Babylonian rabbi, grammarian, and poet, was also the author of what could be considered the first major work of medieval Jewish philosophy, *The Book of Beliefs and Opinions*. Addressing the issue of the aim of creation, Saadia writes:

---

7 See *Midrash Rabbah im kol ha-Mefarshim*, 2 vols. (Jerusalem, n.d.) (Bereshit, XI 6).

8 *Midrash Tanhuma* (Warsaw: Y.G. Munk Press), 187.3 (Tazria V, pp. 19a–b).

9 See, for example, Judah Halevi, *The Kuzari*, trans. Hartwig Hirschfeld, revised by Lisa Greenwald (Jerusalem: Sefer ve-Sefel Publishing, 2003), III 11 (pp. 127 and 131 in Hirschfeld's translation) and V 10 (pp. 236–237 in Hirschfeld). Halevi, however, notes that "we may not be aware of the use of most" things in nature (*Kuzari*, V 10 [p. 236 in Hirschfeld]).

10 See, for example, Moses Maimonides, *Guide of the Perplexed*, trans. Shlomo Pines [henceforth: Pines], 2 vols. (Chicago: University of Chicago Press, 1963), III 13 (Pines 449) and Crescas, *Or ha-Shem*, II 6 (p. 226 in Fisher's edition). Avicenna, Averroës, and Aquinas endorsed this claim as well. See Robert Pasnau's contribution to this volume; Jeffrey K. McDonough, "The Heyday of Teleology and Early Modern Philosophy," *Midwest Studies in Philosophy* 35 (2011): 184; and Stephan Schmid, "Finality without Final Causes? Suárez's Account of Natural Teleology," *Ergo* 2 (2015): 396.

Even though creatures are many in number, nevertheless we need not be confused in regard to which constitutes the goal of creation.... When we find the earth in the center of the heaven with the heavenly spheres surrounding it on all sides, it becomes clear to us that the thing which was the object of creation must be on the earth. Upon further investigation of all [of the world's] parts we note that the earth and water are both inanimate, whereas we find that beasts are irrational. *Hence only man is left, which gives us the certainty that he must unquestionably have been the intended purpose of creation.*[11]

Judah Halevi, an early twelfth-century Spanish philosopher and physician, and an astounding poet, also argued that "it is clear that domestic animals were created for the benefit of man"[12] and that "the world was but completed with the creation of man who forms the heart of all that was created before him."[13] Anthropocentric teleology which suggests that the world was created for the sake of man is also present in the early writings of Moses Maimonides (1135 (1138?)–1204).[14] Thus, in the preface to his *Commentary on the Mishnah*, written in his twenties, Maimonides notes: "The purpose of the world and everything that is in it, is just: a wise and good individual man."[15] Maimonides's views on this issue will change dramatically. In the twenty-fifth chapter of the

---

11 Saadia Gaon, *The Book of Beliefs & Opinions*, trans. Samuel Rosenblatt (New Haven, CT: Yale University Press, 1948), Treatise IV, Exordium (pp. 180–181 in Rosenblatt's translation); Saadia Gaon, *Emunot ve-Deot*, translated into Hebrew by Judah Ibn Tibbon (Constantinople, 1562), 42a–b. Italics added.
12 Halevi, *Kuzari*, V 8 (p. 231 in Hirschfeld).
13 Halevi, *Kuzari*, IV 15 (p. 201 in Hirschfeld). For Crescas too the purpose of the material world is the human race. See Crescas, *Or ha-Shem*, II 6 3 (p. 265 in Fisher's edition).
14 For anthropocentric teleology in Aristotle, see *Politics* 1256b11–21 and Rich Cameron, "Aristotle's Teleology," *Philosophy Compass* 5, no. 12 (2010): 1104. The latter text also addresses the Stoic endorsement of anthropocentric teleology. For early modern defenses of divinely ordained anthropocentric teleology, see Jeffrey McDonough's discussion of Robert Boyle in his contribution to the current volume.
15 Maimonides, *Haqdamot le-Perush ha-Mishnah* [*Prefaces to the Commentary on the Mishnah*] (Jerusalem: Mossad ha-Rav Kuk, 1961), 77. Cf. 79–81 and Warren Zev Harvey, "Spinoza and Maimonides on Teleology and Anthropocentrism," in *Spinoza's "Ethics": A Critical Guide*, ed. Yitzhak Y. Melamed (Cambridge: Cambridge University Press, 2017), 54.

third and last part of his philosophical magnum opus, the *Guide of the Perplexed*—composed in his fifties—Maimonides writes:

> Know that the majority of the false imaginings that call forth perplexity in the quest for the end of the existence of the world as a whole or the end of every part of it have as their root *an error of man about himself and his imagining that all that exists exists because of himself alone*.[16]

The mature Maimonides clearly rejected global anthropocentric teleology (i.e., the view that man is the end of everything that is), and the elucidation of this misconception was highly significant for his conception of God and the proper role of religion. Still, even *after* the disqualification of anthropocentric teleology, the question of the aim of reality was far from settled. In the lines that follow the passage just quoted, Maimonides hints at a certain principle of plenitude according to which what was "primarily intended" in creation is "the bringing into being of everything whose existence is possible, existence being indubitably good."[17] Maimonides does not elaborate on, or motivate, the claim that existence is "indubitably good," and notably, in *Guide* III 13, the main locus of his discussion of the purpose of reality, Maimonides does not even mention plenitude and the goodness of existence as possible explanantia of reality.

Guide III 13 begins with the following announcement:

---

16 Moses Maimonides, *Moreh Newokhim* [Heb.: *Guide of the Perplexed*], trans. Shmuel Ibn Tibbon with commentaries by Efodi, Shem Tov, Asher Crescas, and Yitzhak Abravanel (Jerusalem, 1960), III 25; Maimonides, *Guide of the Perplexed* (Pines 452): "It should not be believed that all the beings exist for the sake of the existence of man. On the contrary, *all the other beings too have been intended for their own sakes and not for the sake of something else*." Italics added. Cf. Harvey, "Spinoza and Maimonides," 46–47. Harry Austryn Wolfson, *The Philosophy of Spinoza: Unfolding the Latent Process of His Reasoning*, 2 vols. (Cambridge, MA: Harvard University Press, 1934), 2:426, suggests that Maimonides's critique of anthropocentrism is directed, at least in part, against Saadia.

17 *Guide* III 25; Pines 506. Italics added.

> Often the minds of perfect men have grown perplexed over the question of what is the final end of that which exists. Now I will explain that in all schools this question is abolished.[18]

By "all schools" Maimonides refers here to both those who believe in the eternity of the world (e.g., Aristotle), and those who assert that the world was created in time. The primary aim of *Guide* III 13 is to show that according to *both* schools the question about the ultimate end of reality as a whole makes hardly any sense.[19] Maimonides begins his argument by pointing out a few crucial premises which he believes are "clear" and "not in need of demonstration." In order to analyze this crucial passage, I have parsed it into five sections, designated by roman numerals.

> I say then that (i) in the case of every agent who acts with a purpose, the thing he has done must necessarily have some end with a view to which it has been done. According to philosophic speculation, this is clear and is not in need of demonstration. (ii) It is also clear that a thing that has been done in this way with a purpose must have been produced in time after not having existed. (iii) Among the things that are clear also belongs the fact, and this fact universally admitted, that He whose existence is necessary, who has never and will never be nonexistent, does not need an agent, as we have already made clear. (iv) And as He has not been made, no question as to the final end arises with reference to Him. For this reason, one does not ask: What is the final end of the existence of the Creator, may He be exalted?; for He is not a created thing. (v) Through these premises it has become clear that a final end can only be sought with regard to

---

18 *Guide* III 13; Pines 448.
19 In his canonical commentary on the *Guide* of the late fifteenth century, Shem Tov ibn Shem Tov argues that another major aim of *Guide* III 13 is to show that "man is not the aim of reality as it is thought [שאין האדם תכלית המציאות כמו שיחשבו]" (Maimonides, *Moreh Newokhim*, part 3, p. 16b).

all things produced in time that have been made through the purpose of an intelligent being. I mean to say that with regard to that which has its beginning in an intellect, one necessarily must seek to find out what its final cause is. On the other hand, one must not, as we have said, seek the final end of what has not been produced in time.[20]

Section (i) seems to make a relatively weak and uncontroversial claim,[21] and so we will not dwell on it. Section (ii) asserts the far stronger and nontrivial claim according to which aim-directed action can take place (a) only in time, and (b) only if the aimed-for state does not exist yet at the time of the action. Both (a) and (b) can be challenged. We may challenge (a) by arguing that *if* one can make sense of actions that are not in time, then we should also be able to conceive of such actions as being aim-directed. In other worlds, the issue here seems to be the possibility of nontemporal action, and this question is orthogonal to the question of the aim-directedness of the action. Point (b) might be challenged by noting that preserving the *current* state of things seems to be an aim just as good as any other one.[22] Section (iii) makes the valid argument that God whose essence *is* existence requires no agent or cause to bring him into existence.[23] From (ii) and (iii) Maimonides infers, in (iv), that insofar as God has not been produced, it is pointless to ask about the aim of God's existence since there is no final end for his existence. In section (v), Maimonides apparently attempts to infer a more general principle from (iv), namely, that one should seek an end for the existence of a thing *if and only if* the thing has been

---

20 Maimonides, *Guide* III 13; Pines 451–452.
21 Unless one reads (i) as stating that all teleology is thoughtful ("have some end with a *view* to which it has been done"). I do not think such a reading is warranted.
22 Obviously, both of these objections are just first moves in debates that require further scrutiny. See the commentary of Shem Tov ibn Shem Tov (Maimonides, *Moreh Newokhim*, part 3, p. 17a) for an attempt to answer the challenge to (b).
23 See Maimonides, *Guide* I 61; Pines 148. Cf. Yitzhak Y. Melamed, "Spinoza's Deification of Existence," *Oxford Studies in Early Modern Philosophy* 6 (2012): 77–84.

produced in time by an intelligent being. The last claim is incompatible with Aristotle's natural, thoughtless teleology (i.e., teleology in plants and the organization of animal limbs that is not guided by a plan of an intelligent creator). The biconditional stated in (v) does not follow from (ii), and as we have already noted, the premises asserted in (ii) are questionable.

Why does Maimonides disregard—indeed deny—the possibility of natural, thoughtless teleology? As we have seen earlier in this book, one strand in Aristotle's discussion of teleological principles in nature (such as "Nature does nothing in vain") suggests that—as a heuristic device—we may conceptualize nature "as an intelligent, creative designer."[24] Maimonides (and virtually almost all medieval philosophers)[25] was reluctant to follow Aristotle on this point, and he seems to have had good reasons for this. If nature is *not* itself an intelligent, creative designer, then what is the point of (mis)conceiving nature as if there were one?[26]

From the premises laid out in the passage I have quoted, Maimonides infers that those—like Aristotle—who believe in the eternity of the world should not seek the ultimate end of reality. Since only things produced in time have ends, and the world is eternal (i.e., has not been produced in time), it is clear that the world has no end.

> For according to Aristotle's opinion, it is not permitted to ask: what is the final end of the existence of the heavens? ... Or What is the final end of this particular species of animals or plants? For all things

---

[24] See Leunissen's contribution to this volume: "Teleology in Aristotle," section 2.5. Cf. Mariska Leunissen, *Explanation and Teleology in Aristotle's Science of Nature* (Cambridge: Cambridge University Press, 2010), 119–121. Some commentators suggest that Aristotle's entire theory of teleology is nothing but a heuristic device (see Leunissen, *Explanation and Teleology*, 23 n. 35 and 112 n. 1).

[25] For a helpful discussion of Aquinas on the same issue, see Robert Pasnau's contribution to this volume.

[26] Thoughtless teleology that is *not* suggested as a heuristic device would most likely appear to Maimonides as a belief in an eerie magic, or miracle, that is not befitting a philosopher like Aristotle.

derive, according to him, from an eternal necessity that has never ceased and will never cease.[27]

In fact, claims Maimonides, Aristotle's willingness to accept teleology among species, so that one species exists for the sake of another, undermines the belief in the eternity of species and provides "one of the strongest proofs for the production of the world in time."[28] Insofar as "purpose can only be conceived with reference to the production in time," it would make no sense to speak about the purpose of species, or reality as a whole, if either was eternal.[29]

Maimonides has no qualms about what he calls "first finality," i.e., the view that "the end of every individual produced in time consists in the perfection of the form of the species."[30] However, since both the world (for Aristotle), and God (for Maimonides and Aristotle) have not been produced in time, the search for the purposes of their existence is futile, as they have none.[31] Notice that, at least in the case of God, it is even improper to say that God's existence is the final end *of itself*. For Maimonides, God exists for the sake of no end.

Turning next to the school of those who assert that the world was created in time, Maimonides notes:

> It is sometimes thought that, according to our opinion and our doctrine of the production in time of the world as a whole after nonexistence . . . it is obligatory to seek out the finality of all that exists. It is likewise thought that the finality of all that exists is solely the existence of the human species so that it should worship God.[32]

---

27 See Maimonides, *Guide* III 13; Pines 449. In Spinoza we will encounter again the claim that eternal necessity does not allow for teleology.
28 See Maimonides, *Guide* III 13; Pines 449.
29 See Maimonides, *Guide* III 13; Pines 449.
30 See Maimonides, *Guide* III 13; Pines 450.
31 Or, as Shem Tov ibn Shem Tov notes: "seeking the purpose for that which has no purpose is complete folly" (Maimonides, *Moreh Newokhim*, part 3, p. 16b).
32 Maimonides, *Guide* III 13; Pines 450–451.

To begin undermining the belief in global anthropocentric teleology, Maimonides asks whether God could not have created humanity without creating all other creatures.[33] If one were to insist that every single feature of reality was necessary for the creation of man, we should—Maimonides argues—question the alleged aim of the creation of humanity, i.e., the worship of God. Clearly, God would not acquire any greater perfection by human worship.[34] Hence, human worship of God must aim at the perfection of humanity, rather than the perfection of God. Still, Maimonides asks:

> What is the final end of our existence with that perfection? Necessarily and obligatorily the argument must end with the answer being given that the final end is: God has wished it so, or: His wisdom has required this to be so. And this is the correct answer.[35]

Taking this cluster of questions as a genuine refutation of anthropocentric teleology, Maimonides concludes:

> For this reason, to my mind, the correct view according to the beliefs of the Law—a view that corresponds likewise to the speculative views—is as follows: it should not be believed that all the beings exist for the sake of the existence of man. On the contrary, all the other beings too have been intended for their own sakes and not for the sake of something else.[36] *Thus, even according to our view holding*

---

33 Maimonides, *Guide* III 13; Pines 451.
34 Maimonides, *Guide* III 13; Pines 451.
35 Maimonides, *Guide* III 13; Pines 451–452.
36 Note that the last sentence seems to indicate that Maimonides rejects not only the strong claim that *all* beings are created for the sake of man, but also the weaker claim that *some* beings are created for the sake of man.

that the world has been produced in time, the quest for the final end of all the species of beings collapses.[37]

A crucial link in Maimonides's argument in the last two excerpts is the assertion that God's will is the *ultimate* explanation for creation, an explanation that *cannot* be elaborated any further ("the argument must end with the answer being given"). Maimonides reasserts this point toward the end of the chapter:

Just as we do not seek for the end of His existence, so we do not seek for the final end of His volition, according to which all that has been and will be produced in time comes into being.[38]

Remarkably, Maimonides's greatest and sharpest critic, Hasdai Crescas (~1340–1410/11) suggested that these claims of Maimonides must be interpreted in a nonliteral manner ("צריך שנפרשהו בדרך רחוק קצת") as merely asserting that "God has no purpose *known to us* [שאין שם תכלית ידוע לנו]."[39] Crescas justifies the need for this nonliteral interpretation by pointing out that, read literally, Maimonides seems to ascribe to God *arbitrary* action "which is the ultimate disadvantage for any intelligent being."[40]

Crescas was not the only philosopher to be disturbed by the claims of *Guide* III 13.[41] In his notes after reading the Latin translation of the

---

37 Maimonides, *Guide* III 13; Pines 452. Italics added. Notice that it is only the quest for *global* teleology that collapses according to the end of the current passage. I am indebted to Jeff McDonough for drawing my attention to this point.
38 Maimonides, *Guide* III 13; Pines 454–455.
39 Crescas, *Or ha-Shem*, II 6 5 (p. 271 in Fisher's edition).
40 Crescas, *Or ha-Shem*, II 6 5 (p. 272 in Fisher's edition). Indeed, in *Guide* I 58 (Pines 136), Maimonides insists that we should conceive of creation as governed "by means of purpose and will."
41 Maimonides's critique of anthropocentric teleology has also been subject to a major attack by the early sixteenth-century Kabbalist Meir ibn Gabbai, who dedicated the entire third part of his chief work, *Avodat ha-Qodesh* [*Service of the Holy*], to this issue. See Meir Ibn Gabbai, *Avodat ha-Qodesh* (Jerusalem, 2010), 123–254.

Guide (Buxtorf, Basel, 1629), Leibniz writes: "He [Maimonides] does not allow it to be said that all things are for the sake of man and man that he might worship God."[42] As we shall see presently, Leibniz was struck by the substantial similarity between the claims of Maimonides, the great rabbinic author, and those of Benedict de Spinoza, in his notorious appendix to Part One of the *Ethics*. Indeed, the concluding paragraph of *Guide* III 13 could be easily misattributed to the great heretic from Amsterdam.

> When man knows his own soul, makes no mistakes with regard to it, and understands every being according to what it is, he becomes calm and his thoughts are not troubled by seeking a final end for what has not that final end.[43]

5.3. Divine Teleology in the Kabbalah

The foundational text of the Kabbalah, the Jewish mystical tradition, is the Zohar [the Book of Splendor]. Traditionally, the Zohar is attributed to the second-century Mishnaic sage R. Shimeon bar Yohai. The book of the Zohar, or rather the Zoharic literature, first appeared in Spain at the end of the thirteenth century. Moshe de Leon (~1240–1305), an important rabbinic and mystical figure with a significant philosophical education, claimed to have discovered the manuscript of the book (though his widow attributed it to him), and within a very short period of time the Zohar achieved canonical status. Kabbalistic thought underwent a major transformation in the mid-sixteenth century through the teachings of Rabbi Isaac Luria (1534–1572) and his disciples.

The philosophical core of mainstream Kabbalah is a system of emanation which is intended to explain and portray in great detail the

---

42 Lenn E. Goodman, "Maimonides and Leibniz," *Journal of Jewish Studies* 31 (1980): 233.
43 Maimonides, *Guide* III 13; Pines 456.

derivation of various layers of reality from the absolutely singular *Ein-Sof* (the infinite), the most sublime and ineffable aspect of God. The Kabbalists, just like Plotinus and the late Platonists, were deeply troubled by the problem of explaining the very first step in this process: why did the absolutely indivisible *Ein-Sof* proceed to emanate anything, and how could the first emanation be any different from the *Ein-Sof*. Some Kabbalists viewed the first act of emanation as brute grace (חסד). Yet many Kabbalists were not satisfied by this explanation. In this brief section I will concentrate on the discussion of divine teleology in one of the most lucid and systematic presentations of Lurianic Kabbalah.

Shomer Emunim (The Faithful, or, the Loyal Guard) was authored by the Italian Kabbalist Yoseph Ergas (1685–1730) and appeared first in Amsterdam in 1736.[44] The book is written in the form of a dialogue between two interlocutors: Sha'altiel (the one who asks about God) and Yehoyada (the one who knows God). Yehoyada is a Kabbalist, while Sha'altiel is a Talmudist, or perhaps a philosopher, who is somewhat skeptical about the Kabbalah and its teachings. In the following exchange, Sha'altiel asks Yehoyada to explain to him "the purpose of God's intention in creating the worlds":

> Doubtlessly, *it cannot be said that the Infinite caused the entire reality in vain and for no purpose at all*. And though I have noticed that the divine R. Isaac Luria pursued this investigation, I was not able to understand his views adequately due to my poor capacities. For he writes that the reason for the creation of the worlds was that God necessarily had to be perfect in all of his actions . . . and if he were not actualizing and realizing all of his powers, he would—as if [כביכול]—not be perfect. And Luria's words are obscure. I failed to understand them. *For they seem to imply that God was more perfect*

---

44 *Shomer Emunim* is one of only three Kabbalistic texts whose study was permitted under the age of thirty (following a mid-eighteenth-century ban on the study of Kabbalah).

with the world than without it. But this cannot be said at all, for the Infinite is perfect in himself and does not require anything else.[45]

Sha'altiel's objection is clearly in place: how can one claim that the aim of creation is the realization of divine perfection while not asserting that God was *imperfect* before creation? Let us look carefully at Yehoyada's answer:

> We can speak of actual purpose [התכלית בפועל] in two distinct manners. According to the one, the agent aims at achieving a purpose that is external to himself, as when one strives to achieve wealth, wisdom, or any other perfection which he lacks. This kind of purpose cannot explain the creation, for the Infinite is not lacking any perfection.... According to the second manner, the agent acts due to the end of his nature and perfection [לתכלית טבעו ושלמותו], as a good and generous person who benefits others due to his nature. It is in this manner that the divine R. Isaac Luria explained the intention of creation. In other words, the *Ein-Sof*, being the absolute good whose simple essence contains latently all perfections before and after creation, wished to create the worlds because it is the way of the good and perfect to benefit and profuse [להשפיע] perfection and reality, and not in order to increase its perfection, since the existence of beings benefiting from the *Ein-Sof* does not increase its perfection.[46]

Yehoyada denies that the *Ein-Sof* acts for an end (or purpose) according to the first manner of understanding end-directed actions. Yet it is not at all clear that his second manner of understanding end-directed actions—action due to the nature, or essence, of the subject—is indeed

---

45 Yosef Ergas, *Shomer Emunim* [Heb.: *The Loyal Guard*] (Jerusalem: Be-Ferush uve-Remez Press, 1965), 63, right column. Italics added. My translation.
46 Ergas, *Shomer Emunim*, 63, left column. Italics added. My translation.

genuine teleology. Consider, for example, the nature of odd numbers. It is indeed due to the very nature of odd numbers that they are not divisible by four, yet it clearly is not the case that odd numbers are not divisible by four because of their aim, purpose, or goal. In other words, acting due to one's nature, or essence, need not be an action involving teleology. Now, Yehoyada (or Ergas), may well respond that some actions due to the nature of the subject constitute genuine teleology (as in the case of the *Ein-Sof*), while other do not (as in the case of odd numbers). Yet it seems that at this point the burden of proof is on Yehoyada's side; he must explain and motivate the distinction between the two kinds of acting due to the nature of the subject (or agent).

If we look carefully at Yehoyada's words, we can detect his rejection of another common Kabbalistic explanation for creation that has been usually stated by the slogan "There is no king without people [אין מלך בלא עם]."[47] According to this view, God had to create the world, since otherwise it would be impossible to ascribe to him kingship, or, if we wish to use more careful and less anthropomorphic language, it would be impossible to ascribe to him any perfection which requires the existence of things outside God's essence (goodness, omnipotence etc.). Presumably, it is in response to such a view that Ergas writes: "the existence of beings benefiting from the *Ein-Sof* does not increase its perfection." In other words, divine perfections, being essential characteristics of God, cannot presuppose creatures without thereby making God ontologically dependent upon creatures.

5.4. Spinoza's Critique of Teleology

Spinoza's critique of teleology in the appendix to Part One of the *Ethics* has been regarded as one of its most stunning features for more

---

47 A similar formula appears in the *Zohar* [Heb: *Book of Splendor*] (Vilnius: Widow and Brothers Romm Print, 1882), Part 3, p. 5a. The view is very common in Hassidic literature. See, for example, Nahman of Bratslav, *Likutei Muharan* (Jerusalem: Makhon Torat ha-Netzah, 1992), §102.

than three centuries of readership. The precise scope of Spinoza's critique of teleology has been a subject of intense and excellent scholarly debate over the past few years.[48] The remaining part of this chapter will attempt to provide an outline of an interpretation of Spinoza's view, situating it in the broader context of this chapter.

Let us begin with a passage from Spinoza's preface to Part Four of the *Ethics*, the other main locus for Spinoza's discussion of teleology. The passage provides a useful overview of Spinoza's stance. I have parsed it into four sections, divided by roman numerals.

> (i) That eternal and infinite being we call God, *or* Nature, acts from the same necessity from which he exists. For we have shown (IP16) that the necessity of nature from which he acts is the same as that from which he exists. (ii) The reason, therefore, *or* cause, why God, *or* Nature, acts, and the reason why he exists, are one and the same. (iii) *As he exists for the sake of no end, he also acts for the sake of no end. Rather, as he has no principle or end of existing, so he also has none of acting.* (iv) *What is called a final cause is nothing but a human appetite insofar as it is considered as a principle, or primary cause, of some thing.*[49]

In (i)–(iii) Spinoza argues that God's actions are *necessitated* by its nature (or, what is the same, its essence), and that for *this* reason it would

---

48 See Don Garrett, "Teleology in Spinoza and Early Modern Rationalism," in *New Essays on the Rationalists*, ed. Rocco J. Gennaro and Charles Huenemann (Oxford: Oxford University Press, 1999), 310–335; Martin Lin, "Teleology and Human Action in Spinoza," *Philosophical Review* 115 (2006): 317–354; McDonough, "Heyday of Teleology"; and John Carriero, "Spinoza on Final Causality," *Oxford Studies in Early Modern Philosophy* 2 (2005): 105–147.

49 *Ethics*, Part IV, Preface (II/206/23–207/5 in Gebhardt's critical edition). Italics added. Unless otherwise marked, all references to Spinoza's *Ethics* are to Curley's translation: *The Collected Works of Spinoza*, 2 vols., ed. Edwin Curley (Princeton, NJ: Princeton University Press, 1985, 2016). For the Latin and Dutch original text, I have relied on Gebhardt's critical edition: Benedict de Spinoza, *Opera*, 4 vols., ed. Carl Gebhardt (Heidelberg: Carl Winter, 1925). I cite the original texts according to the volume, page, and line numbers of this edition. Thus, II/206/23 refers to volume 2, page 206, line 23 in Gebhardt's edition.

be wrong to view God's actions as aim-directed.[50] In (iv) Spinoza begins to explain his own understanding of what is commonly called a "final cause." As we shall shortly see, this last explanation is supposed to complement his genealogy of the common erroneous belief in divine, anthropocentric teleology in the appendix to Part One.

Section (iii) clearly echoes Maimonides's words, "just as we do not seek for the end of His existence, so we do not seek for the final end of His volition,"[51] and Spinoza's insistence that divine actions necessitated by God's nature cannot be aim-directed is quite similar to Maimonides's argument that for Aristotle there cannot be a final end for reality since, "according to Aristotle, all things derive from an eternal *necessity* that has never ceased and will never cease."[52] Still, why precisely does Spinoza think the necessity of God's actions is incompatible with conceiving these actions as aim-directed?

One simple (and adequate) answer is that, for Spinoza, the necessitation of God's actions by his nature makes teleological explanations redundant. Insofar as God's nature—being the *efficient* cause of all things[53]—is the sufficient cause for all of God's actions,[54] teleological explanations appear sterile at best, and misleading at worst. Still, in order to better understand Spinoza's view, we should look carefully at the appendix to Part One of the *Ethics*, where he develops an intricate analysis of the beliefs in divine teleology, human teleology, and free will, as well as the interrelations among these three beliefs. Arguably,

---

50 The contrast between teleology and necessitarianism will be addressed shortly once we turn to discuss Spinoza's claim that the belief in (thoughtful) teleology relies on the erroneous belief in free will.
51 Maimonides, *Guide* III 13; Pines 454–455.
52 See Maimonides, *Guide* III 13; Pines 449. Italics added. Cf. Harvey, "Spinoza and Maimonides," 51–52.
53 See *Ethics*, Part I, Proposition 16, Corollary 1.
54 See *Ethics*, Part I, Axiom 3, where Spinoza stipulates that a cause must be necessary and sufficient for the effect. In "Spinoza's Monster Cause" (an unpublished manuscript), I show that, for Spinoza, *all* causation is efficient, but even if one does not accept this general and strong claim, Axiom 3 is barely intelligible unless read as referring to efficient causation. On the paradigmatic role of efficient causation in Suárez, see Schmid, "Finality without Final Causes."

Spinoza attempts to root out not only belief in divine teleology, but also in human teleology.

Spinoza begins his analysis in the appendix to Part One with the following observations.

> All the prejudices I here undertake to expose depend on this one: that men commonly suppose that all natural things act, as men do, on account of an end; indeed, *they maintain as certain that God himself directs all things to some certain end, for they say that God has made all things for man, and man that he might worship God*.... Of course this is not the place to deduce these things from the nature of the human mind. It will be sufficient here if I take as a foundation what everyone must acknowledge: *that (i) all men are born ignorant of the causes of things, and that (ii) they all want to seek their own advantage, and (iii) are conscious of this appetite.*[55]

This passage too contains clear echoes of Maimonides's discussion of teleology, as the view attacked by Spinoza (and Maimonides)—"they say that God has made all things for man, and man that he might worship God"—is formulated in almost the very same words as those of Maimonides.[56]

Typically for Spinoza, when he launches an argument to prove a thesis which he knows is likely to be highly controversial (and there is no shortage of those), he strives not only to prove his thesis, but also to provide a detailed explanation of why its opposite became so commonly accepted by almost everyone else.[57] Spinoza's main argument for the rejection of teleology—both divine and human—is that the

---

55 *Ethics*, Part I, Appendix; II/78/1-17. Italics added.

56 "It is likewise thought that the finality of all that exists is solely the existence of the human species so that it should worship God." Maimonides, *Guide* III 13; Pines 451.

57 This is indeed a prudent and useful manner to establish controversial claims, though in some cases (not in the case of teleology), Spinoza seems to be so carried away by his attempt to explain the genealogy of his adversaries' error that he forgets the need to establish his thesis first.

"eternal necessity of nature" leaves no room for intentional action out of free will.[58] But why does Spinoza think that intentional action—or, at least, intentional action suited for genuine teleology—requires free will? In order to answer this question, as well as understand his genealogy of the belief in divine teleology, we need to carefully reconstruct his analysis. For Spinoza, the belief in divine teleology is the result of a *pile of errors*, accumulating one above the other; in order to understand the full scale of the problem it is crucial that we should not be satisfied by pointing out just *one* error, but rather make sure that the errors diagnosed so far provide a *complete* explanation of the philosophical blunder at stake.

Spinoza begins his analysis by identifying three universally agreed-upon claims (which he also endorses): "that (i) all men are born ignorant of the causes of things, and that (ii) they all want to seek their own advantage, and (iii) are conscious of this appetite." Relying on this common ground, Spinoza will attempt to show why we develop the false belief in divine teleology. The first layer of error resulting from (i)–(iii) is the false belief in (human) free will. Thus, the passage we just quoted continues:

> From these [assumptions] it follows, *first, that men think themselves free*, because they are conscious of their volitions and their appetite, and do not think, even in their dreams, of the causes by which they are disposed to wanting and willing, because they are ignorant of [those causes]. It follows, secondly, that men act always on account of an end, viz. on account of their advantage, which they want. *Hence, they seek to know only the final causes of what has been done, and when they have heard them, they are satisfied, because they have*

---

58 Spinoza, *Ethics*, Part I, Appendix; II/80/5-9. Next to this chief argument, Spinoza launches two auxiliary arguments. According to the first, teleology "turns nature upside down" by making the finite the end of the activity of the infinite (II/80/10-22). According to the second, teleology "takes away God's perfection. For if God acts for the sake of an end, he necessarily wants something he lacks" (II/80/22-29). Here, I will limit myself to the discussion of Spinoza's main argument.

no reason to doubt further. But if they cannot hear them from another, nothing remains for them but to turn toward themselves, and reflect on the ends by which they are usually determined to do such things; *so they necessarily judge the temperament of other men from their own temperament.*[59]

We develop the belief in free will as a result of the collusion of three elements: (1) the fact that we have desires (or volitions), (2) the fact we are *conscious* of our desires (or volitions), (3) the fact that it is almost impossible for us to have a *complete* knowledge of the *causes* of our desires.[60] Obviously, we may have some knowledge of the causes of our volitions. For example, I may know that part of the reason why I desire garlic ice cream rather than dulce de leche is because I am allergic to milk. However, this knowledge explains (at best) only why I avoid dulce de leche; it does not explain why I always order garlic ice cream (and not onion ice cream). Occasionally, I may try to achieve more substantial self-transparency and attempt to understand the causes underlying some of my more important decisions (or volitions). In such a case, I go to a psychotherapist (or a geneticist) and spend a good couple of months (or years) in trying to understand, as fully as possible, the causes of my volitions. Yet I experience volitions almost every moment of my life, and in almost all of these instances of volition, I have merely an awfully incomplete knowledge of the causes of my volitions. Thus, I hardly ever experience my volitions as fully necessitated by the causal information I have, or, in other words, I experience my volitions as *free*, and not necessitated by previous (efficient) causes. This, in a nutshell, is Spinoza's explanation of how we come to develop the belief in free will.

---

59 Spinoza, *Ethics*, Part I, Appendix; II/78/17-28. Italics added.
60 In the current paragraph I merely attempt to provide an outline of Spinoza's explanation of why we necessarily develop the barely eliminable belief in free will. I discuss in greater detail the relevant texts and address a number of important objections in Yitzhak Y. Melamed, "The Causes of Our Belief in Free Will: Spinoza on Necessary, Innate, yet False Cognitions," in *Spinoza's Ethics: A Critical Guide*, ed. Yitzhak Y. Melamed (Cambridge: Cambridge University Press, 2017), 121–141.

Since this experience of "free" volitions accompanies us throughout our lives, one could see why we are so attached to this false belief. Just think of how you would react to a belief that is reinforced whenever you have volitions, i.e., every second of your life.

The belief in free will is thus the first layer of error in the pile which results in the belief in divine teleology. The second layer is the belief in *human* teleology, i.e., that "men act always on account of an end." Shortly, we will zoom in on the question of why Spinoza thinks that the belief in human teleology results from the belief in free will. For the time being, I only wish to note that according to the earlier passage, the belief in human teleology "follows [*sequitur*]," or results, from the issues previously discussed. The third layer of error is a simple projection. I believe that my actions are free and should be explained by my aims, and I project the same belief onto other agents. In the earlier passage Spinoza discusses the manner in which we project from ourselves to "the temperament of other *men*." A few lines later in the appendix, Spinoza invokes the very same psychological mechanism to explain anthropomorphic thinking, i.e., the way we project from what (we believe) is true about our own psychology to the psychology of the unknown rulers of nature, or the gods.[61]

Let us now look more carefully at the relation between the beliefs in free will and human teleology in the last passage. Why does Spinoza think that the belief in human teleology "follows" from the belief in free will? The crucial sentence in this context is the following: "Hence, they seek to know only the final causes of what has been done, and when they have heard them, they are satisfied [*quiescant*], because they have no reason to doubt further." Teleology provides an easy explanation for the causes of our volitions (and actions), and thus distracts

---

61 "And since they had never heard anything about the temperament of these rulers, they had to judge it from their own. Hence, they maintained that the Gods direct all things for the use of men in order to bind men to them and be held by men in the highest honor.... This was why each of them strove with great diligence to understand and explain the final causes of all things." *Ethics*, Part I, Appendix; II/79/5-14.

us from the challenging, yet absolutely crucial task of uncovering the efficient causes of our volitions. As long as we feel that we are in a state of ignorance about the causes of our volitions, we would still have the urge to look for these causes. Teleological explanations relax—or "satisfy," in Spinoza's language—this urge. They tell me that I pick garlic ice cream because I desired garlic ice cream. Spinoza would not deny that I desired garlic ice cream. Yet he would insist that such desires, just like anything else, cannot arise ex nihilo, and thus must have an efficient cause which produced them.[62]

Still, we may wonder, why not adopt the epistemological virtues of human teleology while rejecting its vices? In such a case we could, for example, view explanations through final and efficient causes as equal and *parallel*. We would be careful to avoid the temptation to be satisfied merely by teleological explanation, but we would still insist that teleological explanations are on equal footing with efficient causation, and cannot be reduced to efficient causation. In order to see why Spinoza rejects this Leibnizian line of thought,[63] we need to return to the very end of the passage with which we began our discussion of Spinoza in this section of the chapter.

> *What is called a final cause is nothing but a human appetite insofar as it is considered as a principle, or primary cause [principium, seu causa primaria consideratur], of some thing.* For example, when we say that habitation was the final cause of this or that house, surely we understand nothing but that a man, because he imagined the conveniences of domestic life, had an appetite to build a house. So habitation, insofar as it is considered as a final cause, is nothing more than this singular appetite. *It is really [reverá] an efficient cause,*

---

[62] In other words, for Spinoza, teleology presupposes free will, which in its turn presupposes the absence of efficient cause.

[63] For a very helpful discussion of Leibniz's "two kingdoms" view, see McDonough, "Heyday of Teleology," 196–199.

which is considered as a first cause, because men are commonly ignorant of the causes of their appetites. For as I have often said before, they are conscious of their actions and appetites, but not aware of the causes by which they are determined to want something. As for what they commonly say—that Nature sometimes fails or sins, and produces imperfect things—I number this among the fictions I treated in the Appendix of Part I.[64]

As far as I can see, Spinoza's main point here is the following. Desires are indeed the causes of our actions (or more precisely, desires are the causes of the mental parallels of the causes of our physical actions).[65] When a desire D causes me to perform act A, the desire is just the efficient cause of the action. Just like any other efficient cause, D itself must have in its turn its own efficient cause. Spinoza does not at all deny that we have desires, but he rejects the very possibility of desires that are "primary causes," i.e., uncaused causes. Just like anything else, desires must have efficient causes. Thus, the picture we get is one in which nature is governed fully under the tyranny of efficient causes. Aim-directed actions, just like memories, are crucial features of certain mental items in these infinite chains of *efficient* causes. The memory I have now of certain events that occurred when I was five years old are likely to influence my actions in the near future. Still, this intentionality toward the past does not violate the strict regime of efficient-causal determinism, nor do I believe that there is some special kind of causation in which my distant past causes me now to act. It is the *recollection*

---

[64] *Ethics*, Part IV, Preface; II/207/3-17. Italics added.

[65] For Spinoza, there is no causal connection between minds and bodies, but rather mental and physical items are two aspects of one and the same thing. See *Ethics*, Part II, Proposition 6 and the scholium to Proposition 7. Thus, strictly, (mental) desires cannot cause physical change. Instead, desires are the causes of the mental aspect of what we perceive as physical change, or action. In *Ethics*, Part III, Proposition 2, scholium, Spinoza designates the terms "decision" (*decretum*) and "determination" (*determinatio*) for the mental and physical aspects of volition, respectively (II/144/3-8). In the following, I will adopt the coarse, non-Spinozist language and refer to desires "causing" action just for the sake of brevity.

of my distant past—which can be weak or strong, adequate or misleading, happy or miserable—and not the distant past itself, that is the cause of my action. The recollection is an efficient cause of my action, and the intentionality toward the past is just a *feature* of this efficient cause. Along the very same lines, Spinoza would argue, intentionality toward the future does not make the future the cause of my action.[66] The intention itself can take as its object past, present, or future states, and these states might be possible, impossible where the impossibility is unbeknown to me, or even transparently impossible ("I wish I could climb tomorrow this Escher-style staircase"). Still, Spinoza would insist, the desire, with its embedded intention, is just an efficient cause.

Before concluding this section, let me note that Spinoza barely engages Aristotle's natural, thoughtless teleology.[67] Given our discussion so far, one can easily see why Spinoza is not impressed by that strand in Aristotle's thought which suggests that, heuristically, we may view the teleological principles of nature *as if* nature has "an intelligent, creative designer." If genuine divine teleology leads us to deep errors and contentment with ignorance, it would seem quite silly to adopt this view as a mere heuristic device (unless our aim is ignorance and erroneous belief). Indeed, in the very last sentence of the passage quoted, Spinoza responds to Aristotle's claim that nature sometimes fails or sins.[68] Spinoza can barely hide his ridicule toward this highly anthropocentric evaluation of the perfection of things.

---

66 Clearly, I can have intentionality toward the future even when this future will never exist (or even cannot ever exist). Thus, even if one holds that the future is as real as the present, ascribing causal powers to the future (rather than to the present desires toward, or anticipation of, the future) seems to be highly problematic.

67 The most common Aristotelean natural, thoughtless teleology that is not presented as a mere heuristic device would most likely appear to Spinoza as a bizarre, redundant, and unmotivated claim, bordering on the occult.

68 See *Generation of Animals* IV.3, 765b5–23, and Mariska Leunissen's fascinating discussion (in her contribution to this volume) of Aristotle's view of females as monsters, i.e., deficient animals that fail to replicate the form of their species.

5.5. Conclusion

Spinoza's attack on teleology is one of his boldest philosophical moves (and this is quite a high bar)—so much so, that, even today, Spinoza's wholesale rejection of teleology (and especially, of human thoughtful teleology), read literally, may strike many readers and scholars as counterintuitive and odd. Spinoza is indeed rarely afraid of challenging his readers' intuitions. Whether Spinoza succeeded in proving that all forms of teleology are erroneous is an evaluation I cannot fully pursue in the current chapter. Still, I hope I have demonstrated that Spinoza's critique of teleology (read according to the letter) is both insightful and powerful. As Warren Zev Harvey has pointed out recently,[69] Spinoza's attack on teleology is at least partly indebted to Maimonides's deep reservations about many aspects of Aristotelean teleology.[70] I have also attempted to show in this chapter that readers who expect to find rabbinic authors endorsing a textbook version of medieval teleology are very likely to return frustrated. As with many other issues of doxa, the rabbinic scholarly discourse was strongly decentralized and poorly regimented. Some of the results of this fortunate chaos has been illustrated in the current chapter.

Acknowledgments

I would like to thank Jonathan Garb, Zach Gartenberg, Warren Zev Harvey, and Jeff McDonough for their exceedingly helpful and generous comments on earlier drafts of this chapter

---

69 See Harvey, "Spinoza and Maimonides."

70 In one of his sermons, Saul Morteira, Spinoza's teacher and rabbi in the Jewish community of Amsterdam, criticized Maimonides's views on divine teleology. See Marc Saperstein, *Exile in Amsterdam: Saul Levi Mortera's Sermons to a Congregation of "New Jews"* (Cincinnati: Hebrew Union College Press, 2005), 92. Morteira's sermons were delivered on the Sabbath in front of the entire congregation. The young Spinoza might have been a member of the audience.

CHAPTER SIX

Not Dead Yet

TELEOLOGY AND THE "SCIENTIFIC REVOLUTION"

Jeffrey K. McDonough

6.1. Introduction

In 1897, James Ross Clemens became seriously ill. He didn't die. Not then at least. Nonetheless, rumors swarmed throughout London that his cousin, Samuel Clemens, had passed away. Samuel Clemens—Mark Twain—was bemused, famously quipping that reports of his death had been greatly exaggerated. To be sure, something had happened, perhaps something important, but nothing as definitive as what was rumored.

It has similarly been thought that the concept of teleology met its fate in the seventeenth and eighteenth centuries with the rise of early modern science. Francis Bacon famously derided the use of final causes in physics as being akin to vestal virgins dedicated to God and accomplishing nothing.[1] It is easy to see in Bacon's quip the suggestion that

---

[1] Francis Bacon, "De augmentis scientiarum," in *Works*, vol. 1, ed. James Spedding, Robert Leslie Ellis, and Douglas Denon Heath (London: Longman, 1858, facsc. repr.

natural philosophers in the early modern period came to see appeals to final causes as unhelpful or simply not explanatory. René Descartes implied that the pursuit of final causes in physics is presumptuous and promised to forgo them in his own investigations of the physical world.[2] It is easy to see in his remarks a slightly different concern—the thought that even if there are final causes in the world, we have no reliable, scientific way of investigating them. Finally, Baruch Spinoza boldly denied that God acts for the sake of ends and suggested that final causes are nothing more than "human fictions" that "turn the order of nature completely upside down."[3] It is easy to imagine that Spinoza's first denial marks a decisive break between a medieval worldview infused with divine purposes and an early modern worldview that became increasingly naturalistic. It is easy to imagine that Spinoza's second denial signals a deep skepticism about the very coherence of final causation and foreshadows a general shift from a focus on final causation in the medieval period to a focus on efficient causation in the early modern era.

Scholars of early modern philosophy have—not unreasonably—devoted much effort to exploring attacks (or apparent attacks) on teleology at the dawn of modern science.[4] It remains a stubborn fact, however, that most natural philosophers in the early modern period

---

Stuttgart-Bad Cannstatt: Friedrich Frommann, 1963), 571, but for a fuller picture see also 570.

2 René Descartes, *Oeuvres de Descartes*, ed. Charles Adam and Paul Tannery (Paris: Vrin, 1978), vol. 9, pt. 2, 15–16; see also vol. 7, 53–63.

3 Benedictus Spinoza, *Opera*, vol. 2, ed. Carl Gebhardt (Heidelberg: C. Winter, 1925), 80. For discussion, see Yitzhak Melamed's chapter on Jewish philosophy in this volume.

4 For extended discussions of teleology in the early modern era, see Vincent Carraud, *Causa sive ratio: La raison de la cause, de Suarez à Leibniz* (Paris: Presses Universitaires de France, 2002); Dennis Des Chene, *Physiologia: Natural Philosophy in Late Aristotelianism and Cartesian Thought* (Ithaca, NY: Cornell University Press, 1996); and Stephan Schmid, *Finalursachen der Frühen Neuzeit* (New York: de Gruyter, 2011). Among much-discussed early modern philosophers, Gottfried Leibniz stands out as a recognized proponent of final causes. For an attempt to situate his views on teleology in the larger landscape of the early modern era, see Jeffrey K. McDonough, "The Heyday of Teleology and Early Modern Philosophy," *Midwest Studies in Philosophy* 35 (2011): 179–204.

remained deeply committed to teleology. Because they are numerous rather than few, it is impossible to relate their story here in the same detail that has been afforded to their more skeptical-sounding counterparts. The three sections that follow will, however, attempt to correct, at least in a small measure, the persistent impression that teleology was simply undermined by the so-called scientific revolution. It will do so by looking at three areas in which teleology was upheld and developed by three pioneers of early modern science. The next section will show how teleological reasoning is woven into the very fabric of William Harvey's revolutionary work in biology. Section 6.3 will take up Robert Boyle's explicit and systematic defense of teleology and especially his effort to reconcile the methods and commitments of the new science with a deep-seated commitment to divine teleology. Finally, section 6.4 will explore Pierre Maupertuis's bold attempt to find a place for teleology in the heart of modern, mathematical physics.

As we will see, in the early modern period, much happened to the concept of teleology, much that was no doubt important. And yet, like James Ross Clemens, teleology didn't just die, not in the early modern era at least. As with Clemens's hale and hearty cousin, rumors of teleology's early demise have been greatly exaggerated.

6.2. William Harvey and Biological Teleology

Born between Bacon and Descartes in 1578, William Harvey rose from a yeoman's background to become the leading anatomist and physiologist of the early modern era. His accomplishments were many. After attending Cambridge, he earned a medical degree at the University of Padua, where he worked closely with the pioneering anatomist and surgeon Hieronymus Fabricius. At the age of twenty-nine, he joined the Royal College of Physicians and soon after was put in charge of St. Bartholomew's Hospital. Later, he would be appointed to the office of Lumleian lecturer and would eventually become "Physician Extraordinary" to King James I. A leading figure of early modern science, Harvey is best known today for his discoveries concerning the heart and the circulation of blood as set out in his masterpiece, *Anatomical Exercises Concerning the Motion of the Heart and Blood in Animals* (*Exercitatio anatomica de motu cordis et sanguinis in animalibus,* hereafter *de Motu Cordis*).[5] A closer look at his work quickly reveals that teleology plays important roles in Harvey's pioneering discoveries; that he draws explicitly teleological conclusions from those discoveries; and that, collectively, his efforts provide a powerful response to the charge that the investigation of final causes must be useless, brash, or both.

In Harvey's day, physiology—the study of the use and function of parts of the body—was still dominated by the second-century work of Galen of Pergamum.[6] Galen sees the heart as standing at the juncture of two otherwise autonomous vascular systems. One system, anchored in the stomach and liver, produces purple, nutritive blood that slowly ebbs and flows through the venal system to the body's extremities, replenishing muscles and bones. The other system is anchored in the lungs and heart. Galen conjectures that some nutritive blood from the venal system is drawn into the right side of the heart, where it seeps through invisible pores in the septum into the left ventricle of the heart. There venal blood is mixed with a vital spirit drawn from the lungs in a process called "concoction." The process of concoction

---

5 William Harvey, *Exercitatio anatomica de motu cordis et sanguines in animalibus* (Frankfurt, 1628). I have generally followed the English translation in William Harvey, *An Anatomical Disputation Concerning the Movement of the Heart and Blood in Living Creatures,* trans. Gweneth Witteridge (London: Blackwell Scientific Publications, 1976). All references are to the English translation. In spite of being a major figure in the scientific revolution, Harvey has long been relatively neglected by historians of philosophy. That tide may, however, finally be turning. For recent work on Harvey and teleology, see, for starters, Peter Distelzweig, "'*Meam de motu & usu cordis, & circuitu sanguinis sententiam*': Teleology in William Harvey's *De motu cordis*," *Gesnerus Swiss Journal of the History of Medicine and Sciences* 71, no. 2 (2014): 258–270; Benjamin Goldberg, "William Harvey on Anatomy and Experience," *Perspectives on Science* 24, no. 3 (2016): 305–323; James Lennox, "The Comparative Study of Animal Development: William Harvey's Aristotelianism," in *The Problem of Animal Generation in Early Modern Philosophy*, ed. Justin E. H. Smith (New York: Cambridge University Press, 2006), 21–46.

6 On Galen's relation to teleology, see Patricia Marechal's essay in this volume.

transforms the venal system's purple, nutritive blood into bright red, vivifying arterial blood. Once concocted, arterial blood ebbs and flows from the left ventricle of the heart through the arterial system to the organs where it is consumed (with any remainder evaporating). For Galen, then, the vascular system is really two vascular systems. Blood gently sloshes through both systems and is continuously produced and consumed. The heart plays a significant but not central role.

Harvey was led to a radically different understanding of the "motions of the heart and blood in animals" by two principal clues, both of which make explicit appeal to teleological reasoning. The first such clue draws on assumptions about the teleological functions of animal parts. Earlier anatomists had discovered that veins contain numerous valves. Galen's followers had supposed that the function of venal valves is to counteract the force of gravity. As venal blood slowly ebbs and flows through the venal system, valves, they supposed, are needed to prevent it from pooling in the lowest extremities of the body. This Galenic account, however, struck Harvey as untenable. It was known, for example, that valves in the jugular vein are—in a person standing— oriented down, not up. They thus seem to guarantee that blood flows with gravity, not against it. Reflecting on orientation of jugular valves, Harvey concludes, "The discoverer of these valves did not rightly understand their use.... For their use is not to prevent the whole mass of the blood from falling downwards by its own weight into the lower parts of the body."[7] To this negative assessment, Harvey adds a positive discovery. He notes that venal valves are in general oriented in such a way as to guarantee the flow of blood toward the heart and away from the body's extremities. After conducting numerous investigations, including dissections of a wide variety of animal species, he concludes that venal "valves were made entirely lest the blood.... should not go from the center of the body to the extremities, but rather from the

---

7 Harvey, *de Motu Cordis*, 101.

extremities to the center."[8] Venal valves, in Harvey's opinion, don't function to counteract gravity, they function to ensure that blood in the veins always flows toward the heart.

Harvey's second clue appeals to quantitative results backed up by teleological considerations—considerations invoking the purposes for which bodily parts were formed or created. Having witnessed countless vivisections and butcherings, Harvey was struck by the sheer quantity of blood that must pass through a beating heart. On the basis of rough calculations, he reckons, for example, that if it is supposed, conservatively, that "in a man there is sent forth at every beat of the heart... one dram which cannot possibly return to the heart by reason of the hindrance of the valves," and that "[t]he heart in one half hour makes above a thousand pulses," it can be deduced that in a half hour a "quantity of blood, is passed through the heart into the arteries, that is, always in a greater quantity than can be found in the whole of the body."[9] These quantitative estimates are supported, according to Harvey, by physiological—that is teleological—considerations. Harvey argues that the "abundance of blood passing through the heart out the veins into the arteries" is witnessed by "the symmetry and great size of the ventricles of the heart and of the vessels which go into it and go out from it (for Nature who makes nothing in vain would not have allotted to those vessels so comparatively large a size to no purpose)."[10] Harvey is using teleological considerations—what the ventricles of the heart are good for, their purpose—to support his quantitative estimations. Those quantitative estimations, Harvey concludes are, in turn, inconsistent with Galenic theory, according to which blood is continuously produced and consumed.[11] For Harvey, this is all more evidence

---

8 Harvey, *de Motu Cordis*, 104, 102.
9 Harvey, *de Motu Cordis*, 79, see also 105.
10 Harvey, *de Motu Cordis*, 74–75.
11 Harvey, *de Motu Cordis*, 80.

that a new theory is needed, a theory according to which blood is not constantly generated and destroyed but rather recycled.

Spurred by physiological and quantitative clues, and assured by innumerable dissections, observations, and experiments, Harvey accordingly first formulated, then confirmed to his own satisfaction, just such a new theory. Putting his "trust in the love of truth and in the integrity of learned minds," Harvey dares to put forward his "opinion concerning the circulation of the blood and to state it formally to all men":

> [T]he blood passes through the lungs and heart by the pulse of the ventricles, and is driven in and sent into the whole body and there creeps into the veins and porosities of the flesh, and through the veins themselves returns from all parts, from the circumference to the centre, out of the tiny veins into the greater, and from thence comes into the vena cava and at last into the auricle of the heart, and in so great abundance, with so great an outflowing and inflowing, from hence through the arteries thither, from thence through the veins hither back again ... it must of necessity be concluded that the blood is driven into a round by a circular motion in living creatures, and that it moves perpetually.[12]

Details remained to be worked out. What is the exact function of the blood itself? What is the exact mechanism by which it passes from the arteries to the veins? Nonetheless, Harvey's central thesis is of course correct: blood is forcefully circulated by the heart through a single circulatory system that includes both the veins and arteries. His understanding of the operations of the heart and circulatory system was a revolution in early modern science, comparable in its significance to Newton's theories in mechanics. Indeed, insofar as it eventually helped to loosen the grip of Galen's influence on biology and medicine, its

---

[12] Harvey, *de Motu Cordis*, 74, 107.

FIGURE 1

FIGURE 2

FIGURE 3

FIGURE 4

practical implications were perhaps even greater. Newton's discoveries quickly led to improvements in astronomy and mechanics. Harvey's, however, spurred the advancement of modern medicine and public health.

Teleology thus played a central role in the discovery of one of the most important and far-reaching theories of early modern science. In Harvey's work, however, teleology is not limited to the process of discovery. Rather, he also aims to draw conclusions that are themselves teleological. Some of these conclusions assign teleological functions to animal parts and processes. They specify the purposes of animal parts and activities. So, for example, in the second chapter of *de Motu Cordis*, Harvey tells us that "the *proper* movement of the heart is not the diastole but systole," that is, that its proper, essential function is to pump blood out rather than to draw blood in.[13] The fifth chapter of *de Motu Cordis* is entitled "Of the Action and Function of the Movement of the Heart." In it, Harvey tells us "one of the [characteristic] actions of the heart is the very transmission of the blood and its propulsion to the extremities by the intermediacy of the arteries."[14] Again, the thought is teleological: one of the functions of the heart is to push the blood through the arteries into the extremities of the body. In the eighth chapter, he describes the heart as "this familiar household god" and attributes to it the functions of "nourishing, cherishing and quickening."[15] In the thirteenth chapter, he discusses of the "uses" of the valves. In the fourteenth, he declares that driving the blood in a circular motion is "the action or function of the heart, which by pulsation it performs."[16] In such passages, we see Harvey drawing explicitly teleological conclusions. We see him assigning proper functions to animal parts and processes.

---

13 Harvey, *de Motu Cordis*, 34, emphasis added.
14 Harvey, *de Motu Cordis*, 51–52.
15 Harvey, *de Motu Cordis*, 76.
16 Harvey, *de Motu Cordis*, 107.

Other conclusions drawn by Harvey assign teleological origins to animal parts and processes. They specify why animals have the particular parts and processes that they do have. In the final chapter of *de Motu Cordis*, he argues that "because more perfected creatures need a more perfected aliment and a more abundant innate heat ... it was fitting and reasonable that these animals should have lungs and a second ventricle."[17] He tells us, for example, "Nature being perfect and divine and making nothing in vain, neither gave a heart to any animal where there was no need, nor made it before it could be of any use."[18] He argues that "since Nature who is perfect makes nothing in vain and in all her works suffices every need, the nearer the arteries are to the heart, the more they differ from veins in their constitution."[19] Finally, he concludes that "it were very hard for anyone to explain by any other way than I have done for what cause all these things were so made and appointed."[20] For Harvey, biological parts and operations not only have teleological functions, they also have teleological origins. The heart, for example, not only has a purpose, namely, circulating the blood: it is present in cordate creatures because of its purpose. Hearts are for the sake of circulating blood, and creatures have hearts because they are for the sake of circulating blood.

The roles of teleological reasoning in Harvey's discovery of the circulation of the blood, as well as the teleological conclusions he drew from his momentous discovery, provide the basis for a powerful reply to the charges raised against teleology by Bacon and Descartes. One distillation of Bacon's quip about vestal virgins is that teleology—like a virgin dedicated to God—is useless. It is easy to be sympathetic with Bacon's complaint. When we are told that bones are for the sake of supporting the body and that the earth is for the sake of supporting creatures, we

---

17 Harvey, *de Motu Cordis*, 122.
18 Harvey, *de Motu Cordis*, 128.
19 Harvey, *de Motu Cordis*, 130.
20 Harvey, *de Motu Cordis*, 133.

seem to learn nothing and to gain no advantage.[21] Harvey, however, has a powerful reply. For surely a response to Bacon's charge does not require one to show that *every* appeal to final causes is useful. And, indeed, in his "introductory discourse" to *de Motu cordis*, Harvey savages the teleological conclusions of many of his predecessors. No, a proper reply to Bacon's charge only requires producing evidence that teleological reasoning can be useful in some cases, that it can, in some cases, get results. And that is exactly what Harvey does in his *de Motu cordis*. We've seen already how considerations of function played a role in the two major clues leading to Harvey's discovery of the circulation of blood. But even those clues don't tell the whole story. Harvey's masterpiece is laced through with teleological hypotheses and principles: hypotheses, for example, concerning the function of the valves of the heart, the thickness of the arteries near the heart, and the thinness of arteries at the body's periphery; principles, for example, such as the maxim that similar structures should be presumed to have similar functions and that nature does nothing in vain.[22] If Bacon's charge is that teleological reasoning cannot be *useful* in the pursuit of science, Harvey's work provides a devastating rebuttal.

Harvey's work also represents a powerful response to the central thrust of Descartes's criticism of final causes, namely, that it would be presumptuous to speculate concerning them. Again, it is easy to be sympathetic with the charge. Granted that our bones prop up our bodies, how do we know that that is their function? Granted that the earth supports the creatures living on it, how do we know that it even has a function? Again, however, we should be clear about the rules of the game. Surely, the defender of teleology needn't rebut the radical skeptic. In order to defend teleology, she needn't refute general arguments intended to show that we have no knowledge or justified beliefs at all. Rather her goal—qua defender of teleology—must be to show

---

21 Bacon, "De augmentis scientiarum," 569.
22 Harvey, *de Motu Cordis*, 16–17, 128.

that evidence can be amassed for teleological conclusions in essentially the same way that it can be amassed for nonteleological conclusions. In the context of early modern science, that means above all showing how evidence in the form of observations and experiments can be marshaled in support of an interlinked set of hypotheses some of which are teleological in nature.

With his *de Motu cordis*, Harvey again rises to the challenge. His account of the motion of the heart and blood contains a complex web of interlinked hypotheses, including, for example, that the chief action of the heart occurs during contraction, that the function of the mitral valves of the heart is to prevent the backflow of blood driven out of the heart during contraction, and that arteries are thickest near the heart in order to prevent their being ruptured when engorged with blood surging out the mitral valves. Harvey understood all of these hypotheses as involving appeals to final causes, and—with the possible exception of the hypothesis concerning the chief action of the heart—we should too. Can evidence be marshaled in their favor? Of course. The thickness of the arteries near the heart is evident to the naked eye and can be compared directly with their relative thinness at the body's extremities. Harvey convincingly argues that the function of the mitral valves can be confirmed by experiment—for example, by probing the valves or trying to force water against their closure. The chief action of the heart is—Harvey acknowledges—difficult to discern because the hearts of warm-blooded animals beat so quickly. But the lion's tail can be twisted here as well, in part, for example, by observing hearts just before they expire, by looking at the hearts of cold-blooded animals, which generally beat more slowly, and by making inferences from the nature of the muscle fibers constituting the heart.[23] None of this evidence, of course, is absolutely conclusive. Real evidence seldom is. But Harvey is nonetheless surely right to see it as evidence for his teleological hypotheses.

---

23 Harvey, *de Motu Cordis*, 86–87, 129.

Indeed, it is as good or better than most of the evidence for any interesting hypothesis in early modern science.

Harvey's *de Motu cordis* thus represents an ambitious defense of teleology along two main fronts. First, and perhaps foremost, it is ambitious in its conclusion. Above all, Harvey's efforts radically reshaped our understanding of the physiology of the central components of the cardiovascular system. The structure and location of the parts of the cardiovascular system were, in general, already well known. Harvey didn't discover the general structure or location of the heart, liver, lungs, arteries, veins, etc. He didn't even discover the presence of valves or blood in the arteries. What he offered was a better understanding of the *function* of all these parts, of *why* they are so structured and located. Second, Harvey's *de Motu cordis* is ambitious in its efforts to combine the full rigor of the new science with the ancient investigation of ends and functions. Although not alone in this endeavor, Harvey helped to popularize and reinforce techniques in the investigation of ends and functions of animal parts that seem obvious only in hindsight: careful observation, comparative study, experimental variation. In doing so, he married early modern physiology to the methods of the new science. In spite of occasional reservations—such as those of Bacon and Descartes—it has, in fact, been a long and happy union.[24]

6.3. Robert Boyle and Divine Teleology

Robert Boyle, the father of modern chemistry, was as much a leading figure of the "scientific revolution" as William Harvey. Born in Ireland in 1627, Boyle received a privileged education at the hands of private tutors and at Eton College. After his father passed, Boyle devoted himself to scientific research. In 1654, he set up shop at Oxford and, with the aid of Robert Hooke, began experimenting with air pumps. In the

---

24 On the place of teleology in modern science, see Patrick's Forber's essay in this volume.

course of defending his work, Boyle articulated the law that still bears his name, that is, "Boyle's law." Many additional discoveries followed, and Boyle became a recognized spokesperson for the new mechanical philosophy. Like most natural philosophers in the early modern era, however, Boyle's commitment to religion remained broad and deep. He contributed funds to missionary work and translations of the Bible. Having helped to found the Royal Society, he turned down its presidency on theological grounds. In his will, he endowed a series of lectures—now known as the Boyle Lectures—to defend the Christian religion against "notorious infidels, namely, atheists, deists, pagans, Jews and Muslims." No one might be more aptly described as a man of the science *and* religion of his day than Boyle.

In 1688, Boyle published what is perhaps the most important, explicit treatment of teleology by a leading figure of the scientific revolution: *A Disquisition about the Final Causes of Natural Things: Wherein it is inquired, Whether, and (if at all) with what Cautions, a Naturalist should admit them?* (hereafter *Disquisition*).[25] The defense it mounts, Boyle tells us, is "now the more seasonable" because "two of the chief sects of the modern philosophizers do both of them, upon differing grounds, deny, that the naturalist ought at all to trouble or busy himself about final causes."[26] The two sects Boyle has in mind are Epicureans and Cartesians. Epicureans "banish the consideration of the ends of things; because the world being, according to them, made by chance, no ends of any thing can be supposed to have been intended."[27] Cartesians, in contrast, allow that the earth has not been

---

25 Robert Boyle, *The Works of the Honorable Robert Boyle*, ed. Thomas Birch, new edition, 6 vols. (London, 1772; reprint Hildesheim: Georg Olms, 1966), 392–344. For recent work on Boyle and teleology, see, for starters, Laurence Carlin, "The Importance of Teleology to Boyle's Natural Philosophy," *British Journal for the History of Philosophy* 19, no. 4 (2011): 665–682; James G. Lennox, "Robert Boyle's Defense of Teleological Inference in Experimental Science," *Isis* 74, no. 1 (1983): 38–52; Timothy Shanahan, "Teleological Reasoning in Boyle's Disquisition about Final Causes," in *Robert Boyle Reconsidered*, ed. Michael Hunter (New York: Cambridge University Press, 1994), 177–192.

26 Boyle, *Disquisition*, 393.

27 Boyle, *Disquisition*, 393.

made by chance, but nonetheless "suppose all the ends of God in things corporeal to be so sublime, that it were presumption in man to think his reason can extend to discover them."[28] One sect, Boyle declares, thinks it is "impertinent for us to seek after final causes," the other "presumptuous to think we might find them."[29]

In responding, Boyle draws a distinction between two kinds of teleological reasoning. What he calls *physical reasoning* begins with ends and draws conclusions about the natures of the things that have those ends. In cases of physical reasoning, Boyle tells us, "upon the supposed ends of things men ground arguments, both affirmative and negative, about the peculiar nature of things themselves; and conclude, that this affection of a natural body or part ought to be granted or that to be denied, because by this, and not by that, or by this more than by that, the end, designed by nature, may be best and most conveniently attained."[30] Physical reasoning, in short, moves from the fitness of creatures (or parts of creatures) to conclusions about their natures and ends. Ears are for the sake of hearing, so the tiny bones of the ear must have a function that promotes hearing. What Boyle calls *metaphysical reasoning* begins with the fitness of things to certain ends and draws conclusions concerning God's intentions in creating those beings. In this case, Boyle tells us, "from the uses of things men draw arguments, that relate to the Author of nature, and from the general ends He is supposed to have intended in things corporeal: as when from the manifest usefulness of the eye, and all its parts, to the function of seeing, men infer, that at the beginning of things the eye was framed by a very intelligent Being, that had a particular care, that animals, especially men, should be furnished with the fittest organ of so necessary a sense as that of sight."[31] Metaphysical reasoning, in short, moves from the

---

28 Boyle, *Disquisition*, 393.
29 Boyle, *Disquisition*, 393.
30 Boyle, *Disquisition*, 420.
31 Boyle, *Disquisition*, 420.

fitness of creatures (or parts of creatures) to the divine reasons for their existence. Ears are good for hearing, so God gave us ears for the sake of hearing.

Boyle draws a further distinction between two kinds of physical reasoning, namely, positive and negative physical reasoning. He maintains that both are permissible. As an example of a positive physical reasoning, Boyle offers Harvey's own work as an example. Boyle had met Harvey not long before the elder man's death and asked him what had put him on to the idea of the circulation of the blood. On the basis of their conversation, Boyle reports:

> [W]hen he [Harvey] took notice, that the valves in the veins of so many parts of the body were so placed, that they gave free passage to the blood towards the heart, but opposed the passage of the venal blood the contrary way; he was invited to imagine, that so provident a cause as nature had not so placed so many valves, without design; and no design seemed more probable, than that since the blood could not well, because of the interposing valves, be sent by the veins to the limbs, it should be sent through the arteries, and return through the veins, whose valves did not oppose its course that way.[32]

Harvey's report provides Boyle with a prime example of what he sees as positive physical teleological reasoning. On Boyle's rendering, Harvey was led to positively attribute a particular function to the venal valves on the assumption that the human body is well designed. The venal valves are so well suited to directing the flow of blood from the limbs to the heart that it may be surmised that it is indeed the nature of venal valves to have precisely that end. The inference here is from positive suitability to positive purpose.

---

[32] Boyle, *Disquisition*, 427.

Boyle also provides an example of negative physical reasoning. Earlier physiologists had supposed that the seat of vision is to be found in the crystalline humor (that is, the lens) of the eye. Boyle suggests that the physiologist Christof Scheiner was able to refute this view by arguing that the crystalline humor is not well suited to perform the requisite functions of the eye and that furthermore the retina is so suited:

> Thus, though anatomical and optical writers, as well as the schools, did for many ages unanimously conclude the crystalline humour to be the principal seat of vision; yet the industrious Scheiner, in his useful tract, intituled Oculus, does justly enough reject that received opinion, by shewing, that it suits not with the skill and providence of nature, to make that part the seat (or chief organ) of vision, for which it wants divers requisite qualifications, especially most of these being to be found in the retina.[33]

Whereas Harvey had moved from the fitness of the valves to a conclusion concerning their positive function, Scheiner, on Boyle's telling, moves from the lack of fitness of the crystalline humor, and the greater fitness of the retina, to the conclusion that the crystalline humor does not have the function of serving as the seat of vision. Whereas Harvey's inference was from suitability to purpose, Scheiner's inference is from lack of suitability to lack of purpose.

Although Boyle defends physical reasoning at some length, his principal aim in the *Disquisition* is to champion the legitimacy of metaphysical reasoning about ends. In setting out the conditions under which metaphysical teleological reasoning may be pursued, Boyle distinguishes four kinds of ends. (1) *Universal ends* concern the creation of the universe as a whole. These are, Boyle tells us, the "grand and general ends of the whole world, such as the exercising

---

33 Boyle, *Disquisition*, 427.

and displaying the Creator's immense power and admirable wisdom, the communication of his goodness, and the admiration and thanks due to Him from his intelligent creatures, for these his divine excellences, whose productions manifest his glory."[34] (2) *Cosmic ends* concern the movement and apparent design of celestial bodies. These are "ends designed in the number, fabric, placing, and ways of moving the great masses of matter, that, for their bulks or qualities, are considerable parts of the world . . . so framed and placed, as not only to be capable of persevering in their own present state, but also as was most conducive to the universal ends of the creation, and the good of the whole world, whereof they are notable parts."[35] (3) *Animal ends*, which—as the label suggests—"concern the parts of animals, (and probably plants too) which are those, that the particular parts of animals are destinated to, and for the welfare of the whole animal himself, as he is an entire and distinct system of organized parts, destinated to preserve himself and propagate his species, upon such a theatre (as the land, water, or air) as his structure and circumstances determine him to act his part on."[36] (4) Finally, *human ends* concern the ends of nature occurring specifically for the sake of human beings, that is, the ends "that are aimed at by nature, where she is said to frame animals and vegetables, and other of her productions, for the use of man."[37] Such human ends, Boyle tells us, may themselves be distinguished into two kinds: on the one side, ends that are for the sake of our minds, that is, ends that increase our awe, wonder, and appreciation of the divine, and on the other side, ends that are for the sake of our bodies, that is, ends that contribute to our preservation and propagation.[38]

---

34 Boyle, *Disquisition*, 395–396.
35 Boyle, *Disquisition*, 396.
36 Boyle, *Disquisition*, 396.
37 Boyle, *Disquisition*, 396.
38 Boyle, *Disquisition*, 396.

Boyle maintains that metaphysical reasoning can legitimately be applied with respect to all four kinds of ends. As an example of metaphysical reasoning applied to cosmological ends, Boyle maintains that "the sun, moon, and other celestial bodies, excellently declare the power and glory of God."[39] Boyle's favorite examples of metaphysical reasoning, however, involves animal ends, and in particular the eye. In a characteristic passage, he writes:

> The eye (to single out again that part for an instance) is so little fitted for almost any other use in the body, and is so exquisitely adapted for the use of seeing, and that use is so necessary for the welfare of the animal, that it may well be doubted, whether any considering man can really think, that it was not destinated to that use.[40]

The passage underscores a difference in aim between Harvey's *de Motu Cordis* and Boyle's *Disquisition*. Although Harvey believes in divine teleology, his principal aim in *de Motu Cordis* is to establish the ends of bodily parts such as the heart, valves, and veins. He aims, for example, to show that the function of the heart is to circulate blood. Boyle, conversely, believes in physical teleology—he agrees that the function of the heart is to circulate blood. His principal aim in the *Disquisition*, however, is to defend metaphysical reasoning—to argue, for example, that the eye not only has the function of seeing, but that it was indeed designed in order to see. The divine teleology largely in the background in Harvey's *de Motu Cordis* takes center stage in Boyle's *Disquisition*.

Boyle's extended defense of metaphysical reasoning may serve as a reminder that the vast majority of the proponents of the new mechanical science saw it as thoroughly consistent with the postulation of divine teleology. It is possible today to imagine the mechanist's universe as an impersonal, autonomous world. A world of billiard-ball-like

---

39 Boyle, *Disquisition*, 444.
40 Boyle, *Disquisition*, 425.

interactions: the movement of one lifeless part mechanically, efficiently causing the movement of another lifeless part, a world with no need nor place for God. To the early modern mind, however, things were likely to seem very different. The thought of the world as a grand machine—one with obvious efficiencies and countless intricacies—naturally conjured the further thought of a grand designer. If the world is like a wondrous clock, surely there must be a wondrous clockmaker. Thus, where we might be tempted to see mechanism as a step in the direction of a secular worldview, early modern naturalists like Boyle were more apt to see it as providing further reason for a providential worldview. For Boyle and his like, religion and science were mutually supportive. Religion leads us to expect a well-designed world with purposes hidden around every corner. Science shows that that expectation is met.

Boyle's defense of final causes goes beyond Harvey's in several respects. It goes beyond it in its focus. Teleology per se is not a topic of Harvey's *de Motu Cordis*. Harvey's work draws teleological conclusions, but its central topic is the movement of the heart and blood. In contrast, teleology per se is the central topic of Boyle's *Disquisition*. Its central aim is to categorize teleological reasoning and explicitly defend its legitimacy as far as possible. Boyle's work also goes beyond Harvey's in the scope of the teleological reasoning it defends. In *de Motu Cordis*, Harvey is almost exclusively concerned with the functions of animal parts and organs. As we've seen, Boyle cites Harvey's own work as part of his defense of what he calls physical reasoning, and his favorite examples of teleology similarly involve animal parts and organs. In keeping with his aim of defending teleology per se, however, Boyle offers a much wider range of cases, and moves beyond animal parts and organs to treat universal and cosmological ends as well. Finally, and most importantly, Boyle explicitly defends not just physical reasoning but also what he calls metaphysical reasoning about final causes. The divine teleology that hums in the background of Harvey's *de Motu Cordis* becomes a central theme in Boyle's *Disquisition*. Where Harvey generally takes divine teleology for granted, Boyle gives it a rigorous, sustained defense.

6.4. Pierre Louis Maupertuis and Formal Teleology

Born seventy-one years after Boyle, in Saint-Malo, France, Pierre Louis Maupertuis rose to become the foremost French proponent of Newtonianism in the eighteenth century. Good, but not brilliant, at mathematics, Maupertuis cultivated his native talents and social position well enough to secure an adjunct position at the Academy of Sciences in Paris in 1723. Thirteen years later, he led a daring expedition to Lapland to verify the Newtonian view that the earth is flattened at the poles. The wild success of his expedition gained him favor with Frederick the Great, and he was appointed to serve as the president of the Berlin Academy of Sciences from 1745 to 1753. His most daring adventures behind him, and his pioneering work on genetics still ahead, in 1746, Maupertuis published a short work in the *History of the Royal Academy of Sciences and Belles Lettres* entitled *Les loix du mouvement et du repos déduites d'un principe metaphysique* (*The Laws of Motion and Rest Deduced from a Metaphysical Principle*, hereafter *The Laws*).[41] He described the piece to Leonard Euler, his colleague at the Berlin Academy, as "a dissertation on final causes and the abuse that

---

41 Pierre Maupertuis, "Les loix du movement et du repos, déduites d'un principe de métaphysique," in *Histoire de L'Académie Royale des Sciences et Belles-Lettres* (Berlin, 1746 [1748]), 267–294. For recent work on Maupertuis and teleology, see, for starters, J. Christiaan Boudri, *What Was Mechanical about Mechanics? The Concept of Force between Metaphysics and Mechanics from Newton to Lagrange* (Dordrecht: Kluwer, 2002); Helmute Pulte, *Das Prinzip der kleinsten Wirkung und die Kraftkonzeptionen der rationale Meckanik: Eine Untersuchung zur Grudlegungsproblematik bei Leonhard Euler, Pierre Louis Moreau de Maupertuis und Joseph Louis Lagrange* (Stuttgart: Franz Steiner Verlag, 1989); Ansgar Lyssy, "L'économie de la nature—Maupertuis et Euler sur le principe de moindre action," *Philosophiques* 42, no. 1 (2015): 31–51.

some physicists have made of them."[42] It represents yet another surprising twist in the long history of the concept of teleology.

The Laws begins with a critique of earlier attempts to defend final causes. Maupertuis makes a show of not criticizing arguments by figures such as Cicero and Aristotle, "drawn from the beauty, order, and understanding of the universe." Given the science of their time, such historical figures are, in Maupertuis's opinion, "too little acquainted with Nature, to be entitled to admire" it.[43] Instead, Maupertuis sets his sights on the great Newton and the "crowd of physicists, after Newton, [who] have found God in the stars, in insects, in plants, in water."[44] His criticisms focus on two kinds of argument in particular, arguments that Boyle would have identified as metaphysical reasoning about cosmic ends and metaphysical reasoning about animal ends.

As an example of metaphysical reasoning about cosmic ends, Maupertuis highlights an argument suggested by Newton in the "queries" appended to his *Opticks*.[45] According to Maupertuis:

> This great man [Newton] believed that the motions of celestial bodies demonstrate well enough the existence of the One who governs them. Six planets, Mercury, Venus, the Earth, Mars, Jupiter and Saturn, revolve around the Sun. All move in the same direction, and describe nearly concentric orbs: while another species of celestial object, the Comets, describing very different orbits, move in all directions, and roam all regions of the sky. Newton believed that such uniformity could only be the effect of the will of a Supreme Being.[46]

---

42 Letter from Maupertuis to Euler, May 22 [1746], *Archives de l'Académie Royale des Sciences*, Paris, cited in Mary Terrall, *The Man Who Flattened the Earth* (Chicago: University of Chicago Press, 2002), 270.
43 Maupertuis, *The Laws*, 269.
44 Maupertuis, *The Laws*, 270.
45 See Query 31 in Isaac Newton, *Opticks, or A Treatise on the Reflections, Refractions, Inflections and Colours of Light*, based on the 4th ed. (London, 1730) (New York: Dover, 1952).
46 Maupertuis, *The Laws*, 269–270.

The form of the argument is familiar. The movement of the six planets seems too uniform and harmonious to be due to chance alone. The effect appears designed, and the most reasonable conclusion is that it is the intended end of a cosmic designer. To this familiar, intuitive argument, Maupertuis adds a touch of mathematical sophistication. Anticipating the feel of contemporary fine-tuning arguments, he suggests that the plane in which the planets move is so narrow that the probability that all the planets should be contained in it is 1,419,856 to 1![47] The implication, of course, is that it is all but certain that the orbits of the planets have a cosmic end.

Maupertuis is willing to concede that, if Newton is right in assuming that "all the celestial bodies attracted towards the Sun, move in the void," then their current trajectories are highly improbable.[48] They are a long shot on a cosmic scale. He pauses to note, however, that even so, the probability of the coincidence is not nil. Even if Newton's assumptions are right, the coincidence of the trajectories of the planets might be due to chance, and so "it cannot be said that this uniformity is the necessary effect of choice."[49] But this is really just skirmishing—a prelude to Maupertuis's main point. For, he asserts, we simply do not know the true physical causes of the uniformity of the motions of the planets. Perhaps Newton is wrong on that front. Perhaps the planets are carried along in fluid vortices, as Descartes had previously suggested. In that case, "the uniformity of their trajectories does not seem inexplicable; it no longer requires this singular chance or choice; and proves no more the existence of God, than would any other movement imparted to Matter."[50] The odds of the motions of the planets might be a million and half to one given Newton's assumptions. Nonetheless, they might be highly probable, or even necessary, if given their true causes.

---

47 For contemporary versions of the fine-tuning argument, see the essays in Neil Manson, *God and Design: The Teleological Argument and Modern Science* (New York: Routledge, 2003).
48 Maupertuis, *The Laws*, 271.
49 Maupertuis, *The Laws*, 271.
50 Maupertuis, *The Laws*, 271.

Turning from planets to animals, Maupertuis allows that the "argument drawn from the suitability of the different parts of animals with their needs appears to be more solid."[51] Concerning animals, he asks, rhetorically, "are not their feet made for walking, their wings for flying, their eyes for seeing, their mouths for eating, other parts for reproducing their ilk?"[52] Even here, however, Maupertuis is ultimately critical. On defense, he offers clear anticipations of thoughts that would be worked out with much greater care by Darwin in the next century. Maupertuis asks if the following might not be the case:

> Hazard ... had produced an innumerable multitude of individuals: a small number were found in such a manner that the parts of the animal could satisfy its wants; in an infinitely greater number, there was neither convenience nor order, all these perished: Animals without mouths could not live, others who lacked organs for generation could not perpetuate themselves; the only ones which have remained, are those in which order and convenience are found."[53]

On offense, Maupertuis takes a different tack, effectively accusing his opponents of cherry-picking their evidence. If the presence of thick skin on the rhinoceros is evidence *for* design, why is its absence on the turtle not evidence *against* design?[54] Maupertuis suggests that we should grant that the serpent's being "covered with a hideous and scaly skin" helps it survive.[55] But how can this fact be admired as evidence of the design of a wise and benevolent creator when the snake's skin seems merely to preserve "an animal whose tooth kills man"?[56] Generalizing in a way that recalls modern-day attacks on the argument from design,

---

51 Maupertuis, *The Laws*, 271.
52 Maupertuis, *The Laws*, 271.
53 Maupertuis, *The Laws*, 272.
54 Maupertuis, *The Laws*, 272–273.
55 Maupertuis, *The Laws*, 274.
56 Maupertuis, *The Laws*, 274.

Maupertuis concludes that "[t]he evils of all kinds, the disorder, vice, grief" seem as prodigious as their contraries and are "difficult to reconcile with the empire of" "a wise and mighty Being."[57]

Having heaped abuse on his predecessors in the first part of *The Laws*, Maupertuis turns, in the second part, to a positive defense of teleology rooted in his principle of least action. That principle states, "In collisions of bodies, motion is distributed in such a way that the quantity of action, once the change has taken place, is as small as possible," and that "in a state of rest, bodies in equilibrium must be situated such that if they are given some small motion, the quantity of action will be a minimum."[58] Maupertuis's principle has the implication, for example, that a ray of sunshine will travel along the quickest path from the sun to a viewer's eye regardless of whether it travels straight through the air, is reflected by a flat mirror, or is refracted by a glass of water. It has the implication that the momentum of two lumps of clay will be the same before and after they collide. It has the implication that the kinetic energy of two billiard balls will be the same before and after they collide. It has the implication that two children of different weights will balance on a teeter-totter if they each sit at the right distance from its center. Maupertuis was justly proud of his articulation of the principle of least action. It was a bold and fruitful attempt to unify the laws of physics in a single, exceptionally elegant principle. But how does it lend support to teleological reasoning?

In *The Laws*, Maupertuis suggests that the principle of least action provides a new basis for an argument for divine teleology. As the new science revealed elegant, general laws of nature, it was an irresistible move by devout believers to suggest that those elegant, general laws provide evidence of God's wise design and governance of the world. Just as Boyle infers providential ends from the apparent design of animal parts, Maupertuis would infer providential ends from the elegance

---

57 Maupertuis, *The Laws*, 275.
58 Maupertuis, *The Laws*, 286.

of the most basic law of nature. In pursuing this rather well-trodden line of thought, Maupertuis could see his principle of least action as providing two specific advantages over earlier efforts.

First, Maupertuis suggests that the principle of least action provides an improved foundation for supporting divine teleology because his principle far exceeds its rivals in unifying the laws of nature. He argues, for example, that within the domain of physics, his principle surpasses Descartes's laws in grounding accurate rules of collision, and that it surpasses Leibniz's laws in applying to both elastic and inelastic bodies.[59] Indeed, Maupertuis suggests that the principle of least action might be applied to all phenomena with full generality—not only to colliding bodies and cases of equilibrium, but also to "the movement of animals, the vegetation of plants, the revolutions of the stars."[60]

Second, Maupertuis suggests that the principle of least action—presumably in contrast to other laws of nature—can be deduced directly "from the attributes of an all-powerful and all-wise being."[61] He doesn't, of course, show in detail how such a deduction would go. Perhaps, however, we can see the grounds for his optimism. Laws such as Galileo's law of falling bodies or Newton's second law of motion are elegant and powerful. But they suggest no intuitive connection in their content to the possible ends of a divine designer. Why should a wise designer seek to make bodies fall with constant acceleration or guarantee that the product of a body's mass and acceleration is directly proportional to the forces to which it subjected? The principle of least action, however, does, at least at a first pass, suggest just such an intuitive link. We can easily imagine that a wise designer would aim for the sort of universal efficiency seemingly promised by the content of Maupertuis's principle of least action.

---

59 Maupertuis, *The Laws*, 283–286.
60 Maupertuis, *The Laws*, 286.
61 Maupertuis, *The Laws*, 279.

In *The Laws*, Maupertuis himself thus emphasizes how the principle of least action might lend support to divine teleology—to what Boyle calls *metaphysical* reasoning about ends. But Maupertuis's principle is striking in part because it might also seem to lend support to conjectures about ends falling within nature itself, to what Boyle calls *physical* reasoning about ends. Maupertuis closes *The Laws* by showing how the principle of least action could be applied to a small handful of elementary cases. With his unrivaled mathematical skills, Euler subsequently extended the principle's applications to a much wider range of examples. In doing so, he became convinced that "nothing whatsoever takes place in the universe in which some relation of maximum and minimum [i.e., "least" in Maupertuis's sense] does not appear."[62] In this universal result, Euler saw conclusive evidence of teleology operating within the world itself. By Euler's lights, it is clear that natural phenomena develop in such a way as to realize maxima and minima—they unfold in order to realize determinate outcomes. Those outcomes may be taken to be the ends of the physical processes that lead to them. A ray of light may reflect at such and such an angle in order to travel along the quickest path. Two billiard balls might rebound in such and such a way in order to minimize their overall "action." Euler thus maintains that "there is absolutely no doubt that every effect in the universe can be explained as satisfactorily from final causes, by the aid of the method of maxima and minima, as it can from the efficient causes themselves."[63] This line of thought is distinct from the line just attributed to Maupertuis. Whereas Maupertuis inferred the existence of divine ends from the principle of least action, Euler infers the existence of ends within nature itself. On Euler's view, it seems, any world governed by the principle of least action would have physical ends even if it were not the product of divine choice. The phenomena of such a world—of a world like ours—would be teleological in the sense that they would

---

62 Terrall, *Man Who Flattened*, 278.
63 Terrall, *Man Who Flattened*, 278.

come about for the sake of precise, predictable ends. More than two thousand years after Aristotle's *Physics*, we seem to have returned to a kind of immanent teleology.[64]

Maupertuis's defense of final causes is no less ambitious than the defenses offered by Harvey and Boyle. As we've seen, *The Laws* begins with a critical, incisive attack on earlier attempts to defend teleological reasoning in the sciences. Maupertuis is openly dismissive of arguments that seek to support divine teleology by appeal to either cosmological phenomena or the functions of animal parts. Indeed, he even offers a prescient argument for how the apparent design of organisms might come about through a process of blind natural selection. And yet it is clear that such criticisms are merely a propaedeutic to an even more audacious attempt to defend teleology on the basis of the principle of least action. Maupertuis saw his new principle not only as providing novel foundations for physics and natural philosophy more generally, but also as providing a novel basis for divine teleology. Surely such an elegant and universal principle could only be the product of a wise and benevolent designer. Furthermore, the principle itself suggested to many that teleology must operate within the order of nature. Just as I might go to the store in order to buy milk, or a dog might dig in the backyard to find a bone, so a physical particle might, it seems, follow a particular path in order to minimize or maximize its action. Maupertuis's principle thus held out the promise that a home might be found for teleological reasoning even in the heart of the mathematical physics of the new science.

6.5. Conclusion

Often portrayed as a victim of the scientific revolution, teleology was, in fact, widely upheld by leading figures of early modern science. As

---

[64] For discussion of Aristotle's views on teleology, see Mariska Leunissen's chapter in this volume.

we've seen, Harvey championed teleology above all in the domain of biology. There he made a powerful case that the attributions of functions to animal parts and organs could not only be made rigorous but also prove fruitful in the pursuit of scientific discovery. Boyle defended the legitimacy of teleology above all in the domain of natural theology while making a systematic, positive assessment of the place of final causes in the worldview of early modern natural philosophy. Finally, Maupertuis, with Euler's assistance, made a surprisingly powerful pitch for locating teleology at the foundations of physics, setting the stage for novel arguments in support of both providential and natural ends. Despite rumors to the contrary, teleology was alive and well in the early modern period. Reservations expressed by the likes of Bacon, Descartes, and Spinoza converted few at the time, and primarily served to rally others to take up their quills in defense of teleological reasoning.

To say that teleology survived, even flourished, with the new science, however, is not to say that the concept did not evolve during the period. No universal assertions are warranted here. If we restrict ourselves to the English-inspired tradition to which Harvey, Boyle, and—to a slightly lesser extent—Maupertuis belonged, two broad, general trends might nonetheless be noted. First, the investigation of final causes became increasingly continuous with the critical methodology of early modern natural philosophy. Harvey, Boyle, and Maupertuis all thought that attributions of final causes could not rest with everyday experiences or common sense. Harvey performed countless dissections, vivisections, and experiments to discover and test the functions he ascribes to animal parts and organs. Boyle cites, often in exhausting detail, studies drawn from throughout the full range of early modern science. Even while championing the legitimacy of final causes against Cartesians and Epicureans, he repeatedly cautions his fellow natural philosophers to shun arrogance and presumption and to "ground all things upon as solid reasons as may be had."[65] Finally, Maupertuis proved willing—even eager—to turn the critical reasoning so indicative of the new science against the teleological claims of his predecessors, even as he sought to provide new foundations for final causes in mathematical physics. Having developed a critical approach to the study of nature, early modern natural philosophers such as Harvey, Boyle, and Maupertuis couldn't but help to apply the same standards of reasoning to their investigations of final causes.

Second, within the English-inspired tradition, focus shifted from perennial metaphysical debates surrounding final causes to their explanatory potential. The late scholastic philosopher and theologian Francisco Suárez overlapped with Harvey for almost four decades. A reader of his *Disputationes Metaphysicae* will be treated to discussions of teleology, for example: "Whether the end is a true cause?" "What the nature of causing or the causality of the final cause is or consists in?" "What the proximate nature of causing in the final end is?"[66] Such foundational metaphysical questions are simply absent from Harvey's *de Motu Cordis*, Boyle's *Disquisition*, and Maupertuis's *The Laws*. In focusing their attention on whether and how attributions of final causes might be held to the rigors of the new science, the English-inspired tradition by and large simply ceased to discuss—perhaps ceased to worry—about the vast majority of metaphysical questions that had seemed so pressing to scholastic figures such as Suárez. It was progress in the spirit of Newtonian quietism—progress that delivered explanatory payoffs without fussing over their metaphysical foundations. It was also a development that almost begged for someone to make a clean break. That almost begged for someone to explicitly embrace the utility of teleological reasoning while denying that we can have any deep

---

65 Boyle, *Disquisition*, 399.
66 Francisco Suárez, *Disputationes Metaphysicae*, 2 vols. (reprint Hildesheim: Georg Olms, 2009), Disputation 23.

knowledge of the metaphysical basis of teleology itself. Having been raised in the very non-English tradition of Leibnizian metaphysics, Immanuel Kant would awake to that call and—as the next chapter will show—answer it with enormous implications for the historical development of the concept of teleology.

Reflection III
THE END OF POETRY
TELEOLOGY IN PHILIP SIDNEY'S SONNETS

Kathryn Murphy

The thirty-fourth poem in Philip Sidney's sonnet sequence *Astrophil and Stella* (pub. 1591, composed c. 1581) opens by asking after the teleology of poetry: "Come, let me write. And to what end?"[1] English Renaissance poems beginning "come" or "let" have a tendency to endorse erotic pleasure, and fend off censorious bans on self-delighting activity: "For God's sake hold your tongue, and let me love"; "Come live with me and be my love"; "Let me not to the marriage of true minds / Admit impediments."[2] But Sidney quickly dispels the mood of invitation with a querulous voice which asks after the larger purpose to which writing may be put: "And to what end?"

Sonnet 34 rehearses various answers. Sidney begins by suggesting that the suffering lover writes "to ease / a burdened heart," purging difficult emotions through catharsis. And depicting pain might bring others pleasure, since "Oft cruel fights well pictured forth do

---

[1] References to *Astrophil and Stella* are to Sidney, *The Major Works*, ed. Katherine Duncan Jones, rev. ed. (Oxford: Oxford University Press, 2008), by poem number.

[2] John Donne, "The Canonization"; Christopher Marlowe, "The Passionate Shepherd to His Love"; William Shakespeare, Sonnet 116.

please." This versifies an argument from Aristotle's *Poetics* which suggests that "even when things are painful to look upon … we take pleasure in viewing highly realistic images of them."[3] In the context of the *Poetics*, a technical discussion of the high genres of tragedy and epic, this account is the beginning of an answer to the perennial question of why the contemplation of suffering causes pleasure. Sidney's sonnet, however, is erotic lyric, and such grandiose justification is dismissed again by the teleological voice, which suspects love poems of being mere fripperies: "But will not wise men think thy words fond ware?"

Some wise men did. Francis Bacon claimed that "Poesie" was "rather a pleasure, or play of the imagination, than a worke or dutie."[4] It had no end or purpose. Sonnet 34 offers minor defenses against this charge, proposing private solace or pleasure as justifications. An extended response appears in Sidney's *Defence of Poesy*, which asserts more ambitious aims. Sidney begins, again, with Aristotle. He points to the derivation of "poet" from Greek *poiein*, "to make," which allows him to associate poetry as verbal art with the discussion of *poiesis* in the opening sentences of the *Nicomachean Ethics*, where Aristotle establishes that all arts and actions aim at some good; but that a "certain difference is found among ends," so that the end of medicine is health, the end of shipbuilding a boat, etc. Sometimes such ends are organized hierarchically, so that some arts are done for the sake of others, and are thus subordinate. The best of all arts must thus be that to which all others are directed: for Aristotle, this is politics.

This may seem a strange place to begin an apology for poetry. Nonetheless, Sidney summarizes Aristotle's discussion closely.

---

[3] Aristotle, *Poetics* 1448b10f, trans. Anthony Kenny, in *Poetics* (Oxford: Oxford University Press, 2013), 20.

[4] Francis Bacon, *The Tvvoo Bookes of Francis Bacon. Of the proficience and aduancement of Learning*, ed. Michael Kiernan (Oxford: Clarendon Press, 2000), 75.

Astronomy, music, natural philosophy, and mathematics are, Sidney suggests,

> serving sciences, which, as they have each a private end in themselves, so yet are they all directed to the highest end of the mistress-knowledge, by the Greeks called *architektonikē*, which stands as I think in the knowledge of a man's self, in the ethic and politic consideration, with the end of well-doing and not of well-knowing only—even as the saddler's next [*sc.* immediate] end is to make a good saddle, but his further end to serve a nobler faculty, which is horsemanship, so the horseman's to soldiery, and the soldier not only to have the skill but to perform the practice of a soldier.[5]

The equestrian examples are Aristotle's; and "architectonic" is Aristotle's word for the overarching art or kind of *poiesis* to which all other human arts and activities are bent. Against those who suggest that poetry is mere pointless play, Sidney suggests that it is in fact the art most fit to bring about "the ending end of all earthly learning," which he designates "virtuous action," by spurring men to virtuous emulation. Poetry, he argues, is better than history because historians are yoked to the historical record, while poets can address the probable, ideal, and exemplary. This is why Aristotle claimed, in the *Poetics*, that poetry was more philosophical than history: because it traffics in universals. But for Sidney, unlike Aristotle, poetry is also better than philosophy, which offers only barren universal precepts, while poets can move and delight the reader toward practicing virtue.

Sidney's argument, however, raises a problem of theory and practice—of how the *Defence* might be squared with *Astrophil*

---

[5] Sidney, *The Defence of Poesy*, in *Sidney's "The Defence of Poesy" and Selected Renaissance Literary Criticism*, ed. Gavin Alexander (London: Penguin, 2004), 13. Cf. Aristotle, *Nicomachean Ethics*, in *The Complete Works of Aristotle: The Revised Oxford Translation*, ed. J. Barnes (Princeton. NJ: Princeton University Press, 1984), 1094a10–15.

and Stella. The *Defence* uses Plato's dialogues and Xenophon's *Cyropaedia* as its prime examples of poetry, not erotic lyric. Since sonnets are concerned with seduction and self-involved complaint at a lover's disdain, how can they build the polis?

We might glimpse the beginnings of an answer in the ways in which Aristotle's hierarchy of ends is visible not just in how Sidney argued about poetry, but how he wrote it. *Astrophil and Stella*'s first sonnet begins, like Sonnet 34, with the pleasurable representation of pain:

> Loving in truth, and fain in verse my love to show,
> That she (dear she) might take some pleasure of my pain;
> Pleasure might cause her read, reading might make her know;
> Knowledge might pity win, and pity grace obtain;
>   I sought fit words to paint the blackest face of woe.

The lines are full of teleology: of actions done in order to win or obtain. The first line sets as its goal mimesis, or representation, the definitive character of poetry, according to the *Poetics*. The second line, introduced by "That" in the teleological sense of "in order to," subordinates that goal to another: the lover's pleasure in the representation of painful things. Even this is not the ending end: the pleasure she takes might cause her to "read," which would lead to edification, which would lead to pity, which might transform her behavior, leading her to be gracious to the poet.

This is structurally similar to Sidney's articulation of Aristotle's example of bridle-making as subordinate ultimately to soldiery: a sequence of substitutions leads from a proximate aim through a hierarchy of ever nobler ends. Sidney uses the same structure in the *Defence* when he declares that poets

> do merely make to imitate, and imitate both to delight and teach, and delight to move men to take that goodness in hand, which

without delight they would fly as from a stranger, and teach to make them know that goodness whereunto they are moved [which is] the noblest scope to which ever any learning was directed.[6]

Again, a poet's making has an immediate end of mimesis or imitation, but this is swiftly turned to other purposes: poets make to imitate, but imitate to delight and teach; and they delight and teach in order to teach men to know and enact goodness, the "noblest scope," or ending end.

In Sonnet 1 and the two passages from the *Defence*, the pattern is expressed by the same rhetorical figure: what is called in Latin *gradatio*, literally "walking," or, in Greek, κλῖμαξ (climax). Sidney's contemporary George Puttenham described it as a figure which "goeth ... by strides or paces. It may as well be called the climbing figure, for *climax* is as much to say as a ladder."[7] It expresses causal relationships through a sequence of two-term phrases, in which the second term in the first phrase becomes the first term in the second, the second term of the second phrase the first of the third, etc. Puttenham offered a common example unpacking the paradox "Peace brings war, and war brings peace":

Peace makes plenty, plenty makes pride,
Pride breeds quarrel, and quarrel brings war,
War brings spoil, and spoil poverty,
Poverty patience, and patience peace[.]

This causal concatenation is superficially similar to Sidney's use of *gradatio*. But in fact his use of the figure differs significantly, in that for Sidney, the first action, whether mimesis or writing or

---

6 The Defence of Poesy, 13. Cf. Aristotle, *Nicomachean Ethics*, 1094a10–15.
7

saddle-making, is completed in order to bring about the second: a teleological chain.

Sidney's examples of *gradatio*, like Puttenham's, can be collapsed into a summary sentence which leaps straight from the first action to the last. In the case of Sonnet 1, this would read, "The poet writes in order to obtain pity and grace from his mistress." This is a basic summary of the ostensible maneuvers of much courtly love poetry, where what "pity" and "grace" would most literally mean is the loved one granting the lover's desires. That *gradatio* is also known as "climax" makes the possibility of sexual punning rife. The notorious fact that in Shakespeare and English Renaissance poetry "to die" and "to end" mean "to reach orgasm" likewise suggests an erotic teleology. The "end" for erotic verse, it seems, is consummation.

But sonnet sequences were rarely written—if ever—for the beloved they purport to address, but for an audience of subtle readers. *Astrophil and Stella* is not a persuasion toward an actual consummation; instead, its mimesis should delight and move the reader toward something else. It is this structure of the substitution of ends which *Astrophil and Stella* repeatedly mimics. Rhyming metrical poetry inevitably foregrounds endings which are not ends: each line, each completed rhyme, each couplet or stanza concludes, but each also heralds the next. It is in the nature of the structure of a sonnet sequence that the close of an individual poem is a stopping point on the way to the next. Sidney's erotic lyrics are a minor mimesis of the larger concerns of a structure of postponed gratification, a ladder of ends, which enacts the architectonic teleology which he reworked from Aristotle.

CHAPTER SEVEN

"The Revised Method of Physico-Theology"

KANT'S REFORMED TELEOLOGY

Paul Guyer

7.1. Introduction

Teleological thinking—thinking that considerations of purposiveness are ineliminable from our comprehension of nature—might be thought to have been banished by the combined efforts of Descartes, Spinoza, and Hume.[1] Descartes insisted that "It is not the final but

---

[1] Citations from the *Critique of Pure Reason* are located by the pagination of the first edition of 1781 ("A") and the second edition of 1787 ("B"). Citations from all other works by Kant are located by volume and page number from the *Akademie* edition: *Kant's gesammelte Schriften*, ed. Royal Prussian (later German, then Berlin-Brandenburg) Academy of Sciences, 29 vols. (Berlin: Georg Reimer [later Walter de Gruyter & Co.], 1900–). The following abbreviations and translations are used here: *Only Possible Basis for a Demonstration of the Existence of God* (*OPB*), from Kant, *Theoretical Philosophy, 1755–1770*, ed. David E. Walford (Cambridge: Cambridge University Press, 1992). *Critique of Pure Reason* (*CPuR*), ed. Paul Guyer and Allen W. Wood (Cambridge: Cambridge University Press, 1998). *Groundwork for the Metaphysics of Morals* (*G*)

efficient causes of created things that we must inquire into," thus that "When dealing with natural things we will, then, never derive any explanations from the purposes which God or nature may have had in view when creating them."[2] Spinoza held that all of nature flows from God with absolute necessity, but that it makes no sense to think of God, who is identical with nature, as having anthropomorphic faculties such as intellect and will, and therefore "Not many words will be required ... to show that Nature has no end set before it, and that all final causes are nothing but human fictions."[3] And Hume seems to have established beyond doubt—if we can say that about Hume!—that thinking of nature as the product of purposive design is unacceptable anthropomorphism from the point of view of religious orthodoxy and ungrounded analogy from the point of view of a rigorous empiricism.[4]

As Jeffrey McDonough has shown in his chapter, the qualms of these philosophers by no means sufficed to eliminate teleological thinking from early modern science. Scientists made good use of the concept of *function* in their work, as when William Harvey determined that it is the function of the valves in veins to keep venous blood flowing back toward the heart for its subsequent recirculation (after, as was later determined, its oxygenation). What was controversial, rather, was

---

and *Critique of Practical Reason* (*CPrR*), from Kant, *Practical Philosophy*, ed. Mary J. Gregor (Cambridge: Cambridge University Press, 1996). *Critique of the Power of Judgment* (CPJ), ed. Paul Guyer (Cambridge: Cambridge University Press, 2000). *Religion within the Bounds of Mere Reason* (*RBMR*), from Kant, *Religion and Rational Theology*, ed. Allen Wood and George di Giovanni (Cambridge: Cambridge University Press, 1996). Also referred to, without abbreviations: Kant, *Correspondence*, ed. Arnulf Zweig (Cambridge: Cambridge University Press, 1999); Kant, *Anthropology, History, and Education*, ed. Günter Zöller and Robert B. Louden (Cambridge: Cambridge University Press, 2006).

2 René Descartes, *Principles of Philosophy*, Part One, §28, in *The Philosophical Writings of Descartes*, trans. John Cottingham, Robert Stoothoff, and Dugald Murdoch, 2 vols. (Cambridge: Cambridge University Press, 1985), vol. 1, 202.

3 Benedict de Spinoza, *Ethics*, Part One, Proposition 17, Scholium I, and Part I, Appendix, in *The Collected Works of Spinoza*, ed. and trans. Edwin Curley, 2 vols. (Princeton, NJ: Princeton University Press, 1985 and 2015), vol. 1, 426 and 442.

4 David Hume, *Dialogues Concerning Natural Religion*, Parts 10 and 11, in Hume, *The Natural History of Religion and Dialogues concerning Natural Religion*, ed. A. Wayne Colver and John Valdimir Price (Oxford: Clarendon Press, 1976), especially 227 and 241.

the assumption that any such function had to be the product of intentional and intelligent *design*, and thus the inference from functionality in nature to the existence of God as its ground—what McDonough calls the "metaphysical" interpretation of teleology, which he has shown was vigorously defended by Robert Boyle in spite of all his other contributions to the emergence of modern science. This is the form of teleology that philosophers such as Descartes, Spinoza, and Hume criticized, by Hume especially in his posthumous *Dialogues concerning Natural Religion* (published in 1779, translated into German in 1781), the core argument of which, however, was already stated in his *Inquiry concerning Human Understanding* (1748). That work had been translated into German as early as 1754 and was known to Kant as a young man.

But for all that Hume awoke him from a "dogmatic slumber," Kant grew up in an intellectual world dominated by Leibniz, Christian Wolff, and Alexander Gottlieb Baumgarten, all of whom held that it was not merely permissible but indispensable to conceive of the world and therefore everything in it as the purposive expression of God's beneficence—for them, that stood to reason, in technical terms was the only possible explanation of the Principle of Sufficient Reason. Kant could and did not simply reject this way of thinking. Instead, over a period of more than twenty-five years from *The Only Possible Basis for a Demonstration of the Existence of God* of 1763 to the *Critique of the Power of Judgment* of 1790, he transformed it from a metaphysical certitude about the world as it is independent of our own way of thinking about it to a characteristic feature of human psychology, inescapable and beneficial but not warrentedly assertible about reality as it is independent from our representation of it. Of course, Kant transformed *all* metaphysical certitudes about objective reality into inescapable features of the human *representation* of reality, so at one level his reform of teleology does not differ from his reform of metaphysics itself. But among the characteristic features of the human representation of reality, Kant came to distinguish between the indispensable conditions of representing objects at all—the pure forms of intuition and conceptual thought, space, time, and the categories—and natural tendencies of human thought that are not indispensable for representing objects at all but that, if properly applied, are beneficial for the successful conduct of both scientific inquiry and morality. This is Kant's distinction between the constitutive and the regulative principles of human thought, and Kant's reform of teleology consists in reassigning it from the realm of constitutive principles where his German predecessors thought it fit to the newly discovered realm of regulative principles. Kant did this both for the concept of function as applied to organisms and their organs and for the further thought that both organisms and the world as a whole have been designed by an intelligent designer and for an overarching purpose.

This did not happen in a single step, and my use of Kant's phrase "the revised method of physico-theology" as the title of this chapter is a little misleading. For this phrase comes from Kant's early work *The Only Possible Basis*, and at this stage of his thought Kant was revising popular ways of conceiving of the expression of divine purposiveness in the world, as taking the form of frequent intervention in the operation of the laws of nature, into a conception of much of the purposiveness of nature as built into the very laws of the possibility of things that are grounded in God. Some of the rules for the revised method of physico-theology that Kant described at this early point in his career are continuous with the "maxims" of the "power of judgment" that he would later identify (*CPJ*, Introduction, section V, 5:184), but in 1763 Kant still conceived of these rules as grounded in metaphysical certitude about the nature of God. It would take him until 1790 to fully transform these rules into regulative principles grounded in an *idea* of the systematicity of nature grounded in divine intelligence and will. Thus Kant's reform of teleology took place in two steps.

Before I describe these steps in more detail, it is also important to observe that there are two aspects to Kant's reformed teleology, namely, that his conception of philosophical *method* as well as of the *content* of philosophy is thoroughly teleological.[5] Kant believes that we should proceed on the supposition that every way in which it is natural for us to think must have some proper function, even if that is not the one that we unreflectively assign to it. One task for philosophy is to figure out what the right use of any natural predisposition is. This thought bears some analogy to Kant's supposition in his moral theory that our natural predispositions, even our "animal" ones—hunger, sex drive, etc.—all have some potentially good role, though we can easily pervert them by raising them to the level of self-conceit and subordinating morality to self-love. The difference is that the teleological presupposition of philosophical method is a regulative principle, while the requirement not to let natural predispositions subordinate morality to self-love is a categorical imperative.

7.2. The Teleological Method of Philosophy

For that matter, a clear example of Kant's teleological method for philosophy itself can be found at the outset of his exposition of his mature moral philosophy. Kant opens the 1785 *Groundwork for the Metaphysics of Morals* with the assertion that the only thing that is "good without limitation" is a good will (*G*, 4:393). He then argues for his assertion from the assumption of "the principle that there will be found in" an "organized" or living being "no instrument for some end other than what is also most appropriate to that end and best adapted to it" (4:395), that is, every organ or capacity in an organism is purposive or has some function for which it is well adapted. He then argues that since our faculty of reason does *not* seem especially well adapted for our "*preservation . . . welfare . . .* in a word . . . *happiness*," all of which are better served by mere instinct, but yet must be well adapted for

---

[5] See my "Kant's Teleological Conception of Philosophy and Its Development," *Kant Yearbook* 1 (2009): 57–97. That entire issue of *Kant Yearbook* is devoted to Kant's teleology. See also Courtney D. Fugate, *The Teleology of Reason: A Study of the Structure of Kant's Critical Philosophy* (Boston: Walter de Gruyter, 2014).

some purpose, "the true vocation of reason must be to produce a will that is good, not perhaps *as a means* to other purposes, but *good in itself*" (4:396). The premise that the production of happiness or the production of a good will are the two mutually exclusive candidates for the purpose of reason might seem problematic, but given the breadth of Kant's conception of happiness, as the maximal possible satisfaction of all of one's particular, "empirical" or "material" ends (see *G*, 4:418 and *CPrR*, 5:22), perhaps this can be defended. But our present concern is only with the status of Kant's teleological principle, which he simply assumes. He attempts no proof of it, so perhaps we must regard it as only a regulative principle for the practice of philosophy itself, to be employed as long as we can in the absence of any proof that it is *not* sound. Perhaps that is the best that we can hope for in a fundamental principle of philosophical method, since any attempt to prove it would itself be a piece of philosophy potentially relying upon it.

Be that as it may, the entire structure of Kant's critical philosophy and not just his initial exposition of the fundamental principle of morality (which is in any case only a "transition from common rational to philosophical moral cognition" [*G*, 4:393] and not yet a proper "metaphysics of morals" [4:406] grounded on a "critique of pure practical reason" [4:446]) is constructed in accordance with the teleological principle that although our own reason may lead to fallacious results under certain circumstances, even to entirely "natural" illusions, it nevertheless has an indispensable function for which it is well suited if only we understand it properly. Thus the overarching argument of the *Critique of Pure Reason* is that human reason produces ideas of the "unconditioned"—ideas of a simple, substantial, immortal soul, of a determinate world-whole (whether finite or infinite), and of a God who is the ground of all possibility as well as actuality—that exceed the limits of confirmation by our senses and thus cannot provide theoretical cognition, or which even lead to theoretical contradiction, but that nevertheless must have some proper function, which turns out to be the dual function of serving as regulative principles for the conduct of theoretical inquiry and as postulates of pure practical reason to make the pursuit of our necessary moral goals rational. Kant emphasizes the second of these purposes rather than the first in this seminal statement in the Preface to the second edition of the first *Critique*, written when he was in the throes of expounding his moral philosophy, between the composition of the *Groundwork* in 1784 and that of the *Critique of Practical Reason* in 1787:

> Hence a critique that limits the speculative use of reason is, to be sure, to that extent **negative**, but because it simultaneously removes an obstacle that limits or even threatens to wipe out the practical use of reason, this critique is also in fact of **positive** and very important utility, as soon as we have convinced ourselves that there is an absolutely necessary practical use of pure reason (the moral use), in which reason unavoidably extends itself beyond the bounds of sensibility, without needing any assistance from speculative reason, but in which it must also be made secure against any counteraction from the latter, in order not to fall into contradiction with itself. (*CPuR*, B xxv)

In the body of the work, however, Kant devotes more space to the teleology of the regulative principles of theoretical inquiry (in the Appendix to the Transcendental Dialectic) than he does to the teleology of practical reason (which is more fully developed in the *Critique of Practical Reason* and subsequent works). But both functions are equally emphasized in the following passage in which Kant is explaining the generation of the "transcendental concepts of reason" before his detailed account of the impossibility of using them directly for knowledge of objects in the body of the Transcendental Dialectic:

> Although we have to say of the transcendental concepts of reason: **They are only ideas**, we will by no means regard them as

superfluous and nugatory. For even if no object can be determined through them, they can still, in a fundamental and unnoticed way, serve the understanding as a canon for its extended and self-consistent use, through which it cognizes no more objects than it would cognize through its [own] concepts, yet in this cognition it will be guided better and further. Not to mention the fact that perhaps the ideas make possible a transition from concepts of nature to the practical, and themselves generate support for the moral ideas and connection with the speculative cognitions of reason. (*CPuR*, A 329 / B 385–386)

What is crucial about this passage is its claim that even though the attempt to use the unconditioned ideas of reason for direct knowledge of objects in the absence of anything unconditioned in sensibility is unsuccessful, still these ideas cannot simply be "superfluous and nugatory," because unless proven otherwise we must assume that nothing in nature is superfluous and nugatory—and reason is as much as part of our nature as any of other faculties.

There is no room here for a detailed account of Kant's diagnosis of the natural illusions that arise from treating the ideas of pure reason as if they were ordinary concepts of pure reason, nor is this section the proper place for a more detailed account of his conception of the natural and proper regulative and practical functions of these ideas.[6] I will just conclude the present section by citing Kant's remark in the introduction to the Appendix to the Transcendental Dialectic, "On the regulative use of the ideas of pure reason":

Everything grounded in the nature of our powers must be purposive and consistent with their correct use, if only we can guard against

---

6 For further discussion of and references on these two issues, see Paul Guyer, *Kant*, 2nd ed. (London: Routledge, 2014), chapters 3 and 6.

a certain misunderstanding and find out their proper direction. Thus the transcendental ideas too will presumably have a good and consequently **immanent** use, even though, if their significance is misunderstood and they are taken for concepts of real things, they can be transcendent in their application and for that very reason deceptive.... Accordingly, I assert: the transcendental ideas are never of constitutive use, so that the concepts of certain objects would thereby be given.... On the contrary, however, they have an excellent and indispensably necessary regulative use, namely that of directing the understanding to a certain goal. (*CPuR*, A 642–644 / B 670–672)

Once again, Kant combines the language of necessity with the language of supposition: he "asserts," but does not prove, that the ideas of reason have a necessary and indispensable regulative function in the conduct of inquiry by the understanding, that they "presumably" have such a function. The methodology of philosophy cannot itself be philosophically proven, but if the teleological method for philosophy can find a function for every one of our natural capacities instead of leaving some of them idle, like a Scrabble player who uses up all her tiles rather than having to deduct points for leftovers at the end of the game, that is surely a recommendation in its favor.

To be sure, Kant's assumption that nothing natural is essentially wasteful may not fit into our present conception of nature as full of evolutionary dead-ends and wastelands in an ordinary sense, or we may find distinguishing between what is useful and wasteful in nature altogether too anthropocentric for our taste. But the Leibnizian-Wolffian-Baumgartian background that Kant took for granted is very different from the Darwinian background that most of us now take equally for granted, and a teleological method for philosophy itself must have seemed entirely natural to him. But let us now turn from the teleological method of his philosophy to its teleological content.

7.3. Kant's Initial Revision

As was noted at the outset, Kant used the phrase "revised method of physico-theology" in his 1763 book *The Only Possible Basis for a Demonstration of the Existence of God*. The revision that he had in mind in that work was building teleology into God's role as the ground of all *possibility* rather than finding it in separate acts of the divine will manifested in the choice to bring particular objects or events into existence—in other words, he locates teleology primarily in the fundamental laws of nature rather than in any miraculous interventions in nature. The general laws of nature that are built into its very possibility, Kant insists, can explain most of the ways in which nature is also purposive. However, highly purposive but apparently contingent arrangements of organs in organisms—plant and animal life—seem to call for a special explanation from the will of a divine author. Kant will continue into the third *Critique* to regard purposiveness in organisms as requiring special treatment, but his second major reform in teleology will be to transform the assertion of an intelligent authorship for organic purposiveness from a metaphysical speculation into a psychological predisposition of human beings. This can be seen as his response to the metaphysical teleology defended by Robert Boyle (although there is no reason to suppose that Kant was familiar with this work by Boyle).

The argument of *The Only Possible Basis* is that neither the ontological argument from the mere concept of God to his actuality nor the cosmological argument from the actual existence of anything finite to the existence of an infinite God can work, so that the only possible basis for a proof of divine existence is that in which the "internal possibility of all things ... presupposes some existence or other" (*OPB*, 2:159–160), but in particular that of a *single* being grounding *all* possibilities—God. Kant views this approach to divine existence as solving an obvious problem in the Leibnizo-Wolffian philosophy, namely that it treats the constraints on the best of all possible worlds as if they arose from outside of God, but he also sees it as grounding a revised method of teleology. Instead of thinking that any evidence of purposiveness in nature is evidence of divine creation or intervention, Kant argues that most of the apparent purposiveness of nature can be regarded as the natural outcome of the operation of the laws of nature that are inherent in the very possibility of nature itself, as grounded in God's existence but not in intentional acts of his will that can only be understood anthropomorphically. The sea breezes that cool shores during the day but not at night do not have to be explained as the product of special divine intentions, aimed at making living by the shore pleasant for human beings, but as the natural outcome of differential heating and cooling of land and water (*OPB*, 2:98). The fact that rivers do not everywhere spread out over plains, rendering the plains unfit for human habitation and cultivation and the rivers unfit for navigation, does not have to be explained by divine intervention aimed at benefiting human commerce, but can be explained by a natural mechanism by which streams erode particles from their mountainous sources and then deposit them to build up their own banks (*OPB*, 2:128–131). Thus features of nature that are in fact very useful to us humans do not have to be explained by miracles but can be explained by the "necessary and most general laws of motion" (*OPB*, 2:98) and other fundamental laws of nature grounded in its very possibility. Thus too natural events that seem contrapurposive to humans, such as earthquakes and hurricanes, do not have to be explained as lapses in divine benevolence or even as specific acts of divine retribution, but can likewise be understood as natural outcomes of the fundamental laws of nature. Both the purposive and contrapurposive effects of nature, as we see them, are consequences of the "essential order of nature" (*OPB*, 2:107), which is itself grounded in the nature of God, but not in intentional interventions by a quasi-human God. Of course, the "general dependency of the essences of things upon God is . . . always a major ground for regarding the consequences as on the whole appropriate and in harmony with the rule of the best" (*OPB*, 2:111), but there is no need to picture God in anthropomorphic terms; all the work is done by his role as the ground of possibilities or essences.

On the basis of this argument Kant recommends what are really two revised methods of "physico-theology," one a method for the conduct of scientific inquiry and one a method for conceiving of God himself. The former is simple:

> In the procedure of purified philosophy there prevails a rule which, even if it is not formally stated, is nonetheless always observed in practice. The rule maintains that in investigating the causes of certain effects one must pay careful attention to maintaining the unity of nature as far as possible. In other words, the rule maintains that one must derive a variety of effects from a single cause which is already known, and not immediately suppose the existence of new and diverse operative causes to explain different effects because of some seemingly important dissimilarity between them.[7] Accordingly, it is presumed that there exists a great unity in nature, in respect of the adequacy of a single cause to account for many different kinds of consequences. (*OPB*, 2:113)

Kant does not yet use the term "regulative principle," but this prescription has the form of one: its status is that of a presumption rather than an assertion, and it does not say that a single cause of diverse phenomena will always be found, but only that the search for a single cause should always be pursued. In the terminology of Kant's later account of the regulative principles of scientific inquiry in the Appendix to the Transcendental Dialectic of the first *Critique*, this is a prescription of "homogeneity" in causal explanation, although there Kant speaks of "systematicity" as well as the "projected unity" of nature (*CPuR*, A 647 / B 675) and accompanies the prescription of the pursuit of

---

[7] Kant would certainly have been familiar with Maupertuis's "law of least action," as described by McDonough, and would have had that sort of law in mind in the present passage.

homogeneity of principles with prescriptions of specificity of kinds and affinity or continuity between more specific and more generic classifications and explanations (*CPuR*, A 657–658 / B 685–686). But at the early stage of *The Only Possible Basis*, he is content to hold that the idea of God as the unitary basis of everything possible in nature rationalizes the scientific practice of seeking unifying explanations of diverse phenomena.

Kant's fuller exposition of the "rules of the revised method of physico-theology" later in *The Only Possible Basis* includes a fuller statement of the method of scientific inquiry but also rules for thinking about God himself. Kant states six rules, the first three of which expand upon the presumption of the unity of nature—not only should we always seek it, but we should correspondingly presuppose that it is greater than initially meets the eye (*OPB*, 2:126). But we should also recognize that there are "artificial" and "*contingent* connections of the world" from which "one will infer the existence of a Being who has originated the manner in which the universe is assembled," as well as the "*necessary* unity of the world," from which "one will infer the existence of that self-same Being, construed as the Author even of the matter and fundamental stuff of which all natural things are constituted" (*OPB*, 2:126–127). So insofar as there are things in nature that seem contingent rather than necessary, we still have to conceive of God in more anthropomorphic terms as a designer as well as, in more purified form, the ground of all possibility—but Kant's message seems clear, always to push the search for necessary connections in a unified nature as far as possible, and thus push the latter as well as the former conception of God as far as possible also.

The threat to Kant's conception of the unity of nature, however, is the case of organisms, plant and animal life. His sees two main obstacles to including organisms in a unitary model of scientific explanation along mechanical lines, like those by which he explains sea breezes and the formation of riverbanks. First, he finds it hard to conceive how the "uniting together of various characteristics in an animal, for example," particularly the "uniting together of useful properties," can be explained by purely mechanical means. In the case of a spider, the union of "the different eyes by means of which it watches out for its prey, the wart from which the spider's thread is drawn out as through a nipple, the delicate claws and even the balls of its feet by means of which it sticks the thread together or holds on to it," constitutes a "system" that allows the spider to function successfully (*OPB*, 2:119)—achieve its purposes, as we might say, from our point of view—but seems hard to explain by any straightforward mechanical process such as the deposition of silt at the side rather than the middle of a stream. Second, Kant finds it difficult to conceive of a "mechanical explanation" of how any organism, whether spider or yeast (*OPB*, 2:115), can reproduce its own kind. He is familiar with two models of reproduction, of course, preformation and epigenesis, on the first of which all future generations are encapsulated in the seeds of the first generation, and on the second of which new generations are formed from contributions by both parents, but in either case some sort of divine intervention in the mechanical laws of nature seems necessary. So organisms seem to Kant to call for the traditional rather than revised conception of God as intervening in nature rather than simply grounding it. Organisms themselves constitute unities—for example, an animal's "organs of sense perception are connected with the organs of voluntary movement" so as to allow it to function successfully, as we saw in the case of the spider, but in this case "one would have to be of an ill-natured disposition . . . not to recognize the existence of a Wise Author, who had so excellently ordered the matter of which the animal was constituted" (*OPB*, 2:125).

7.4. Kant's Subjectivist Teleology in the *Critique of the Power of Judgment*

The special case of organisms is missing from the *Critique of Pure Reason*, as is generally the subject of teleology, although not the teleological method of philosophy itself. This is hardly to say that the first *Critique* does not drastically revise Kant's earlier position. It does so most decidedly, demoting the previous proof of the existence of God as the ground of all possibility to a mere idea of reason of the ground of a sum total of possibilities that can never be determinately conceived, and correspondingly changing the imperative to seek unity among the laws of nature from a revised method of *theology* to a regulative ideal—more precisely, the three regulative principles of homogeneity, specificity, and continuity comprising the ideal of scientific systematicity. But the challenge of understanding organisms returns to prominence in Kant's final *Critique*, although no more than in his work of more than a quarter-century earlier does this case exhaust his reformed teleology. Rather, the third *Critique* considers a teleological approach to natural law in general in its Introduction and the special case of organisms in its second half, the "Critique of the Teleological Power of Judgment," but adds an aesthetic theory that represents another special case of teleological thinking in its first half and concludes with suggestions about a teleological view of human history that are further developed in even later work by Kant, notably his 1793 book *Religion within the Boundaries of Mere Reason*. There are thus four distinguishable aspects of Kant's reformed teleology in the *Critique of the Power of Judgment*, although in all four cases teleology is treated as a distinctive feature of human experience rather than a metaphysical certitude. These four cases are (1) our system of scientific *concepts*, or our conceptions of laws of nature, (2) our aesthetic experience and judgments of taste, (3) our judgments about purposiveness in organisms, and (4) our judgment that nature as a whole—the objects of nature rather than our concepts of nature—forms a system with the full realization of human morality as its ultimate goal.[8] The third of these topics is especially relevant to the question of whether the concept of

---

8 For a similar analysis of the complex topics of the third *Critique*, although in the form of an analysis of Kant's multidimensional conception of "reflecting judgment" rather than teleology, see my "Kant's Principles of Reflecting Judgment," in *Kant's Critique of the Power of Judgment: Critical Essays*, ed. Paul Guyer (Lanham, MD: Rowman & Littlefield, 2003), 1–61.

function is necessary in order to understand at least organic nature (William Harvey's question), while the first and last bear on the metaphysical question of whether we must infer an intelligent ground of nature (Robert Boyle's question).

7.4.1. System of Scientific Concepts

Kant's brief treatment of the ideal of systematicity in scientific cognition in the Introduction to the third *Critique* is overtly teleological in a way that the treatment of this topic in the Appendix to the Transcendental Dialectic of the first is not. In the first *Critique*, Kant wavers between treating the systematic unity of scientific laws, as explicated by the ideals of homogeneity, specificity, and continuity, as a desideratum of the faculty of reason, which always seeks maximal ("unconditioned") unity, that can be *added* to the understanding's requirement that individual laws be true (*CPuR*, A 645 / B 673), and as a *necessary condition* of the truth of our claims to know particular laws of nature, and thus as a condition of the possibility of experience itself (A 651 / B 679), although he offers no explanation of the latter suggestion. In the first draft of the Introduction to the third *Critique*, Kant suggests that the assumption of the systematicity of particular laws of nature—for example, particular causal laws, as opposed to the general law that everything in nature has some cause, which is supposed to have been demonstrated entirely a priori in the second "Analogy of Experience" of the first *Critique* (A 188–211 / B 233–256)—can provide encouraging *assurance* that such laws can be found and a *method* for finding them (*CPJ*, First Introduction, section V, 20:211–212). Kant characterizes this assumed systematicity of nature as an assumption of the "purposiveness" (*Zweckmäßigkeit*) of nature, not in the traditional senses that nature has some purpose of its own or that it serves any particular *practical* purposes of human beings, but rather in the sense that it is well suited for our own *cognitive* aims (First Introduction, section V, 20:216). He says here that "we call purposive [*zweckmäßig*] that the existence of which seems to presuppose a representation of that same thing," which would seem to entail the existence of a representation of all of nature and of a representer capable of such a representation, that is, God, not us, whether individually or collectively, for such a representation would seem to exceed all human powers. But he does not explicitly link the idea of the cognitive purposiveness of nature for us to an idea of God, and instead says that "the end is not posited in the object at all, but strictly in the subject and indeed in its mere capacity for reflecting." In the published version of the Introduction, however, Kant both suggests a further role for the idea of a complete system of particular laws of nature and links it more explicitly to the idea of a designer of nature, or God. His first point is that particular laws of nature, "which can only be known to [us] empirically" and which from our point of view would therefore seem merely contingent, must nevertheless be able to be thought "as laws (i.e., as necessary), because otherwise they would not constitute an order of nature" (*CPJ*, Introduction, section V, 5:184). Yet we cannot cognize them as necessary on the basis of our inductive evidence for them, even when they take on the form required by the synthetic and entirely a priori principles of judgment (the Analogies of Experience and their fellows), conceived of as the laws for "the possibility of a nature (as object of the senses) in general" (*CPJ*, Introduction, section IV, 5:180).[9] Instead, Kant suggests, we

---

9 Following James Kreines, James Messina calls this interpretation of Kant's account of the origin of particular laws of nature and our knowledge of them the "Derivation Account," and attributes it to Michael Friedman. He contrasts it to the "Best Systems Account," which he attributes to Philip Kitcher. This comes closer to the interpretation presented here, which I have also expounded in "Kant on the Systematicity of Nature: Two Puzzles," *History of Philosophy Quarterly* 20 (2003): 277–295, reprinted in Paul Guyer, *Kant's System of Nature and Freedom: Selected Essays* (Oxford: Clarendon Press, 2005), 56–73. Messina proposes a 'Necessitation Account" as an alternative to both of these, on which the necessity of particular laws arises from the essences or natures of natural kinds. He finds this position in Kant's *Only Possible Basis* but argues that Kant continues to hold it throughout his work; see Messina, "Kant's Necessitation Account of Laws and the Nature of Natures," in *Kant and the Laws of Nature*, ed. Michela Massimi and Angela Breitenbach (Cambridge: Cambridge University Press, 2017),131–149. (Kreines's paper is "Kant on the Laws of Nature and the Limitation of Our Knowledge," *European Journal of Philosophy* 17 [2009]: 527–558.) I think that Messina's interpretation of the *Only Possible Basis* is threatened by Kant's argument there for the existence of God as the ground of all *possibilities*, which Kant treats as *laws of nature* giving rise to natural kinds rather than as essences of kinds themselves, and that

ground our conception of the necessity of particular laws of nature in their membership in a *system* of laws:

> [T]he sort of principle that is expressed in the following propositions: that there is in nature a subordination of genera and species that we can grasp; that the latter in turn converge in accordance with a common principle, so that a transition from one to the other and thereby to a higher genus is possible; that since it seems initially unavoidable for our understanding to have to assume as many different kinds of causality as there are specific differences of natural effects, they may nevertheless stand under a small number of principles with the discovery of which we have to occupy ourselves, etc. (*CPJ*, Introduction, section V, 5:185)

Kant's idea, at least in the second part of this passage, in which he is clearly talking about species and genera of particular causal *laws* (like those of combustion or photosynthesis) and not of natural *kinds* (like lions and tigers), seems to be that such laws, otherwise known only inductively, can be lent a kind of necessity, which they must have, by being placed within a system in which they would have *deductive* relations, deriving from higher-level laws and in turn entailing lower-level laws. But since we cannot fully cognize such a system ourselves, and a fortiori cannot produce it ourselves, yet must also conceive it as actually existing, not merely as an ideal, in order to ground the necessity of particular laws, we must conceive of it as conceived and imposed upon nature by an intelligence greater than our own:

> Now this principle can be nothing other than this: that since universal laws of nature have their ground in *our* understanding,

---

his argument for continuity does not do justice to Kant's new argument in sections IV–V of the Introduction to the *Critique of the Power of Judgment*, to be expounded here.

which prescribes them to nature (although only in accordance with the universal concept of it as nature), the particular empirical laws, in regard to that which is left undetermined in them by the former, must be considered in terms of the sort of unity they would have if an understanding (*even if not ours*) had likewise given them for the sake of our faculty of cognition, in order to make possible a system of experience in accordance with particular laws of nature. (*CPJ*, Introduction, section IV, 5:180; emphases added)

The human "power of judgment must thus assume it as an a priori principle for its own use that what is contingent for human insight in the particular (empirical) laws of nature nevertheless contains a lawful unity, not fathomable by us, but still thinkable, in the combination of the manifold" of particular laws "into one experience" of systematicity "possible in itself" and actually conceived by God (*CPJ*, Introduction, section V, 5:183–184)—yet at the same time "This agreement of nature with our faculty of cognition is presupposed a priori by the power of judgment in behalf of its reflection on nature in accordance with empirical laws, while at the same time the understanding recognizes it objectively as contingent" (5:185). That is, we must occupy the complex position of conceiving of particular laws of nature as part of a system of laws designed and instituted by God in order to be able to conceive of them as necessary, yet at the same time recognize that our idea of God is indeed our own idea, the existence of the object of which we have no right to assert on theoretical grounds (although we will eventually acquire such right on practical grounds). In sum, Kant's position that we form an idea of God and the system of natural laws that he intends is a revision of his earlier method of *teleology*, while his insistence that this idea is presupposed by our power of judgment for its reflection on nature but is not a sound theoretical assertion for our understanding is a revision of his earlier method of *theology*.

7.4.2. Aesthetic Experience

Kant links aesthetic experience and judgment to the general theme of teleology in two ways.[10] First, he characterizes our pleasure in aesthetic experience (paradigmatically, the experience of beauty) as our response to "the purposiveness of the object, which is not grounded on any available concept of the object and does not furnish one," but instead consists in an apparently contingent "agreement of the object with the faculties of the subject" (*CPJ*, Introduction, section VII, 5:190). Since the aesthetic experience is not a response to any *concept* of its object, it cannot be a response to any *concept of a particular purpose* of the object (*CPJ*, §4, 5:207–209); therefore Kant characterizes the purposiveness of the aesthetic object as "perceived in it **without representation of an end**" (*CPJ*, §17, 5:236). This leads to its common characterization as "purposiveness without purpose," although Kant's own preferred expression is that aesthetic purposiveness or beauty is "the form of the purposiveness of an object" (*CPJ*, §17, 5:236 and *CPJ*, §11, 5:221) or "the subjective purposiveness in the representation of an object without any end" (5:221) or "the merely formal purposiveness in the play of the cognitive powers" (§5:222). The last phrase points toward Kant's theory that the actual source of our pleasure in beauty is the "free play" between imagination and understanding, which satisfies the understanding's ambition for "lawfulness" (*CPJ*, General remark following §22, 5:241) or unity or coherence in our experience without dependence upon the understanding's usual means for securing unity, namely concepts, a fortiori concepts of purpose. Kant claims that

> The consciousness of the merely formal purposiveness in the play of the cognitive powers of the subject in the case of the representation

---

10 Kant's letter to Karl Leonhard Reinhold of December 28 and 31, 1787, suggests that his recognition of a connection between aesthetic and teleological judgment was the occasion for his composition of a third *Critique*, but hardly makes clear precisely what connection he had in mind. See *KGS*, 10:513–516; in Kant, *Correspondence*, letter 83, 271–273.

through which an object is given is the pleasure itself, because it contains a determining ground of the activity of the subject with regard to the animation of its cognitive powers, thus an internal causality (which is purposive) with regard to cognition in general, but without being restricted to a particular cognition, hence it contains a mere form of the subjective purposiveness of a representation in an aesthetic judgment. (*CPJ*, §12, 5:222)

That is, the free but lawful play of our cognitive powers triggered by our experience of a beautiful object is purposive for those cognitive powers insofar as it satisfies our general interest in lawfulness, but this play is subjectively purposive in not being founded in any other sort of purposiveness.[11]

Although in Kant's account of our sense of the necessity of particular laws of nature there is a rapid inference to the idea if not the assertion of a superhuman intelligence as the source of these laws and, as we will see, there is a similar move in his account of our comprehension of organisms, in his initial account of aesthetic experience there is no tendency to interpret the subjective purposiveness of such experience as the product of an intention of any intelligent agent other than ourselves. However, in a later stage of Kant's exposition, he introduces the idea of an "intellectual interest" in natural beauty, grounded in the interest of our reason that its ideas, specifically those connected with "moral feeling," also have "objective reality," which leads to a general interest "that nature should at least show some trace or give a sign that it contains in itself some sort of ground for assuming a lawful correspondence of its products with our satisfaction" that is also satisfied by the existence of natural beauty (*CPJ*, §42, 5:300). Kant speaks here of *nature* satisfying our interest, not of God doing so, but still seems

---

[11] For a brief defense of my general approach to Kant's conception of the free play of our cognitive powers, see Paul Guyer, "The Harmony of the Faculties Revisited," in *Values of Beauty: Historical Essays in Aesthetics* (Cambridge: Cambridge University Press, 2005), 77–109.

to be suggesting a teleological interpretation of aesthetic judgment even though aesthetic judgment itself is not literally teleological: we take nature's satisfaction of our own subjective purposiveness as itself a sign of a kind of purposiveness or concern for our interests on the part of nature—although of course, since Kant's theory of aesthetic judgment is part of his theory of reflecting judgment, this interpretation of nature's purposes must be taken in a "reflective" rather than "constitutive" mode. In that way, Kant seems to be describing a characteristic tendency of human thought, not an objective, metaphysical fact.

7.4.3. *The Teleological Judgment of Organisms*

But the delicate status of teleological judgment is clearer in the case of Kant's account of the teleological judgment of organisms in the third *Critique*. Kant resumes several of his long-standing views about organisms, adds some new challenges, and, as in the Introduction, transforms his earlier theology into a doxologically complex position. In his early work, it will be recalled, Kant thought that both the apparent contingency of the complex but purposive structures of organisms and their ability to reproduce could not be explained as ordinary consequences of the general laws of nature grounded in the basic possibilities for existence grounded in turn in the being of God, but instead required the intentional action of God. In the third *Critique*, Kant incorporates the puzzle of reproduction into a threefold classification of organic features, borrowed from Buffon,[12] that cannot be readily explained on the mechanical model of the determination of whole by parts:[13] the

---

12 For discussion of Kant's debt to Buffon, see Catherine Wilson, "The Building Forces of Nature and Kant's Teleology of the Living," in Massimi and Breitenbach, *Kant and the Law of Nature*, 256–274.

13 For this interpretation of what Kant means by the kind of mechanical explanation that he denies is available to us in the case of organisms, see work by Peter McLaughlin, including *Kant's Critique of Teleology in Biological Explanation: Antinomy and Teleology* (Lewiston, ME: Edwin Mellen Press, 1990), especially 163–169, and "Mechanical Explanation in the 'Critique of the Teleological Power of Judgment,'" in *Kant's Theory of Biology*, ed. Ina Goy and Eric Watkins (Berlin: Walter de Gruyter, 2014), 149–165.

growth and self-repair of individual organisms as well as the preservation of the species through reproduction are held to require determination of parts by the whole (*CPJ*, §64, 5:371–372), in a way that we humans can understand only through the conception of an antecedent *representation* of the whole determining the parts, as a human builder's antecedent representation of a structure to be built determines his acquisition of the parts that he then assembles into the planned whole— although organisms are "self-organizing" (§65, 5:374) in accordance with an idea of the whole that is somehow internal to the organism, so "Strictly speaking, the organization of nature is therefore not analogous with any causality that we know" (5:375).

Initially, Kant stresses that the determination of the parts of an organism by its whole rather than the other way around provides a strictly regulative principle for the reflecting power of judgment, basically a heuristic principle that encourages us to look for the functions of particular organs, indeed of every organ in an organism, even parts that might seem to be explicable in purely mechanical terms ("such as skin, hair, and bones"; §66, 5:377), and he apparently denies that the "occasion" that natural science "provides for the **teleological** judging of its objects" leads to "the consideration of God, and thus [to] a **theological** derivation" (§68, 5:381). However, after making the points that a teleological outlook on any part or function of an organism naturally leads us to a teleological outlook on every aspect of the organism, just mentioned, but also leads us to look at the whole of nature as teleologically organized, and thus disposes us to look for purposive connections among mountains and rivers (§67, 5:377) and even between humans and vermin (5:379), and further leads us to look back at "beauty in nature," originally described as not objectively purposive, as "an objective purposiveness of nature in its entirety, as a system of which the human being is a member" (5:380) (as already suggested under the rubric of the "intellectual interest" in natural beauty), Kant suggests that teleology does lead to theology after all. He hints at this even before he denies it, when he says that "once we have discovered in nature a capacity for bringing forth products that can only be conceived by us in accordance with the concept of final causes... the former idea already, as far as its ground is concerned, leads us beyond the sensible world, and the unity of the supersensible principle must then be considered as valid... not merely for certain species of natural being but for the whole of nature as a system" (§67, 5:380–381). That is, we can after all conceive of the ground of the whole that determines the parts of an organism only as the idea of that whole in the mind of a superhuman creator, and then inevitably conceive of that creator as having an intelligent and beneficent plan for the whole of the natural world. And Kant then extends this thought in the "Antinomy" of the teleological power of judgment that he next constructs.

Kant states that the thesis that "All generation of material things is possible in accordance with merely mechanical laws" and the antithesis that "Some generation of such things is not possible in accordance with merely mechanical laws" would be a straightforward contradiction, but that there is no contradiction between the "**first maxim** of the power of judgment" that "All generation of material things and their forms must be judged as possible in accordance with merely mechanical laws" and the "**second maxim**" that "Some products of nature cannot be judged as possible according to merely mechanical laws (judging them requires an entirely different law of causality, namely that of final causes" (*CPJ*, §70, 5:387) because the first of these is a merely regulative principle "that I **should** always **reflect** on [things] **in accordance with the principle of mere mechanism** of nature" and is only a recommendation to "research the latter, as far as I can" that is not contradicted by the resistance of some things in the end to mechanical explanation. Some interpreters have accepted the shift from constitutive to regulative as a sufficient resolution of the antinomy,[14] but the claim that *all* things can be judged in accordance with the principle of

---

14 Notably Lewis White Beck, *Early German Philosophy: Kant and His Predecessors* (Cambridge, MA: Harvard University Press, 1969), 486.

mechanism and *some* cannot is as much of a contradiction as the claim that all things are possible in accordance with mechanism and some are not. Moreover, Kant *follows* the section just cited with a "preparation for the resolution of the above antinomy (*CPJ*, §71, 5:388–389), implying that the contrast between constitutive principles and regulative maxims was not yet the resolution. The resolution seems instead to be what follows, namely, the suggestion that "theism," the explanation of the entire sensible world as the product of an "intentionally productive (originally living) intelligent being" (*CPJ*, §72, 5:392), is at least a way of conceiving of the world made possible for us by transcendental idealism's distinction between the sensible and the supersensible, which makes it possible for us to conceive of the whole world as the product of intelligent design even though we know that we have no way to know that this is so, that is, "dogmatically establishing" it (*CPJ*, §73, 5:395). This two-level resolution of the antinomy, which has the same form as all of Kant's resolutions of antinomies in the critical philosophy, allows him to reconcile the two maxims by holding that at one level the maxim of mechanical explanation may be pushed as far as possible while at another level we can suppose—though not prove—that intelligent intentionality is at work, achieving its purposes *through* the mechanisms discovered at the first level.

If Kant's resolution takes this form, however, then there is a danger, one that should have been apparent since he first extended our teleological outlook on organisms to the whole of nature, namely that the unique status of organisms as self-organizing beings, or as Kant also calls them, "natural ends" that are both **"cause and effect"** of themselves (*CPJ*, §64, 5:370), namely, that the special character of organisms will become irrelevant to his reformed teleology and, as we have now seen, theology. For the picture would now be that we could extend mechanical explanation to any length, even to the explanation of the purposive structures of organisms such as the multiple eyes of the spider and organisms' capacities for growth, self-repair, and reproduction—as indeed we suppose we have done with post-Darwinian biology—and yet still allow ourselves to gratify our natural tendency to teleology by positing a supersensible purpose being worked out through all of this. The special status of organisms would be a ladder that could be dropped away once we have reconciled the possibility of unrestricted mechanical explanation with the continuing coherence of teleology.

Perhaps to forestall this outcome, Kant has added one point to his account of organisms in the third *Critique* that was not present in his earlier accounts. This is the claim that *inertia* is the "essential characteristic" of matter but incompatible with the nature of organisms: subject to inertia, ordinary matter is "lifeless," incapable of self-originating motion, while self-originating motion, whether in the form of transforming lifeless food into living matter by digestion or quickening mere matter in reproduction, is characteristic of living things—and incapable of mechanical explanation. However, Kant himself will eventually undercut this argument for the special status of living matter by his arguments for the necessity of the "ether," a *self-moving* form of *matter* that permeates the entire universe and prevents the necessity of explaining the existence of motion in a universe otherwise governed by the law of inertia by means of some *external* jump-start—a deficiency of Newtonian physics in his view. This is an idea that appears early in Kant's thought and then again in the late drafts of an unfinished restatement of transcendental idealism that we know as the *Opus postumum*—and which may explain why Kant continued to obsess about how to understand the relation between the inorganic and the organic until the end of his days.[15]

Even if Kant's claim about the special difficulty of understanding organisms has become problematic, however, there can be no doubt that he used this claim to point to the room that transcendental idealism has made for the *idea* of teleology if not the dogmatic assertion of

---

15 For discussion of Kant's late theory of the ether, see my "Kant's Ether Deduction and the Possibility of Experience," in *Akten des Siebenten Internationalen Kant-Kongresses*, ed. Gerhard Funke (Bonn: Bouvier Verlag, 1991), vol. 2, pt. i, pp. 119–132, reprinted in *Kant's System of Nature and Freedom*, 74–85.

it. Before we leave the third *Critique*, we must look at the final use that he made of this room within this work. This is his argument that only the full realization of human morality can play the role of a "final end" of nature. The argument, expounded under the rubric of a "Doctrine of Method" for the Critique of the Teleological Power of Judgment, takes the following form. It begins with two assumptions: that our experience of organisms as "natural ends" inevitably leads us to try to think of the whole natural world as if it were purposive, and further that we inevitably look for some *external* purpose of the world, that is, we do not just look at it as if it were some single well-functioning organism, but look for some point for the existence of this organism. Further, we naturally tend to take *ourselves* as the point of the existence of the universe, to look at ourselves "as the ultimate end of the creation here on earth, because [we are] the only being[s] on earth who form a concept of ends for" themselves (*CPJ*, §82, 5:426–427). Put another way, having been led from the thought of organisms as designed to that of the whole world as designed, we inevitably raise the question of the goal of that design—we cannot imagine a rational but pointless design of the universe. (This is Kant's deepest objection to Spinoza; *CPJ*, §73, 5:393.) However, our experience—of pestilence, flood, and all the rest (*CPJ*, §83, 5:430)—does not allow us to think that our *happiness* can be the goal of nature and its designer, or at least not the *direct* goal. Instead, we must conceive of something of unconditional value as the ultimate end of the existence of nature, and further of something that we can ourselves give to nature as "a relation to an end that can be sufficient for itself independently of nature" (*CPJ*, §83, 5:431). In the language of Kant's *Groundwork*, the only candidate for such an end would be the realization of a good will—which, remember, he described in teleological terms as the only possible goal of our natural possession of the faculty of reason; in the *Critique of the Power of Judgment*, the goal is described as human *freedom*, which however is fully realized only in action in accordance with the moral law and also, in accordance with an argument that Kant takes for granted in the present text, has as its complete object the *highest good*, which includes happiness but only as conditioned by the moral law (*CPuR*, A 811 / B 839 and *CPrR*, 5:110–111) and as the product of morality (*CPuR*, A 809–810 / B 137–138).

> Now we have in the world only a single sort of beings whose causality is teleological, i.e., aimed at ends and yet at the same time so constituted that the laws in accordance with which they have to determine ends is represented by themselves as unconditioned and independent of natural conditions but yet as necessary in itself. The being of this sort is the human being, though considered as noumenon: the only natural being in which we can nevertheless cognize, on the basis of its own constitution, a supersensible faculty (**freedom**) and even the law of the causality together with the object that it can set for itself as the highest end (the highest good in the world). (*CPJ*, §84, 5:435)

While other teleological theologies in eighteenth-century Germany saw the purpose of human existence as the reflection of the glory of God,[16] for Kant God's purpose in creating the world is ultimately creating a being who must realize the value of freedom for itself, perhaps exercising freedom in a way that it makes no sense to conceive of a perfect and immutable being doing for himself.[17] And this means that the ultimate end of nature is something that, in Kant's view, cannot be accomplished within nature itself, for as the last passage makes clear, in his view the exercise of freedom is something noumenal, something that underlies the order of nature which is itself thoroughly deterministic—just as, in Kant's solution to the antinomy of teleological judgment, the purposive design of nature must be its ground but

---

16 See Christian Wolff, *Vernünfftige Gedancken von den Absichten der natürlichen Dinge*, andere Auflage (Frankfurt am Main: Renger, 1726), chapter 2, §§8–22.

17 For a detailed exploration of Kant's views about the coherence of any concept of divine rather than human freedom, see Christopher J. Insole, *Kant and the Creation of Freedom: A Theological Problem* (Oxford: Oxford University Press, 2013).

not any part of nature. Nature can prepare the way for the exercise of human freedom, in the form of the culture of human discipline (*CPJ*, §83, 5:432), and its outcome can, indeed must, take place in nature, in the form of happiness as one part of the highest good conditioned by morality as the other part; but freedom itself is noumenal.

This means that the metaphysics as well as the epistemology of Kant's reformed teleology is complex. Epistemologically, we are according to Kant naturally disposed to believe in the purposiveness and therefore the design of nature although we know that we cannot know that to exist. The metaphysical content of that belief is that the end of nature is something, namely our own freedom, that stands outside of nature and grounds it, but also has effects upon it. And theologically, for that matter, that our noumenal free choice is the ground of some substantial part of nature (see *CPrR*, "Critical Elucidation," especially 5:97–98) risks blurring the boundary between ourselves and God. But one might well argue that Kant's "Copernican revolution" in philosophy has done that from the outset. The Prussian king Friedrich Wilhelm II and his councilor Wöllner, who banned Kant from further publication on religion in 1794, might have thought precisely that.

7.5. Kant's Teleology in History and Religion

This allusion to the controversy over Kant's religious views prompts me to conclude with a final comment about the teleological tone of Kant's philosophy of history and religion. Kant's philosophy of history, as displayed in such an early work of the critical period as his 1784 essay "The Idea of History with a Cosmopolitan Aim" as well as a later work such as the 1795 essay *Toward Perpetual Peace*, clearly has a teleological tone, but one that remains within the epistemological constraint of psychological presupposition rather than metaphysical assertion or dogma. In these works, Kant argues that in order for it to be rational for us to work toward the full realization of human potential and the ultimate realization of justice, namely the prevalence of peaceful resolution of international disputes across the globe, we have to believe that nature makes the realization of these goals *possible*—for it would be the height of irrationality for us to strive to realize a goal, no matter how important, that we antecedently know cannot be realized. As Kant puts it in the earlier essay, history must be able to be written in a way that "opens a consoling prospect into the future (which without a plan of nature one cannot hope for with any ground), in which the human species is represented in the remote distance as finally working itself upward toward the condition in which all the germs nature has placed in it can be fully developed and its vocation here on earth can be fulfilled."[18] Or perhaps this puts the psychological point a little more strongly: in order for us to be able to work for our moral goals, from the full development of our own capacities to world peace, we not merely have to believe that their realization is possible, but also have to be able to have reasonable hope in their realization. But either way, we do not have to believe that nature *guarantees* the realization of these goals, and indeed if we did believe that *nature* guarantees their realization, that would threaten our own *freedom* in bringing them about.

In his philosophy of religion, however, Kant appears to threaten this carefully qualified teleology. In the third part of his *Religion within the Boundaries of Mere Reason*, published (with considerable trouble with the authorities) in 1793, Kant argues that the rational core of true religion is the moral law and the postulates of pure practical reason, that is, the belief in human freedom, the existence of God, and human immortality; and the only service that God, who has no needs of his own, could possibly want from us is our fulfillment of the moral law from the motive of our own respect for it (e.g., *RBMR*, 6:141–142). Everything else in religion, all historical belief, sacred texts, and observances other than morality itself, is mere "ecclesiastical faith" (6:102–103). Now ecclesiastical faith might seem

---

18 Kant, "Idea for a Universal History with a Cosmopolitan Aim," Ninth Proposition, 8:30, in *Anthropology, History, and Education*, 119.

harmless, for it does not necessarily stand in the way of the proper practice of morality. But Kant believes that it all too easily degenerates into what he calls "counterfeit service" to God based on the belief that it is the performance of religious ceremonies rather than a "good life-conduct" that can make us "well-pleasing to God" (*RBMR*, 6:170). Thus Kant believes that in the course of human history ecclesiastical faith and its practices *could* and *should* fade away. The remarkable thing, however, is that Kant goes further and states several times that the practice of ecclesiastical faith *will* disappear in the course of human history and that at some point human beings will actually practice morality out of respect for the moral law alone in the recognition that this is all that God can possibly want from us. For example, he writes,

> It is therefore a necessary consequence of the physical and, at the same time, the moral predisposition in us—the latter being the foundation and at the same time the interpreter of all religion—that in the end religion will gradually be freed of all empirical grounds of all determination, of all statutes that rest on history and unite human beings provisionally for the promotion of the good through the intermediary of an ecclesiastical faith. (*RBMR*, 6:121)

Kant gives no argument for this confidence, and it is hard to see how he could argue for it given the radical view of human freedom that he has expounded in the first part of the *Religion*, namely that freedom consists in the ability to choose between good and evil, and that we *always* have that freedom—having once chosen evil, we always remain free to choose good, but likewise even having once chosen good, we still remain free to choose evil, and must always be alert for the possibility of overconfidence in our own moral reform and the possibility of moral regress or relapse. If that is so, then it is hard to see how there could be anything that in Kant's view could guarantee the replacement of the counterfeit service of ecclesiastical faith with the genuine morality of true religion. As Kant himself tells it, the genuine morality of Jesus of Nazareth relapsed into an ecclesiastical faith not much better than others within a few generations (*RBMR*, 6:130–131). It seems that Kant has been overcome by his antipathy to the counterfeit service of organized religion and his hope for a purer morality.

Perhaps Kant's lapse is also a sign of how delicate his reformed teleology really is, how hard it is to maintain the psychological disposition to believe that nature not only has a goal but is also progressing toward that goal and yet to avoid dogmatic assertion that nature will realize its goal. But we could not expect simplicity from Kant on any subject, except perhaps on the content of the moral law and our freedom to live up to it.

Nor would Kant's reformed teleology prove stable. In the immediate aftermath of Kant, something like Friedrich Schelling's *System of Transcendental Idealism* (1800), which argues that we must see human intellect as a product of nature while at the same time seeing nature as a product of human but possibly also greater than human intellect, might be seen as an attempt to carry on Kant's way of thinking. But, as James Kreines will argue in the next chapter, Schelling's erstwhile disciple Georg Wilhelm Friedrich Hegel will take a more critical stance toward Kant's reformed teleology. On the one hand, he will argue for the metaphysical reality of purposiveness within nature, in organisms, especially when seen as species rather than merely as aggregates of individuals, but also in human beings. On the other hand, he will, according to Kreines, reject all belief in an external designer of nature, even in the regulative rather than constitutive mode allowed by Kant. The latter part of Hegel's position would seem to have triumphed in the modern worldview, although there are certainly some serious scientists who are still willing to believe that the laws that provide ultimate explanations within nature are themselves the product of something intelligent outside of nature. The former question, whether purposiveness or functionality within nature, for example, within the physiologies of organisms, should be considered ontologically real or only part of our human way of looking at things, is still debated within philosophy of science and biology, so it is by no means clear that Kant's position on this issue has gone down for the count.

CHAPTER EIGHT

Hegel

THE REALITY AND PRIORITY OF IMMANENT

TELEOLOGY

James Kreines

Hegel defends a teleological metaphysics.[1] But he is entirely dismissive of views on which the universe—or nature, or anything insofar as it is

---

1 See especially the prominence, in Hegel's *Science of Logic*, of chapters called "Teleology" and "Life," falling on either side of the all-important transition to the final, concluding section, "The Idea," and on this my paper: J. Kreines, "Hegel: Metaphysics without Pre-critical Monism," *Bulletin of the Hegel Society of Great Britain* 57–58 (2008): 48–70. In what follows, references to the German text of Hegel's self-standing *Logic* are to the critical edition, *Gesammelte Werke* (Meiner, 1968–). Other references to the German are to the writings contained in the *Werke in zwanzig Bände* and are by volume: page in that edition, ed. E. Moldenhauer and K. Michel (Frankfurt am Main: Suhrkamp, 1970–1971). I cite the *Encyclopedia* by § number, with 'An' indicating *Anmerkung* and 'Zu' indicating the *Zusatz*. I also use the following abbreviations for translations (altering where necessary) and other editions: *EL*: *Encyclopaedia Logic*, trans. T. F. Geraets, H. S. Harris, and W. A. Suchting (Indianapolis: Hackett, 1991). *PN*: *Hegel's Philosophy of Nature*, trans. W. Wallace and A. V. Miller (New York: Oxford University Press, 1970). *VGP*: *Lectures on the History of Philosophy*, trans. E. S. Haldane and Frances H. Simson, 3 vols. (Lincoln: University of Nebraska Press, 1995). *VPA*: *Aesthetics: Lectures on Fine Art*, trans. T. M. Knox, 3 vols. (Oxford: Clarendon Press, 1975). *WL*: Hegel's *Science of Logic*, trans. A. V. Miller (London: George Allen & Unwin, 1969). *KU*: *Critique of the Power of Judgment*, trans. Paul Guyer

natural—is akin to an artifact, in having a purpose or telos in virtue of the work of an external designer, or any kind of external imposition.[2] Hegel, then, accords a great deal of importance to a distinction between immanent and external teleology. We can best approach his aim here by comparing two familiar claims about the fate of teleology after Aristotle and moving into early modern metaphysics. The first claim is that, while it would be too simple to say that most philosophers come to deny teleology altogether, there is a strong trend toward skepticism more specifically about *immanent* teleology—and with it the possibility of "unthoughtful" teleology, or teleology without dependence on intelligent agents representing goals.[3] The second claim is that this shift away from immanent teleology is, in comparison with the Aristotelian background, a downgrade or limitation of the status of teleology in metaphysics.[4] A central aim of Hegel's metaphysics is to reverse these trends, in both respects: he aims to defend the reality immanent teleology—and, in so doing, to reorient philosophy around a metaphysical priority of the teleological over the nonteleological.

In some respects, this is to advocate a return to views that Hegel sees in Aristotle. But what Hegel is doing—with respect to teleology, and consequently with respect to his metaphysics more generally—is also shaped in important ways by later philosophical developments, and

---

and Eric Mathews (Cambridge: Cambridge University Press, 2000). (German text from volume 5 of *Gesammelte Schriften* for the published version of the book, and from volume 20 for the "first introduction.") All references to Kant's writings are given by volume and page number of the Akademie edition of Kant's *Gesammelte Schriften* (Berlin: de Gruyter, 1902–).

2 He compares such views to trivialities (*PN* §245Z, 9:14/6; *EL* §205Z; *VPR* 17:520; *VGP* 20:23) and superstitions (*VGP* 20:88, *VPG* 3:186).

3 On "unthoughtful teleology" in early modern philosophy see Don Garrett, "Teleology in Spinoza and Early Modern Rationalism," in *New Essays on the Rationalists*, ed. Rocco J. Gennaro and Charles Huenemann (Oxford: Oxford University Press, 1999), 310–335. On denials of unthoughtful and immanent teleology after Aristotle, see the chapters by Pasnau and Melamed in this volume.

4 Versions of both are present, for example, in Anneliese Maeir, "Das Problem Der Finalkausalität Um 1320," in *Metaphysische Hintergründe Der Spätscholastischen Naturphilosophie* (Rome: Edizioni di storia e letteratura, 1955), 273–299 and Jeffrey McDonough, "The Heyday of Teleology and Early Modern Philosophy," *Midwest Studies in Philosophy* 35 (2011): 179–204.

especially by Kant. We can in fact best approach Hegel's arguments by seeing them as borrowing considerations from post-Aristotelian forms of skepticism about immanent teleology and turning these to Hegel's opposed purposes. And these kinds of arguments ultimately lead Hegel in some directions that, while influenced by Aristotle, are also distinctively Hegelian. Looking at these arguments and ambitions can help us to ask whether there might be, well after Aristotle, viable routes to a teleological metaphysics, and—if so—where those routes might lead.

8.1. Kant's Analysis and His Case for Subjectivism

It is important to begin by highlighting some features, crucial for Hegel, from Kant's account of teleology in the third *Critique*. Some are features from Kant's analysis of immanent teleology, which Hegel will accept. And some are features of the argument—to be contested by Hegel—for Kant's subjectivism about teleology.[5]

Kant's analysis pursues one of the organizing questions of this volume: What are the conditions required for genuine teleology? More specifically, Kant asks what is required for a genuinely teleological *system*. His analysis is shaped by consideration of examples like the arctic ecosystem, where the presence of "great sea animals filled with oil" is an "advantage" for humans (*KU* 5:369). Kant gives two reasons why teleology cannot be explained by saying that this sort of structure, within which some parts of a whole benefit others, makes for teleology. First, this would not explain natural or immanent teleology—or what it is to be an "end of nature"—because it makes sense "only under the condition that the existence of that for which it is advantageous... is in itself an end of nature" (*KU* 5:368). Second, it would be "bold and arbitrary" (*KU* 5:369) to conclude merely from the fact that sea life

---

[5] For more on Kant's subjectivism, see section 7.4 of this volume.

benefits humans that this is a purpose or teleological function. This is especially clear in light of Kant's connection between teleology and normativity (*KU* 20:240): benefiting humans does not make it the case that sea life, if it starts to evade capture, would be malfunctioning or failing to fulfill its purpose.

Kant draws the conclusion that, for a teleological system, it is not enough to have any given structure, or parts standing in any given relations. Genuine teleology imposes rather a specifically *explanatory* demand concerning *why* a system is structured as it is. I call this Kant's "first requirement," best understood in this way:

R1 The parts must be present *because* of their relations to other parts, or to the roles they play within the whole.

In Kant's terms, a teleological system requires that "parts (as far as their existence and their form are concerned) are possible only through their relation to the whole."[6] To pursue an example of Kant's, one watch gear has a purpose—it is "the instrument for the motion of another" (*KU* 5:374)—insofar as a gear of this form or type is present here *because* of how it relates to the other parts, namely, in a manner that results in reliable indication of the time.

This is, in two respects, an *inflationary* account, in that it takes teleology to always carry a kind of explanatory implication. To appreciate the point, it is crucial that the sense of explanation at stake is not itself deflationary, as for example on a purely pragmatic or interest-relative account of explanation.[7] Kant's argument cuts against this. Consider Kant's example: we could construct a purely pragmatic account of explanation, on which describing the arctic ecosystem in terms of how

---

[6] *KU* 5:373. I defend this interpretation at length in my paper: J. Kreines, "The Inexplicability of Kant's *Naturzweck*: Kant on Teleology, Explanation and Biology," *Archiv für Geschichte der Philosophie* 87, no. 3 (2005): 270–311.

[7] See the chapter by Forber in this volume on the impact of broadly pragmatic accounts of explanation on issues concerning teleology.

its parts benefit humans would count as explanatory in context of the interests of humans living there. But Kant's point is precisely that this *fails* to establish the kind of explanatory relation required for teleology: it is "bold and arbitrary" to take benefit as itself grounds for concluding that sea life is present "**because**" (Kant's emphasis) of that benefit (*KU* 5:369). The argument requires understanding explanation, and teleology with it, in more inflationary terms, as raising metaphysical issues—in the sense of issues about what the world must be like, independent of any varying subjective perspectives and interests, so as to support explanation.[8] It is important to note, first, that the analysis of teleology does not require specifically *causality* in any particular narrow sense, such as a temporally prior efficient cause; as we will see, it is crucial to Kant's purposes that the analysis in itself leaves open the possibility of satisfaction by a kind of a kind of grounding that is not narrowly causal—by "a supersensible real ground for nature" (*KU* 5:409).[9] Second, Kant's inflationism does not contradict but is rather needed in support of his subjectivism: only because teleology cannot *be* merely a perspective, but must raise metaphysical issues, might it follow that we can never have objective knowledge of the metaphysics required for specifically immanent or natural teleology. Deflationism and epistemic restriction are generally opposed philosophical strategies, and Kant generally favors what I call restrictive inflationism.[10]

---

8   This is sometimes called explanatory realism. Note that my formulation would be compatible with the possibility that there are *also*—aside from metaphysical conditions—necessary conditions on explanation that are essentially pragmatic, contextual, or similar.
9   For Kant, *causes* (in the narrow sense involving temporal priority) are restricted to the sensible; a supersensible *ground* would be something else. For *natural* teleology or *inner* purposiveness, as opposed to artifacts, there is a strong limit on our ability to comprehend what the needed ground would be like.
10 I make this interpretive case about Kant on laws of nature in J. Kreines, "Kant on the Laws of Nature: Restrictive Inflationism and Its Philosophical Advantages," *The Monist* 100, no. 3 (2017): 326–341, and on teleology in J. Kreines, "The Inexplicability of Kant's *Naturzweck*: Kant on Teleology, Explanation and Biology," *Archiv für Geschichte der Philosophie* 87, no. 3 (2005): 270–311, sketching the route from teleology to a similar point about Kant on free will in J. Kreines, "Kant and Hegel on Teleology and Life from the Perspective of Debates about Free Will," in *The Freedom of Life*, ed. T. Khurana (Cologne: Walther König, 2013), 111–153.

Now the preceding is so far only Kant's general account of the concept of a teleological system, or what he sometimes calls a "purpose" or "end" (*Zweck*). Kant's aim is to narrow this to an account of specifically *immanent* teleology, or of "inner" as opposed to "external purposiveness," or to narrow from the concept of a purpose or *Zweck* to that of a *natural* purpose, or *Naturzweck*. This requires a second requirement, best understood in this way:

R2 The whole must have its form because of its parts.

That is to say: it must have its form because of what is within, rather than outside, as for example in a designer. Kant himself rolls the two requirements together to yield the requirement of a *reciprocity* between part and whole.[11]

Having noted Kant's analysis, it remains to point out his argument from this to subjectivism.[12] Some post-Aristotelians take considerations similar to Kant's—concerning backward causality and the nature of matter—to justify skepticism in the sense of a denial that there can be any immanent teleology; Kant argues that they support rather skepticism in the sense of the denial of the possibility of *knowledge* of real immanent teleology. (For concision, I refer to both views as different varieties of "skepticism.")

The nub of Kant's argument is this: the complex systems we can know about originate over time. In such a temporal development, we can know why the parts are present only in the sense of knowing efficient causes, beginning temporally prior to the initial formation and development of the system. Since the whole itself is not around temporally prior to serve as efficient cause of itself, we can only know R1 to be met where we know this cause to be an intelligent designer representing a

---

[11] For a *Naturzweck* it is required "that its parts be combined into a whole by being reciprocally the cause and effect of their form" (*KU* 5:373). See also Paul Guyer's chapter in this volume.

[12] On Kant's subjectivism, see this volume, Guyer, section 7.4.

concept of the whole.[13] But then any epistemic reason[14] we could have for thinking a system meets R1, or is a teleological system, could only be a reason for taking it to be an artifact, and denying that it satisfies R2, or that it is *immanent* teleology. Similarly, the complex systems we know about have parts that are ultimately matter, which Kant holds to be itself "lifeless," without "intention" or aim (*KU* 5:394); so any epistemic reason to think that a system has its form because of these parts, or satisfies R2, is reason to deny that it satisfies R1, or is a teleological system at all.

Given our epistemic limits, this is supposed to leave a coherent concept of immanent teleology. The basic idea here is that the analysis does not require that its explanatory demand be met specifically by the sort of temporal, efficient causality of which we can have knowledge; it could, then, be satisfied in some other way, beyond our epistemic limits. So Kant says that something could in principle be a case of immanent or natural teleology in virtue of a "supersensible real ground" (*KU* 5:409) that is unknowable and incomprehensible for us. Kant will argue that we necessarily, and usefully, think of nature in terms of that coherent concept of the immanent purposiveness of a natural purpose (*Naturzweck*). But for understanding Hegel what is crucial is the remaining epistemic limit: the concept *Naturzweck* is "problematic," in that when using it "one does not know whether one is judging about something or nothing" (*KU* 5:397).

---

13 In the order of "real causes," an end or purpose (*Zweck*) cannot precede and thereby influence its own causes, so it can do so only as "ideal" or represented (*KU* 5:372). See also P. Guyer, "Organisms and the Unity of Science," in *Kant and the Sciences*, ed. Eric Watkins (Oxford: Oxford University Press, 2001), 265, and R. Zuckert, "Purposiveness, Time, and Unity: A Reading of the *Critique of Judgment*" (Ph.D. diss, University of Chicago, 2000), 136–140.

14 I mean "epistemic reason" and "reason" (unmodified) here to capture Kant's notion of "objectively sufficient" grounds; Kant's subjectivism allows "subjectively sufficient" grounds for teleology, or grounds relating to our ends, including the ends of reason.

8.2. Raising the Stakes: No Teleology without Immanent Teleology

My main focus throughout this chapter will be Hegel's argument, in response to Kant, for the reality and knowability of immanent teleology, in a part of the *Logic* called "Life." But before getting to this, I want to note why Hegel takes the stakes to be so high in this debate about immanent teleology. In particular, Hegel singles out, in a preceding part of the *Logic* ("Teleology"), the tendency within early modern philosophy toward dismissals of immanent teleology that claim to preserve a place for teleology in cases of intentional action.[15] But Hegel holds that arguments against immanent teleology would, if successful, have to be carried through to an elimination of all teleology altogether.

One place we can see this position of Hegel's is where he interprets Spinoza both as a destination toward which trends of modern philosophy point, and as denying or eliminating all final causes.[16] In both respects, Hegel is influenced by a worry of Jacobi's—extremely prominent at the time—that the trends in philosophy lead to Spinozism in a sense that is supposed to include this view:

> [T]here are only efficient, but no final, causes.... [T]he only function that the faculty of thought has in the whole of nature is that of observer; its proper business is to accompany the mechanism of the efficient causes.... We only *believe* that we have acted out of anger, love, magnanimity, or out of rational decision. Mere illusion![17]

---

15 Even if some also worry about epistemic access to divine intentions, this can be one reason for denying a role for teleology in explanations of nature. For relevant background, see the chapters by Pasnau and McDonough in this volume.

16 For example, Hegel translates Spinoza's denial that God acts "sub ratione boni" as "God acts in accordance with no final causes" (*VGP* 20:178/3:267).

17 F. H. Jacobi, *The Main Philosophical Writings and the Novel "Allwill,"* trans. and ed. G. di Giovanni (Montreal: McGill-Queen's University Press, 1994), 189.

Hegel's view is that arguments against immanent teleology would, if successful, force this conclusion.

There is not enough space here to explain Hegel's arguments for this raising of the stakes. But the gist is as follows: modern philosophers who claim to preserve intentional teleology tend to covertly assume some immanent teleology. For example, if they think of human beings as acting for the sake of subjective or represented ends, they are assuming that human beings have bodies to use as means to their ends—and that these bodies are fit for such use in virtue of being teleological systems with this immanent end or purpose.[18] Of course, we can use artifacts, like a plow, as the means to our ends as well. But in thinking of a plow as a means to use in planting crops, we are thinking of the plow itself as the result of the intentional action of designing and building the plow in the first place. If intentional action does require some teleological system as means, then we can see how the threat of a regress might force us to abandon the idea that teleology could be external teleology all the way down, as it were—to conclude that there must eventually be a means that is a case of immanent teleology.[19] If one had general reasons to deny all such immanent teleology, then this might still leave the possibility of human beings *having* subjective ends: of their representing states of the world as desirable, or to be brought about. But Hegel takes the denial of immanent teleology to threaten the conclusion Jacobi worries about: our subjective representations would just take up a perspective on what is going on in the world, but without any of them having, qua ends or goals, the real explanatory relevance to what happens required to support teleology.[20] So the threat is that there would be no genuine teleology at all. On this kind of view, then, a "subjective end" would have "the form of

---

18 §208 and its *Zusatz*. Hegel's lectures emphasize our hands, for example (*VL* 206/210).
19 See the regress in §211.
20 This depends on the inflationary position on teleology and explanation noted earlier.

objective indifference"; it would be "confronted by an objective, mechanical and chemical world to which its activity relates itself as to something already there" (*WL* 6:447/742).

Now one might object to Hegel's position by appeal to *divine* intentional action. Thus one might think of our bodies in terms of external teleology, as artifacts created by a God for our use, thus supporting the possibility of our intentional action. But the argument above gives us an approach to Hegel's famous antidualist opposition to the metaphysics of a transcendent God. In effect, Hegel holds that God would be in the same position with respect to the argument above: to realize purposes in the world—including the design and creation of artifacts—even God would need means within the world. In a dualist metaphysics, with a God distinct from the world, God could not act within the world, but only observe. Putting Hegel's positive views in these terms raises complexities that go beyond my scope here, but where Hegel expresses himself in terms of positive claims about divine purposes, what he says is that these are realized only through there being cases of immanent teleology—human beings, for example—acting on immanent purposes of their own (§209Zu). Sometimes Hegel expresses the point in terms of the purposes of "reason" rather than a God, and famously refers to the use of systems acting on their own immanent purposes as "the cunning of reason" (*WL* 12:166/663; §209).

Again, there is not enough space to do much by way of explaining Hegel's arguments for this way of raising the stakes; here it is more important to keep in mind that he takes the stakes to be high, in that a denial of all immanent teleology would be a denial of all teleology altogether. Similarly, if we cannot know whether there is any immanent teleology, then we cannot know whether there is any genuine teleology at all, even (as Jacobi worries) in the case of our own actions. So Hegel seeks to defend immanent teleology, which he sees as a return to Aristotle:

Aristotle's determination of life... stands infinitely far beyond the concept of modern teleology which has only the finite, the external purposiveness in view. (§204An)

Hegel sees this not as an isolated issue, but as promising benefits throughout philosophy, and he takes Kant's analysis as essential to this end:

One of Kant's greatest services to philosophy was in drawing the distinction between relative or *external* purposiveness and *internal* purposiveness; in the latter he opened up the concept of *life*, the *idea*, and with that he *positively* raised philosophy. (*WL* 12:157/654)

But Hegel also aims to refute Kant's subjectivism, establishing knowledge of real immanent teleology; with respect to subjectivism Hegel says that, "on the contrary," what really follows from Kant's analysis is rather that "purpose . . . is the truth that exists in and for itself" (*WL* 12:159/656). And so I turn to the explanation of this central argument.

8.3. For Immanent Teleology: The Concept as the Substance of Life

Kant's argument for his subjectivism suggests two obvious openings for defenses of immanent teleology. One would be to contest Kant's analysis in favor of a more deflationary account, on which teleology might be something more like an additional useful perspective we may take on events of sufficient complexity. The other would be to assert knowledge of the reality of precisely what Kant himself thinks required to satisfy the analysis: either intentionally acting intelligent matter (which Kant thinks impossible), or a teleology-supporting supersensible ground of nature (which Kant thinks unknowable). Hegel takes neither obvious route.[21] He argues—in a subsequent part of the *Logic*, "Life"—that Kant's inflationary analysis can (contra Kant) be satisfied without need of any intelligence or supersensible ground of all nature, and can be known by us to be satisfied.

Strictly speaking, the direct focus of Hegel's *Logic* is not on objects like actual living beings, but on "forms of thought," including teleological forms. But while this point is important for some downstream issues concerning the metaphysics of Hegel's idealism, to which I return at the end, here what matters is that "Life" in the *Logic* includes an argument against skepticism about immanent teleology. The best way to approach Hegel's argument is to note how it can appeal to considerations drawn from post-Aristotelian arguments for skepticism about immanent teleology. Such arguments cannot rest on an analysis of teleology that is demanding in an ad hoc sense. So they tend to argue that their analysis captures a natural sense in which artifacts do qualify as teleological, but in a way that then supports skepticism about *immanent* teleology. In Kant's case, artifacts like a watch naturally satisfy R1's demand that parts of a certain form are present only because of "their relation to the whole" (*KU* 5:373). For example, a gear is present because of the way it interacts with other parts, such that the whole reliably indicates the time. In such cases, "the producing cause of the watch" is "a being that can act in accordance with an idea of a whole" (*KU* 5:374). What Hegel is going to argue is that there can be natural cases, without any design, where something natural and not involving representations can substitute for the idea of a designer.

Hegel makes his argument by constructing an analysis of a concept of life, out of three requirements. This is not an attempt to give an a priori logical deduction of the features of real living beings.[22] Nor should it

---

[21] In my "Hegel: Metaphysics" and my "Kant and Hegel." I note arguments for those two contrary readings that I think are worthy of serious consideration and response, in Willem de Vries, "The Dialectic of Teleology," *Philosophical Topics* 19 (1991): 51–70 and K. Düsing, "Die Idee des Lebens in Hegels Logik," in *Hegels Philosophie der Natur*, ed. R. P. Horstmann and M. J. Petry (Stuttgart: Klett-Cotta, 1986), 276–289 respectively.

[22] It is "quite improper" to try to "deduce" the "contingent products of nature" (*PN* §250).

be understood as an attempt to analyze our representation of life. It is a theoretical tool, and its ultimate purpose is to demonstrate that, for anything satisfying the three requirements of his concept of *life*, the nature or substance of tokens will be their type, species, or kind—and that this general type will play the role of a designer's idea, making for teleology without need of external design, or for immanent teleology.

In the self-standing *Logic*, the sections on the three requirements are titled "A. The Living Individual," "B. The Life Process," and "C. Kind (*Gattung*)." *First*, parts must be arranged in a way that benefits the whole; since the whole is made of the parts, Hegel follows Kant in taking this to require that the parts are "reciprocally" (*EL* §218) beneficial. *Second*, Hegel's concept of life demands that a complex system needs "assimilation" (*WL* 12:189/686); it "*preserves, develops,* and *objectifies* itself" (*EL* §219). *Third*, self-preservation is also required in an additional sense: preservation of a species or kind (*Gattung*) through mating (*Begattung*) or the mating or species process (*Gattungsprozess*) (*WL* 12:191/688).[23]

What here is supposed to substitute for a designer's representation of an idea of a whole is the reproductive kind or species. That is, Hegel will employ some inflationary metaphysics, which Hegel takes to descend from Aristotle, to meet Kant's inflationary analysis: a metaphysics on which there are natural kinds, and in which the kind or type can be the very nature or substance of a token, so that the type is what it is to be the token. Hegel sometimes refers to these types as "universals," and sometimes (emphasizing the connection he sees to Aristotle) as "forms." What is crucial here is the idea that, if the type is what the token is, then an organism "produces itself": it "produces itself as another individual of the same *Gattung*."[24] Hegel follows here

---

[23] On translation of Hegel's *Gattung* as "species" and "kind," rather than "genus," see my "Hegel: Metaphysics."

[24] *The Philosophical Propaedeutic*, trans. M. George and A. Vincent and ed. A. V. Miller (Oxford: Blackwell, 1986), 4:32/142.

a position that he sees in Aristotle; thus Hegel's *Lectures on the History of Philosophy* glosses a famous claim in Aristotle:

> That which is produced is as such in the ground, that is, it is an end [*Zweck*], kind [*Gattung*] in itself, it is by the same token prior, before it becomes actual, as potentiality. Man generates men; what the product is, is also the producer. (*VGP* 19:176)[25]

It is important at this point to note some unusual Hegelian terminology for this view. First, Hegel in general calls this type-token connection—where the type is what it is to be the token—"concrete universality." He says that this "contains... the two moments, the objective universal or the *kind*, and the *individualized* universal."[26] Second, Hegel's metaphysics is concerned generally with the just-noted objective universals or kinds. These are neither representations nor mind-dependent in the sense of a representation, or "in" a mind—they are, in the contrasting sense, objective.[27] But, *if* grasped by mind, then this is not by sense perception but conceptual comprehension (*Begreifen*). That is part of the reason why Hegel calls such an objective universal also a "concept" (*Begriff*), or "*objective* concept."[28]

We can now state in Hegel's own terms his central claim about life. In the case of life specifically, the *form* (to put the point in terms of Hegel's reference to Aristotle) or the "concept" is the reproductive kind, or *Gattung*. Thus Hegel's discussion of reproduction refers to "the realized *Gattung* that has posited itself as identical with the concept (*Begriff*)" (*WL* 12:191/688). Hegel's key claim is that the nature or

---

25 E.g., Aristotle, *Physics* in *The Complete Works of Aristotle: The Revised Oxford Translation*, ed. J. Barnes (Princeton, NJ: Princeton University Press, 1984), 198a.

26 *WL* 6:349, 662. See also Hegel's connection between the concrete universal and Kant's analysis of inner purposiveness (*WL* 6:443, 739).

27 E.g., *WL* 21:15/16.

28 E.g., *WL* 12:20/527. For mention of another part of the reason, see the concluding thoughts on Hegel's idealism.

substance of a reproducing organism is its type or concept. So Hegel says that a philosophical position renders immanent teleology an "incomprehensible mystery" *if* it "does not grasp the concept, nor does it grasp it as the substance of life" (*WL* 12:181/678).

What difference does any of this make with regard to arguments for skepticism about immanent teleology? Consider an elm tree. To satisfy Kant's R1, an elm leaf (for example) must be present because of the way it relates to other parts, so as to maintain the whole. And if the elm satisfies Hegel's analysis, then this explanatory demand will be met. For a new leaf (the token) is only possible insofar as a leaf (of this type) relates to the whole elm (of this type) in just this way. For only in this way can the prior token survive and produce the new token. If the very nature or substance of the token is the type, or the token in this sense *is* its type, then the leaf is present because of *its* relation to the whole. Where we have such an organism, "all its members serve only as means to the one end (*Zweck*) of self-preservation" (*VPA* 13:193/1:145).

Why would this be *immanent* teleology? The short story is: it requires no external designer. The longer story is that Kant's R2 requires that the form of the whole be due to its parts, so that the parts reciprocally cause one another. In our elm tree, the parts (tokens) are present on account of the effectiveness of those very parts (type); the effectiveness of those parts (types) itself brings about a new token system. So the inclusion of assimilation and reproduction in the analysis allows us to explain or comprehend the origin of a *Naturzweck*: with these included, "its genesis, which was an act of presupposing, now becomes its production" (*WL* 6:484, 772–773). For example, again where Hegel praises Aristotle, "Leaves, blossoms, roots thus bring the plant into evidence and go back into it." And where some see grounds here for *as if* teleology, there is in fact ground for genuine natural teleology:

> What has here been said is already contained in that which was asserted by those who do not represent nature in this way, but say, "that which is constituted as though it were constituted for an end,

will endure." For this is the self-productive action of nature. In the modern way of looking at life this conception becomes lost... either through a mechanical philosophy... or else theological physics. (*VGP* 19:180/2:176–177)

Thinking in terms of Kant's connection between teleology and normativity, say our token leaf has never assimilated energy well. If it never has, then in what sense is it malfunctioning, or failing relative to *its* purpose?[29] In the sense that its nature or substance is its role in the kind, on account of which it is present. So in the case of life, the possibility of "defect" or malfunction is relative to "the rule, the characteristic of the kind."[30]

Or take the connection between the topic of teleological systems and of behavior: Insofar as the parts of an organism *have* purposes, what they *do* when working together is purposive activity. So Hegel's commitment is "[t]o see purpose as inherent within natural objects" and the (unthoughtful) growth of "the seed of a plant" is "purposeful activity" and "orientated solely towards self-preservation." And Hegel makes the same historical connection:

> *Aristotle* had already noticed this notion of purpose in nature and he called the activity the *nature of a thing*. This is the true teleological view. (*E* §245Z)

This explains how thoughtful teleology is supposed to depend on unthoughtful: Only insofar as there are organisms, with bodies structured by immanent purposes, can it also be the case that some of these organisms can think and represent ends on which the availability of a purposive body as "means" (*WL* 12:162/659) makes possible intelligent action.

---

29 I note contemporary considerations of such cases subsequently.
30 *EN* §368Z. In the English edition this is §370Z.

Finally, in thinking of the whole argument here, recall that Kant himself cedes that we *do* in fact think of life in terms of immanent teleology; Hegel would add that this means thinking of life in terms of concrete universality. This point seems compelling, and in itself compatible with giving arguments for various forms of skepticism about that way of thinking. But arguments that concern teleology, in favor of such skepticism, do not—Hegel has effectively argued—work as advertised. For the arguments concede external teleology, or that artifacts are teleological systems, appealing to the causal role of ideas of a designer. And it turns out that this clears the way to understanding something playing the role of such an idea, without need of external design. So arguments meant to displace or cast doubt on our way of thinking of life in terms of immanent teleology in fact provide resources that support the immanent teleology of life.

8.4. Understanding the Argument via Objections and Replies

In seeking to better understand Hegel's argument, it can help to consider objections and replies.

> OBJECTION: We know (the objection would argue) that nature does not include anything like Aristotelian substantial forms, and so neither Hegel's concrete universality nor immanent teleology resting on them. The argument would be that appeal to anything like substantial forms in nature is explanatorily superfluous, given explicability in terms of motions of material parts alone.
> REPLY: Hegel sees this worry in the early moderns, including Descartes.[31] But note that this is a more general consideration,

---

31 E.g., *VGP* 3:242. On Descartes see, e.g., *Oeuvres de Descartes*, ed. Charles Adam and Paul Tannery (Paris: Vrin, 1978), vol. II, p. 7.

not concerning teleology specifically. As such, Hegel's response is to be found elsewhere, earlier in the *Logic*, in a "Mechanism" chapter.[32] There Hegel makes the case that arguments like the preceding one, for outright rejection of substantial forms, are incoherent. He argues that mechanistic explanation, appealing to motions of matter alone, would ultimately require appeal to something like a form or concept of matter. To argue that there are no such forms would leave nothing, not even matter, of any explanatory relevance to anything else—or, in Hegel's terms, would make "*explain*" into "only an *empty word*" (*WL* 12.135/633).[33] Hegel's position is that, insofar as we cannot in general dismiss forms, no such general dismissal can undercut his view of teleology.

OBJECTION: Hegel's account captures no genuine teleology, specifically because it requires no action of any intelligent agent.

REPLY: Skeptics cannot just *assert or stipulate* that genuine teleology requires an intelligent agent. Skeptics about immanent teleology need arguments for this, and they have them. In Kant's case: genuine teleology requires meeting the explanatory demand, R1, and we can know this to be met only in knowing about an originating intelligent agent. But any such argument commits to a standard of genuine teleology—in Kant's case, R1. Hegel argues that this standard—the one chosen by Kant to ground skepticism—can be met without any intelligent agent, evading the case for skepticism.

---

[32] See my J. Kreines, "Hegel's Critique of Pure Mechanism and the Philosophical Appeal of the *Logic* Project," *European Journal of Philosophy* 12, no. 1 (2004): 38–74, and J. Kreines, *Reason in the World: Hegel's Metaphysics and Its Philosophical Appeal* (Oxford: Oxford University Press, 2015), chapter 1.

[33] Some take Descartes's denial of substantial forms to generate this kind of problem for him, and take him to put God to work in place of eliminated substantial forms. E.g., Garber 2004, 206.

OBJECTION: Hegel captures no genuine teleology, because he does nothing to rule out the possibility that life or a reproducing species could have begun by chance.[34]

REPLY: This is more difficult for Hegel. What I would say on his behalf is this: Kant's argument requires, for a teleological system, that there be a certain kind of reason why it is as it is; it does not disallow any chance in the reason for this reason, and so on *all the way* through a regress of reasons. That would seem ad hoc when considering artifacts: it suggests that we cannot know a watch to be a teleological system even having seen the designer produce it, since we would have to know the cause of the designer, and so on, ruling out any chance all the way back. If Hegel's argument in reply to Kant works, then the immanent teleology of life can be defended without *any* commitment concerning any ultimate origin of life or a species, including any commitment to any historical development toward a supposed broader purpose.

OBJECTION: For all Hegel tells us, the *matter* composing organisms is unintelligent and without purpose; this (the objection holds) rules out genuine teleology.

REPLY: Kant argues by allowing artifacts as teleological systems. Surely the idea is not that the matter composing artifacts must be intelligent or represent ends. Rather, the matter does what it would do anywhere, without regard to purpose; but material parts of certain forms or types are present, in a certain arrangement, on account of an end or purpose. If skeptical arguments cede this possibility of teleological systems without intelligent matter, then the way is open to try to argue that the same is true of living beings, without need of intelligence.[35]

---

34 Cf. Kant at *KU* 5:419.
35 Hegel again interprets Aristotle as holding his view on this (e.g., *VGP* 19:173/2:156).

OBJECTION: Still the teleology would not be *immanent* or *natural*, again because it does not show that the very matter has any purpose.

REPLY: Kant's own R2 is not a constraint requiring anything specifically of constituent *matter*. It cannot be, because Kant's aim is to leave open but unknowable the possibility that, even though matter itself is "lifeless" and without intention, the analysis of immanent teleology might be satisfied in the case of living beings by something that comes *after* the matter in a regress of explanatory grounds—namely, by a "supersensible real ground" (*KU* 5:409) of nature. If that possibility is open, then there is an opening to argue that R2 can also be satisfied also by something that comes *before* the matter in a regress: by parts whose substance or nature is their type, kind, form, or "concept."

OBJECTION: Hegel's defense of teleology—one might argue, now from a contemporary point of view—has been rendered simply and obviously obsolete by subsequent progress in the biological sciences.

REPLY: As far as consideration from a contemporary perspective goes, I have space only for a quick meta-level consideration: There is today among philosophers of biology a debate about whether organisms are cases of immanent teleology. There are those on both sides of the question today who are scientifically well-informed, equally opposed to any place for anything like intelligent design in biology, and so on. So immanent or natural teleology does not seem outdated.

Some may think it obvious that today's neo-teleologists are doing something so different as to be entirely irrelevant to the philosophical evaluation of Hegel's case. I argue elsewhere that there is room for an argument to the contrary.[36] Neo-teleologists, like Kant and Hegel,

---

36 Kreines, *Reason in the World*, chapter 3.

certainly understand teleology as carrying explanatory requirements; and there is room to argue that, regardless of whether they would agree, their way of satisfying those requirements must involve something like metaphysical resources akin to those that Hegel labels "concrete universality." The gist of the argument would be this: Neo-teleology, as in Neander, "makes a trait's function depend on its history, more specifically... on its evolutionary history."[37] And "its history" refers to tokens *via types*:

> Selection is always of types, not tokens. So ... function attributions in biology belong primarily to types ... because it is types, not tokens, that are selected for their effects.[38]

The explanatory requirement is that a trait token must be present in an organism because of *its* effects. But this is not to say that the token trait has effects which then, via backward causation, cause that trait to become present in that organism. Rather, the token is present because of the historical effects of a type of trait in a type of life. So one could argue that holding the trait to be present because of *its* effects is to see this token trait as unified with others of the type—or to see the *type* as the nature unifying all of them. And that is a form of the metaphysics Hegel employs in his response to Kant.

Or consider neo-teleologists on biological normativity. They hold that an organ, for example, can fail relative to its own immanent function. Here they seem to require biological type, with a normative function, to determine the *nature* of a token trait, or *what it is to be* that trait. Consider Neander: "The heart that cannot perform its proper

---

[37] Karen Neander, "Functions as Selected Effects: The Conceptual Analyst's Defense," *Philosophy of Science* 58 (1991): 168.
[38] Karen Neander, "The Teleological Notion of 'Function,'" *Australasian Journal of Philosophy* 69, no. 4 (1991): 460.

function (because it is atrophied, clogged, congenitally malformed, or sliced in two) is still a heart."[39]

Is neo-teleology entirely distinct from Hegel in aiming to *naturalize* teleology? Not if the conception of *nature* at stake is one on which the nature of something is its type, or what Hegel calls the "concept."

Granted, Hegel shares only Neander's focus on history, not any requirement that this be specifically an *evolutionary* history. If Hegel's argument works, then it would show that the resource of concrete universality is enough to defend natural teleology, without need of appeal to a philosophical interpretation of natural selection.

Also granted, Hegel is ignorant of, or contradicts, any number of subsequent scientific results in biology. But, if Hegel's argument appealing to "concrete universality" works, then those others details need not affect the philosophical issue concerning the reality of immanent teleology—even if they are crucially important in any number of other respects.

Finally, there are many important and powerful philosophical worries about contemporary neo-teleology, including those covered in Patrick Forber's chapter in this volume. Here I have only pointed out that, thinking from Hegel's perspective, there is an opening to argue that the philosophical resource he draws on still plays a role in debate within contemporary, scientifically informed philosophy of biology.

8.5. Broader Issues in Hegel's Teleological Metaphysics

There is not enough space to discuss the whole of the metaphysics in which Hegel's account of immanent teleology plays such an important role. But it is worth mentioning some of the directions in which Hegel proceeds from the arguments we have considered.

---

[39] Neander, "Functions as Selected Effects," 180. Cf. Ruth G. Millikan, *White Queen Psychology and Other Essays for Alice* (Cambridge, MA: MIT Press, 1993), 55.

To begin with, Hegel aims to argue for the metaphysical priority of the teleological over the nonteleological. A first sense of metaphysical priority is this: Hegel orients all of metaphysics around explanatory power, and the idea that teleological kinds or concepts are supposed to have greater explanatory power. Nonteleological phenomena, governed by laws of nature or "natural necessity"[40] connecting distinct natures of kinds, have general natures that are merely relational in this sense: it is just the nature of basic kind X to, e.g., attract kind Y; each, then, "is not comprehensible from itself, and the being of one object is the being of another" (*WL* 12:149/646), and so on throughout a whole web of natural necessity. A teleological nature or concept is supposed to be what it is more independently from anything else, and in this sense have more explanatory power in itself. With an organism, for example, many complex features and behaviors are explained by something about its own nature, namely, the way in which, again, "all its members serve only as means to the one end (*Zweck*) of self-preservation" (*VPA* 13:193/1:145). The *Logic* expresses the contrast by saying that "cause" in the sense of "blind necessity" must "pass over into its other and lose its originality," while "[t]he purpose, by contrast, is posited as *in itself* the determinacy . . . does not pass over . . . but instead *preserves itself*" (*E* §204R).

And then there is a second sense of metaphysical priority as well: The nonteleological is itself supposed to be a lesser form of teleology; it is not the case that teleology is a greater or enhanced form of nonteleology. Another way to put the metaphysical point is to say that the nonteleological is what it is only in a way that depends on the teleological; the teleological is more completely what it is in virtue of itself. What it is to be a nonteleological form of explanatory relation is to be an approximation that falls well short of the greater explanatory

---

40 Under "natural necessity" Hegel includes both what he calls "Mechanism" and "Chemism" (*WL* 12:155/652). The specific case I mention here is about "Chemism," or kinds connected by necessary laws.

completeness of the teleological. The downstream epistemological consequence of this metaphysics is that the nonteleological can only be correctly understood by thinking of it in terms of its relation to the teleological. One way Hegel expresses the priority is by saying that teleology is "the truth of mechanism" (*WL* 12:155/652). But the idea is not to eliminate the nonteleological, or to hold that everything (once correctly understood) is teleological; rather, the nonteleological *is*, but it is *what it is* only in this dependent manner.

The best way to briefly consider further this metaphysical priority is to compare an unusual combination of views that Hegel sees in Aristotle: On the one hand, Aristotle defends various kinds of explanatory priority of form over matter. For example, take the claim that this explanatory priority makes form the substance of something:

> [T]he question is *why* the matter is some definite thing; e.g. . . . why is this individual thing, or this body having this form, a man? Therefore what we seek is the cause, i.e., the form, by reason of which the matter is some definite thing; and this is the substance of the thing. (*Metaphysics* 1041b)

On the other hand, Aristotle seems to maintain this priority of form even while recognizing a sense in which it is interdependent on its embodiment, so that form must be embodied (e.g., 1026a), and Platonists are criticized for a contrary kind of separation of forms (e.g., 1086b).

Hegel carries over this general pattern, which he sees in Aristotle's views on form, to Hegel's own view of the "concept" of a thing.[41] And Hegel applies this model to his view of teleology: on the one hand, Hegel's metaphysics accords the teleological the two kinds of explanatory priority over the nonteleological, previously noted. On the other hand, this is not diminished by a kind of interdependence of teleology

---

41 E.g., *WL* 21:15/17 and §24Zu.

and nonteleology, so that the existence of immanent teleology depends, for its realization, on there being some nonteleological elements in which to be realized. This is supposed to not conflict with the metaphysical priority of teleology, because the underlying nonteleological realizers have an "indifference ... to purpose," or to how they are used by teleological systems (*WL* 12.188/685). This Hegelian position on the priority of teleology in metaphysics goes far beyond an account of life and the argument for the reality of immanent purposiveness found in the part of the *Logic* titled "Life." For there are some respects in which life is not, on Hegel's view, the most complete or perfect case of immanent teleology, explanatory power, and metaphysical priority.

First, the case of life in particular is limited because the analysis of life does not require a form of self-consciousness—it does not require that life's concept or kind is "for itself." Hegel proceeds on these grounds from "life" to what he calls "spirit" (*Geist*).[42] "Spirit" is supposed to be another form of immanent purposiveness, but where being "spirit" involves its concept or kind being "for itself," in a way that makes its immanent purpose not just preservation but rather a kind of freedom. The "spirit" following "life" is, then, "*free kind [Gattung] for itself*" (§222). Hegel also argues that human beings are instances of spirit. In our own case, then, self-consciousness is supposed to shape what we are and how we develop though history, giving this development the immanent purpose of a kind of freedom. One way to approach Hegel's position here would be through his influence, via Feuerbach, on the early Marx's position that we are conscious of our universal species or kind in a sense that makes us self-shaping and free:

> Man is a species-being [*Gattungswesen*] not only because in practice and in theory he adopts the species (his own as well as those of other

---

[42] In the *Logic*, see *WL* 12:191/688; *E* §222. In the broader system, see the transition from the *Philosophy of Nature* to the *Philosophy of Spirit*. There are many different accounts of the relation between these treatments in different locations.

things) as his object, but . . . also . . . because he treats himself as a *universal* and therefore a free being.[43]

For Hegel, human history—on a sufficient level of abstraction and distance—is supposed to exhibit a kind of teleology, with the immanent purpose of freedom. But this is a complex issue in Hegel. For, first, this is *immanent* purpose of our own: the idea is not that we are just tools of something external, whether the purposes of a God, or the cosmos, etc. And, second, the influence of this end or telos must somewhat stem from the way in which our concept or kind is "for itself," or self-conscious: this cannot be any kind of mechanism working behind our backs, as it were.

And there is also a respect in which this teleological account of human history still leaves us short of Hegel's arguments for "the absolute," or a kind of absolute case of immanent teleology, with absolute explanatory power. Given the previously noted marriage in Hegel between a priority of teleology and an interdependence with the nonteleological, this absolute will not be a metaphysical foundation, in the specific sense of something existing independently of everything else, providing an independent reason for the existence of everything else, so that everything ends up completely explicable. Hegel sees Spinoza as defending a metaphysical foundationalism: Spinoza's God would be the foundation, in terms of which everything real is completely explicable. But Hegel rejects this kind of view. While Hegel's absolute would be something that is what it is in virtue of itself alone, and something on which everything else depends for its being what it is, the absolute is nonetheless in another sense interdependent on, or reciprocally *mediated* by, everything else. So, in criticizing Spinoza for example, Hegel says that "the absolute cannot be a first, an immediate" (*WL* 11:376/437).

---

[43] Karl Marx, *Economic and Philosophic Manuscripts of 1844*, in *Marx-Engels Collected Works*, vol. 3 (New York: International Publishers, 1975), 275.

We can at least note two ways in which Hegel approaches his absolute. One approach is Hegel's argument that there is a kind of absolute case of "spirit." What this "absolute spirit" is, and how it relates to what Hegel calls "finite spirit," is—given Hegel's antidualism—a difficult topic. A second approach is Hegel's case that the direct object of the *Logic*—a series of "forms of thought"—is itself an absolute case of immanent, teleological development. The final paragraphs of Hegel's system, on "philosophy" as a form of "absolute spirit," argue that these two approaches lead to a "unification," or the same destination—to an absolute case of self-consciousness which is also an absolute case of a form or structure of thought (§§574–577). Hegel here compares this to Aristotle's account of God as thought thinking itself (§577). However difficult these claims are, it is clear that Hegel's metaphysics is some kind of idealism: given the second kind of metaphysical priority, mentioned earlier, in the end everything real is supposed to be what it is in virtue of its relation to something that is at once the absolute case of a kind of self-consciousness and the absolute case of a form or structure of thought.

We should keep the unusual aspects of this philosophy in mind when addressing the common association of Hegel with the view that everything real is completely explicable in virtue of having a place in one teleological process of development throughout history. *On the one hand*, there are clearly senses in which this is not Hegel's view. For Hegel holds that some things exist, but are only incompletely explicable. For example, the nonteleological is only incompletely explicable. It is not the case that there must be a metaphysical foundation, existing independently of any given nonteleological phenomenon, which is responsible for its existence, rendering it completely explicable. And it certainly is not explicable in terms of any historical process, because it has no history. With biological species, there can be historical change in biological species, but without any purpose.[44] Only spirit is

---

44 A biological species can go extinct, without a purpose explaining why (*VGP* 19:175/2:158; and *EN* §339Z, p. 280). In general, "even the species are completely subject to the changes of the

supposed to develop through history in a goal-directed manner. Hegel says, for example,

> Merely animate natures, as mere objects, like other things at lower levels on the scale of being, do not have fate. What befalls them is a contingency.... Only self-consciousness has fate in a strict sense, because it is free. (*WL* 12:141/639)

Finally, even Hegel's account of human history is not itself his account of something completely or absolutely explicable in terms of itself; it is not the absolute. *On the other hand*, there is a sense in which parts of the common suggestion do grasp Hegel's view. For Hegel does hold that anything truly substantial and actual must be something completely intelligible in terms of an immanent purpose of development. This allows that some things fall short of this explanatory completeness to some degree, and are to that degree not truly substantial and actual. This is the point of the famous claim, "What is rational is actual / and what is actual is rational"; the point is not that everything is rational, but that "[a]ny sensible consideration of the world discriminates... what truly merits the name 'actuality'" (*EL* §6).

Finally, I want to end with consideration of the relation between teleology and the good. For Hegel, where something is a case of immanent teleology, it has a purpose, the realization of which is good for it; and where there is a good for something, there is immanent teleology. But to say this is not yet to assign any priority either way. Some read Aristotle as understanding teleology in terms of a prior notion of goodness.[45] This is not Hegel's position. Hegel is rather explaining goodness in terms of immanent teleology, and immanent teleology in

---

external, universal life of nature" (*EN* §368A [in the German edition] = §370A [in the English translation]).

45 On Cooper and Kahn, see Allan Gotthelf, "The Place of the Good in Aristotle's Teleology," *Proceedings of the Boston Colloquium in Ancient Philosophy* 4 (1988): 13–39.

terms of the idea that the substance of something can be its form or "concept." We can see this position in some of the complaints Hegel wants to lodge against philosophies that make an independent goodness prior: First, Hegel takes such views to fall within the scope of his criticisms of portrayals of the absolute as something "immediate" rather than a result: the goodness of *the good*, in such a philosophy, would not be mediated by anything else. Hegel has this worry, for example, about the form of the good as discussed in most of Plato's dialogues (*VGP* 19:68–69/3:56). Second, Hegel considers near the end of the *Logic* the possibility of a philosophy making "the idea of the good" or just "the good" into the absolute. Hegel takes this to separate the good from being; we might compare the *Republic*'s famous line: "[T]the good is not being, but superior to it in rank and power" (509b8). Hegel's worry is characteristic of his antidualism: there will be nothing immanent within the nature of anything in particular that makes "the good" something good *for it*. The result is what Hegel often calls a *mere* ought:

> The good thus remains an *ought*; it exists *in and for itself*, but *being*, as the ultimate abstract immediacy, remains over against it. (*WL* 12:233/731)

In response to that problem, Hegel argues that a better understanding of the absolute requires "a turning back to *life*," to build on the account of *immanent* purposiveness (*WL* 6:548/735).

Is there then, for Hegel, something like a cosmic good, as opposed to what is good for this as opposed to that? As is common with Hegel, we find two sides to the answer: *On the one hand*, there cannot be any such cosmic good. For there are, again, nonteleological elements, for which there is no good at all. *On the other hand*, there is a cosmic good, in this sense: everything, to the degree that it is substantial and actual, approximates an "absolute" that is a complete case of immanent teleology, with the immanent purpose and good of a kind of freedom.

And, further, there is a sense in which everything else is what it is in virtue of its relation to—its approximating but falling short of—this ultimate and complete case of something with an immanent purpose and good. In that sense, then, a kind of freedom is supposed to serve in Hegel's metaphysics as *the* purpose and *the* good.

It has of course not been my focus here to try to take on all of these last and very large issues in Hegel's broader metaphysics; my main focus has instead been Hegel's argument for the priority of immanent teleology over external forms, and his argument defending the reality of immanent teleology. These arguments are shaped by an engagement with strong Kantian arguments. I have focused here on trying to bring out Hegel's best case for a route back to a metaphysics of real and knowable immanent, natural teleology, and on some initial exploration of where that route might lead.

Acknowledgments

Thanks for helpful comments and questions, on this and similar work, to seminar participants and the Radcliffe Institute, to participants in a colloquium presentation at Columbia University, and to Anton Kabeshkin, Karen Koch, Edgar Maraguat, Jeff McDonough, and Dean Moyar.

Reflection IV

DECODING THE TELEOLOGY OF JAZZ

Anna Harwell Celenza

In his *Critique of Judgment* (1790), Immanuel Kant brought together the topics of aesthetics and natural teleology. His goal was to explore our ability to understand both art and nature. Using Kant as a starting point, music critic Barry Ulanov outlined the "teleology of jazz" in a series of articles for *Metronome* magazine in 1949. Ulanov was interested in defending the artistic validity of bebop, a driving, virtuosic music that arose in the 1940s and challenged listeners and performers alike with its complex structure and content. Ulanov argued that like all true jazz, bebop was striving for an "almost unattainable profundity" that was too often overlooked or misunderstood by listeners.

Ulanov's interest in developing a set of standards applicable to the evaluation of jazz appears to have grown out of his frustration over listeners who criticized his assessments of what counted as "good" and "bad" jazz. In April 1949, he published an article titled "Are We Cantankerous? An Examination of Some Criticism of Criticism Explaining Some Changes of Mind and Declaring Some Principles," wherein he explained that while many listeners' tastes were driven by "reader opinion polls" and extramusical characteristics like "a musician's personality," he believed in a disinterested approach to critical judgment.[1] Ulanov claimed that his method of judging "what's good and what's bad" always "begins with a consideration of the nature of the jazz beast and ... winds up somewhere close to the speculative realm of aesthetic philosophy."[2] He described his methodology as relatively straightforward: "One can only look for standards, formulate a working set of values, and really laud those precious few who make similar values the canon of their professional life."[3]

In July 1949, Ulanov laid out his methodology. Like Kant, he recognized the special challenges of evaluating music, a genre that had perplexed thinkers interested in developing general principles of aesthetic judgment for centuries. "Of all the arts, there is none so perplexing as music, none so difficult to write about, none so productive of argument and disagreement."[4] Unlike Kant, however, Ulanov focused his critique on a specific musical genre, instrumental jazz:

Of all the branches of music, there is none about which people get so exercised as jazz, none about which they get so distraught, so determinedly disorganized, none in which they resist disciplined thinking and logical procedure so violently. And yet, of all the arts and all their branches, there is none in which discipline and logic, clarity and orderliness should be easier than jazz.[5]

This "logic, clarity and orderliness" is what inspired Ulanov to embark on the development of what we might call his Critique of

---

[1] Barry Ulanov, "Are We Cantankerous? An Examination of Some Criticism of Criticism Explaining Some Changes of Mind and Declaring Some Principles," *Metronome* 65, no. 4 (April 1949): 15.
[2] Ulanov, "Are We Cantankerous?," 28.
[3] Ulanov, "Are We Cantankerous?," 28.
[4] Barry Ulanov, "What's Hot and What's Not: How to Tell Good from Bad in Jazz," *Metronome* 65, no. 7 (July 1949): 18.
[5] Ulanov, "What's Hot," 18.

a Jazz Aesthetic Judgment. As Ulanov explains: "I have decided at this point... to organize on paper some working criteria for jazz and to follow that with a long, reflective, retrospective view of the achievements of jazz from its beginnings to the present."[6] He then lays out three criteria by which jazz should be judged—freshness, skill, and profundity—and offers descriptions of each criterion firmly rooted in teleology. About freshness he states:

This, of course, is freshness of idea, and another way of putting it is an even more ambiguous debating term in the arts, *inspiration*. How in God's name do you ascertain a musician's freshness or inspiration? Well, one way is to do it in God's name, to insist that what we are talking about is divine fury or a heavenly gift, and while that may be regarded as blasphemy by some, delusion of grandeur by others, and the most shattering nonsense by still others, this approach at least suggests the breadth of the subject.[7]

At this point, Ulanov argues that due to the relative newness of jazz (the first commercial jazz recording was made in 1917), it is possible to "compute mathematically" the complete compass of jazz. "It is altogether possible to name the figures a man plays, to compare his phrases with all those which have gone before and to make a firm quantitative judgment and the beginning of a qualitative one as a result of it."[8] Thus determining the freshness in jazz is quite possible.

Another criterion is skill, which, according to Ulanov, "is the easiest standard to describe." He notes that there is abundant skill among jazz musicians, and that jazz musicians have often relied too heavily on their technical skill. "They have been more interested

---

6 Ulanov, "What's Hot," 18.
7 Ulanov, "What's Hot," 18.
8 Ulanov, "What's Hot," 18.

in achieving great control of their instruments than in controlling greatness; they have become mechanical virtuosi and little else."[9] In the mind of the critic, such intentions do not lead to good jazz. For a work of jazz to be deemed good, it must rise above mere skill and freshness. Indeed, it must contain the third criterion: profundity.

Profundity "is one of those grimly determined words, one that covers a multitude of meanings and can be carried over from one field to another," explains Ulanov.

In jazz, until very recently, it has been almost entirely missing from the verbal discussion, and properly, because until some of the later Ellington, until Charlie Parker and Lennie Tristano, there has been little if anything in jazz that could be called profound. Nonetheless, profundity must be the end purpose of jazz as it is of traditional music, of painting and poetry and the novel. And, if jazz is a *bona fide* form of music, it has, I think a supreme opportunity to achieve that profundity of expression. For I hold with many others that the distinguishing mark of music, as contrasted with the other arts, is its ability to portray states of being rather than *things* with the qualities of those states.[10]

Yet not all music is the same, explains Ulanov:

While traditional music . . . must confine itself to the static, to the written mood, caught once forever, jazz can make an infinite number of grasps at profundity, profundity in its permanent forms and profundity at its most transient, because jazz is by its very nature spontaneous.

---

9 Ulanov, "What's Hot," 31.
10 Ulanov, "What's Hot," 30.

This is an important point for Ulanov: "It [jazz] is an improvised art."[11]

Ulanov declares profundity as the ultimate goal of jazz. But he admits that problems arise when arguing this philosophical point. And here, one fully encounters the teleological foundation of his aesthetic theory:

> In making profundity the goal of jazz, two problems face us. (1) How do you achieve that end? And (2) how do you recognize it when it has been attained? The answers are not easy to find. Of course, part of the procedure is to convince jazz musicians that every profound urge and effort they may feel and make should be expressed in their music, and that their music comes closer to offering them an adequate expression for the intangible integers of sorrow and joy and tragedy and pathos than any other creative outlet they have. . . . If they achieve it [profundity] it will be self-evident, I think, recognizable as such beyond the necessity of argument.[12]

As the months passed, Ulanov continued decoding the teleology of jazz in later articles. For example, in August 1949 he noted that the teleological nature of good jazz is clearly evident to the intuitive, creative critic. "The creative critic is the only functioning critic. His perceptions are such that . . . he can describe the next development in jazz before the musicians have reached it."[13] This is because profound jazz is profound about itself. And in October he linked the teleological nature of jazz to a history of the genre that begins with *skill*, moves on to *freshness*, and reaches its ultimate goal of *profundity*:

---

11 Ulanov, "What's Hot," 30.
12 Ulanov, "What's Hot," 30.
13 Barry Ulanov, "The Function of the Critic in Jazz: He Must Match the Musician, Intuition for Intuition, Tension for Tension, Inspiring Some and Guiding Others," *Metronome* 65, no. 8 (August 1949): 17.

> The jazzman of New Orleans ... led an uncomplicated musical life, with only the blues and a few related tunes to rely upon harmonically and melodically. ... The result was a very narrow avenue for creative imagination: the exploitation of instrumental technique [i.e., skill]. ... The jazzmen in Chicago, Kansas City and New York in the twenties followed somewhat more complex patterns. ... They broadened the emotional and intellectual range of New Orleans jazz [i.e., freshness]. ... It remained, however, for Duke Ellington ... to suggest the profound potential of jazz. And it fell, first to Benny Goodman and his generation, then Coleman Hawkins, Roy Eldridge, Lester Young, Charlie Christian, Charlie Parker and Lennie Tristano, in quick order, to translate the potential into the actual. No longer, then, does the jazzman stand alone, uncluttered technically, emotionally constricted. Behind him is a history and tradition. Before him is an art.[14]

Ulanov wanted his readers to take jazz seriously, and in an effort to lead them down that path, he adopted the guise of a philosopher and proposed a history of jazz that was teleological in nature. As Ulanov described it, jazz went from being merely skillful, to being skillful and fresh, and ultimately skillful, fresh, and profound. His account is also teleological in seeing in profundity an ultimate goal for jazz. Good jazz, according to Ulanov, is jazz that has profundity as its highest end.

---

14 Barry Ulanov, "The Function of the Musician: The What, How, Where and When of the Modern Jazzman, Properly Answered, Point to Maturity, Dignity and Great Resources," *Metronome* 65, no. 10 (October 1949): 16.

CHAPTER NINE

Contemporary Teleology

Patrick Forber

9.1. Introduction

Work on contemporary teleology encompasses a vast conceptual landscape that analyzes and investigates thinking about the nature of design, function, and organization. Contemporary philosophers have analyzed teleology with respect to language, mind, biology, and technology.[1] In fact, it looks like humans are naturally disposed to see

---

[1] Ruth G. Millikan, *Language, Thought, and other Biological Categories* (Cambridge, MA: MIT Press, 1984) uses biological functions to analyze language and mental content. For discussion, see Karen Neander, "Teleological Theories of Mental Content," last edited Spring 2018, in *The Stanford Encyclopedia of Philosophy*, ed. Edward N. Zalta. Tim Lewens, *Organisms and Artifacts* (Cambridge, MA: MIT Press, 2004); and Ulrich Krohs and Peter Kroes, *Functions in the Biological and Artificial Worlds* (Cambridge, MA: MIT Press, 2009) address teleology in technology and investigate the connections to biology. This chapter will focus on teleology in biology and leave these explorations for another time.

Patrick Forber, *Contemporary Teleology* In: *Teleology*. Edited by: Jeffrey K. McDonough, Oxford University Press (2020). © Oxford University Press.
DOI: 10.1093/oso/9780190845711.003.0014

the world as organized in a teleological way.[2] Yet many see a modern challenge to the legitimacy of teleology, a challenge that originated in 1858 with the proposal, by Charles Darwin and Alfred Russell Wallace, concerning the evolution of species by means of natural selection.[3] The volume thus far has demonstrated the deep and nuanced history of thinking about teleology, and this history has set the intellectual agenda for a blossoming of important contemporary work. Since I cannot possibly cover the full picture, I will instead pull on just one thread of the tapestry, examining whether and how teleology might be consistent with contemporary biology.[4]

The biological world looks to be awash with design. Nothing makes this point clearer than dwelling on the finely tuned products of evolution. For instance, consider the Hawaiian bobtail squid. These nocturnal animals have evolved a sophisticated light organ for cultivating bioluminescent symbionts. These bacteria, *Vibrio fisherii*, exist in extraordinarily minute concentrations in the open ocean. Yet bobtail squid, as juveniles, are able to reliably recruit six to twelve bacterial cells from this diverse marine bacterial ecosystem to seed their light crypts. They then use the bioluminescence of their cultivated colony throughout their lives to camouflage themselves against the night sky, effectively hiding themselves from nocturnal predators that hunt from below.[5] Predators have similarly impressive equipment. The peregrine

---

[2] See, for instance, the psychological research of Deborah Keleman, "The Scope of Teleological Thinking in Preschool Children," *Cognition* 70 (1999): 241–272; and Deborah Keleman and E. Rosset, "The Human Function Compunction: Teleological Explanation in Adults," *Cognition* 111 (2009): 138–143.

[3] Charles Darwin and Alfred Russell Wallace, "On the Tendency of Species to Form Varieties; and on the Perpetuation of Varieties and Species by Natural Means of Selection," *Journal of the Proceedings of the Linnean Society* 3 (1858): 45–62.

[4] Many of the canonical contemporary papers are collected in David Buller, ed., *Function, Selection, and Design* (Albany: State University of New York Press, 1999). Justin Garson, *A Critical Overview of Biological Functions* (Dordrecht: Springer, 2016), provides a good and systematic overview of the philosophical issues surrounding biological function.

[5] While this is the presumed evolutionary explanation, investigation continues; for a review of the squid-vibrio system see Margaret McFall-Ngai, "Divining the Essence of Symbiosis: Insights from the Squid-Vibrio Model," *PLoS Biology* 12 (2014): e1001783.

falcon hunts by diving from high above aerial prey, often reaching speeds over 200 mph during its stoop. The structure of their bodies, from skeletal and feather morphology to specialized eyelids and airway construction, look to be specially designed for this high-speed hunting strategy. Recent work modeling peregrine falcon aerodynamics shows that they use the same pure proportional guidance laws to optimize their hunting dives that we program into guided missiles.[6] These traits are evolutionary marvels—they demand explanations capable of demonstrating how and why they are designed to do what they do.

Focusing on examples helps us gain traction on the relationship between teleology and biology. First, they show that biological systems look to be designed, and therefore exhibit teleological organization. The various parts of the squid's light organ and the peregrine's body have functions that contribute to the impressive behaviors that allow for sophisticated camouflage and aerial hunting, respectively. Thus, the crucial concept we need to unpack is that of *biological function*. Further, I say "looks to be designed" because whether evolution actually designs and optimizes organisms for their ecological lifeways turns out to be a matter of significant controversy on both philosophical and biological grounds.[7] Biological functions have histories, and how these histories determine, affect, or undermine the teleological organization, or appearance thereof, that we so readily see in organisms turns out to be the crux of the issue. In this chapter, let me start with a historical approach to the problem of biological function by taking a closer look at some features of the nineteenth-century debate over evolution. Then I will consider two core theories of biological function and discuss the

---

6 Robin Mills, Hanno Hildenbrandt, Graham K. Taylor, and Charlotte K. Hemelrijk, "Physics-Based Simulations of Aerial Attacks by Peregrine Falcons Reveal That Stooping at High Speed Maximizes Catch Success against Agile Prey," *PLOS Computational Biology* (2018): 10.1371.

7 This is the rich and complicated controversy over *adaptationism*. The debate concerns a family of issues about the power and prevalence of natural selection. Some of these issues will emerge subsequently, but I cannot do justice to the literature here. A short overview can be found in Patrick Forber, "Debating the Power and Scope of Adaptation," in *The Philosophy of Biology: A Companion for Educators*, ed. Kostas Kampourakis (Dordrecht: Springer, 2013), 145–160.

state of play in contemporary debates. I conclude with a general concern about the prospects for contemporary accounts of function to succeed in providing a naturalistic theory of teleology in biology.

9.2. Biological Design after Darwin

The origins of the historical challenge that Darwin and Wallace created offer a glimpse at the contours that have developed in the contemporary discussions. In the early nineteenth century William Paley chose the vertebrate camera eye as an obvious instance of design in organisms, using it to illustrate his natural theological argument for the existence of God.[8] The argument is simple, familiar, and has well-known defects.[9] Were we to stumble upon a watch when wandering through the English countryside, we would immediately infer this object had a designer, one who crafted its parts to fulfill particular functional roles that contribute to the smooth working of the timepiece. Paley's argument from design uses an analogy between the vertebrate camera eye and the watch to make the case for the existence of God—just as we correctly infer that the watch had a designer, so, too, should we infer that the complex vertebrate eye had a designer, albeit one more powerful and intelligent.

Darwin was aware of Paley's argument and explicitly attempted to answer this challenge, arguing that evolution by natural selection, through the accumulation of gradual changes over long periods of time, could indeed craft such "organs of extreme perfection." Now we

---

8 William Paley, *Natural Theology, or Evidences of the Existence and Attributes of the Deity, Collected from the Appearances of Nature*, 12th ed. (London: Rivington, [1802] 1809).
9 David Hume, in *Dialogues Concerning Natural Religion* (Indianapolis: Hackett, [1776] 1980), provided the definitive dismantling of the design argument before Paley's famous version even appeared. Elliot Sober gives a sharp contemporary analysis of Paley's argument and puts the defects in the clearest possible terms in his "The Design Argument," in *The Blackwell Guide to the Philosophy of Religion*, ed. William E. Mann, 117–147 (Hoboken, NJ: Wiley-Blackwell, 2004) and *Evidence and Evolution: The Logic behind the Science* (Cambridge: Cambridge University Press, 2008).

consider his attempt to be a resounding success, but the implications for the existence of teleological organization in biology are less clear. Some think Darwin eradicated teleology, demonstrating that evolution by natural selection generates "the appearance of design as if by a master watchmaker" and creates the "illusion of design and planning."[10] Yet others see a vindication. Darwin, through a "strange inversion of reasoning" has shown how there can be "competence without comprehension" and therefore how cumulative selection processes produce design without designers.[11]

The radical interpretation that Darwin eradicated teleology is probably mistaken. Functional ascriptions are simply too useful for parsing and explaining the biological world—how would we talk about the squid's light organ and the falcon's hunting strategy without them? However, the motivation for rejecting teleology in biology comes from an important contrast between Darwin's proposal and another influential evolutionary theory in the nineteenth century, that of Jean-Baptiste Lamarck. Most associate Lamarckian evolution with the inheritance of acquired characteristics. Lamarck thought that organisms, through dealing with their external circumstances, developed adaptive changes that were then passed on to their offspring.[12] Yet that was only part of the overall view. The primary process responsible for evolutionary change, according to Lamarck, was "le pouvoir de la vie," or the capacity for life.[13] This involved the action of postulated internal fluids

---

10 Richard Dawkins, *The Blind Watchmaker: Why the Evidence of Evolution Reveals a Universe without Design* (New York: Norton, [1986] 1996).
11 Daniel C. Dennett, *From Bacteria to Bach and Back: The Evolution of Minds* (New York: Norton, 2017).
12 Indeed, Dawkins, *Blind Watchmaker*, identifies this feature of Lamarckian evolution as the key contrast to Darwinian evolution and its eradication of the teleology so common to Lamarckian accounts. Perhaps unsurprisingly, the controversy continues. Some argue that contemporary biological mechanisms, such as plasticity and learning, create patterns similar to the inheritance of acquired characteristics, though in ways compatible with Darwinism. See Eva Jablonka and Marion J. Lamb, *Evolution in Four Dimensions: Genetic, Epigenetic, Behavioral, and Symbolic Variation in the History of Life* (Cambridge, MA: MIT Press, [2005] 2014).
13 Jean-Baptiste Lamarck, *Zoological Philosophy*, trans. Hugh Elliot (New York: Hafner, [1809] 1963).

that drove evolution toward increasing complexity. Thus, for Lamarck, evolution was goal-directed: the internal fluids push a lineage toward the complex, and external circumstances direct adaptive change. Darwin famously disagreed.[14] Yet this raises a puzzle for teleology in biology: if the evolutionary process is not goal-directed, if there is no inherent drive toward complexity or improvement, then how can there be teleological organization in biology?

Rather than eliminate teleology from biology, most contemporary philosophers attempt to *naturalize* it: to analyze teleology, and the corresponding notion of biological function, in a way consistent with the natural sciences, especially evolutionary biology. An important element of contemporary debates concerns whether competing accounts can succeed in this project of naturalization. As I see it, a completely naturalized account of biological function should meet three desiderata. First, such an account should show how functional ascriptions are determined by the biological facts, and not make constitutive appeals to investigator interests, perspectives, or preferences. By *constitutive* appeal, I have in mind the case where an analysis requires some specification of our explanatory query or interests for a functional ascription to be true. Of course, our interests and questions may determine which of a host of compatible explanations we should provide in particular contexts, for there are different sorts of questions we may ask of the same structure or trait.[15] We might want an evolutionary explanation for the origin of some behavior, or we might want a biomechanical explanation for how it's produced. With respect to the squid, the first would involve a phylogenetic

---

14 Darwin's letter to Charles Lyell, March 12–13, 1863. Darwin objects to Lyell's comparison of evolution by natural selection to Lamarck's evolutionary theory, claiming that such a comparison mistakenly "implied a necessary progression" to his own evolutionary theory.

15 Niko Tinbergen, "On the Aims and Methods in Ethology," *Zeitschrift für Tierpsychologie* 20 (1963): 410–433, identifies four questions for behavioral ecology that provide a nice illustration of this sort of explanatory sensitivity. A contemporary extension to this division of explanatory labor is provided by Patrick Bateson and Kevin N. Laland, "Tinbergen's Four Questions: An Appreciation and an Update," *Trends in Ecology and Evolution* 28 (2013): 712–718.

sequence of forms that show how the light organ evolved to cultivate bioluminescent symbionts to use as camouflage from predators, whereas the second would concern biochemical reactions involved in quorum sensing and luminescence among the *V. fisherii*, and how the light organ maintains the colony by flushing excess bacteria. Which questions we ask would determine which explanation is appropriate, but the correct explanations would be true, and still count as explanations, independent of the questions we ask. If we need to make a constitutive appeal to our perspective, interests, or explanatory queries, then functional ascriptions will, to some degree, be projected onto the biological world by us.[16] In short, functions would be compact ways of answering questions and satisfying curiosities, not mind-independent features of the biological world, though they would draw upon historical and causal facts.

A second, and related, desideratum is that a naturalized account should explicate the connection between functional ascriptions and explanation in a satisfactory way. A point of consensus in the contemporary literature is that functions play an explanatory role, perhaps several different roles, in the biological sciences, and any analysis of function should demonstrate how and when they fulfill their explanatory role(s).[17] Finally, the analysis of function should ground two important distinctions, one between function and accident (or mere effect), and another between normal (or proper) function and malfunction. These are crucial distinctions that philosophical accounts

---

[16] The pragmatic account of explanation given by Bas Van Fraasen, *The Scientific Image* (Oxford: Clarendon Press, 1980), would, on this approach, make such a constitutive appeal. Explanations only count as such relative to a question that specifies the contrast class. So a proposed hypothesis may count as an explanation for me, but not for you, if we are asking suitably different questions.

[17] There is some discussion over whether a philosophical account should provide a conceptual analysis of how folk use the term "function" versus a theoretical definition capable of best systematizing the way the term is used in the sciences. While it is important, I will set this issue to the side; see Ruth G. Millikan, "In Defense of Proper Functions," *Philosophy of Science* 56 (1989): 288–302; and Karen Neander, "Functions as Selected Effects: The Conceptual Analyst's Defense," *Philosophy of Science* 58 (1991): 168–184.

aim to capture, and failure to do so would be a strike against any proposed account.

Before I turn my full attention to the contemporary debates, let me return to Darwin, for he had another, prescient comment about functions. In the chapter "Difficulties on Theory," where Darwin discusses the challenge posed by "organs of extreme perfection," he reflects on how evolution can change the function of particular organs:

> Although the belief that an organ so perfect as the eye could have been formed by natural selection, is more than enough to stagger any one; yet in the case of any organ, if we know of a long series of gradations in complexity, each good for its possessor, then under changing conditions of life there is no logical impossibility in the acquirement of any conceivable degree of perfection through natural selection. In the cases in which we know of no intermediate or transitional states, we should be very cautious in concluding that none could have existed, for the homologies of many organs and their intermediate states show that wonderful metamorphoses in function are at least possible. For instance, a swim-bladder has apparently been converted into an air-breathing lung. The same organ having performed simultaneously very different functions, and then having been in part or in whole specialised for one function; and two distinct organs having performed at the same time the same function, the one having been perfected whilst aided by the other, must often have largely facilitated transitions.[18]

There are two striking observations to make here. First, notice that Darwin uses the term "function" to identify the role various organs play in the current biology of an organism. This is an ahistorical teleological notion that ostensibly depends on how an organism lives and

---

[18] Charles Darwin, *The Origin of Species*, 2nd ed. (Oxford: Oxford University Press, [1859] 1998), 166–167.

how its parts contribute to its lifeway. Second, Darwin makes the case that evolutionary history can layer, change, erase, or modify the functions an organ performs so that it may have multiple functions at once or different functions at different times. This historical dependence complicates any analysis of biological function. There are, of course, philosophical issues associated with gaining epistemic access to evolutionary history. This is one of the sources of the controversy over design within evolutionary biology, a point to which I will return.

There is also a deeper layer of philosophical controversy over whether we should use evolutionary history in our analysis of biological function at all—that is, whether the function of some structure or trait may be determined by what it evolved to do, rather than what it does now. On historical approaches, evolution by natural selection for a specific consequence or effect of some structure or trait determines its function. Whether the trait still performs that function is a contingent matter. Current use and evolutionary origin may (and often do) coincide, but they may not.[19] The squid's light organ provides camouflage against the night sky, and the consensus is that evolution by natural selection shaped the organ to do this. Yet the peregrine falcon's feathers, while recently evolved to suit the aerodynamic needs of its high-speed hunting strategy, may have originated for a different purpose, that of thermoregulation for the ancient ancestors of Aves.[20] When evolution by natural selection layers or changes function, the question of how to incorporate history into an analysis of biological function becomes more complicated. Perhaps ancient history fixes the function and later

---

19 This methodological point lies at the core of Gould and Lewontin's "Spandrels" critique of adaptationism, but the point has a long history. Nietzsche, *Genealogy*, II 12, makes the same claim when thinking about the origins of punishment; for discussion see Patrick Forber, "Biological Inheritance and Cultural Evolution in Nietzsche's Genealogy," *Journal of Nietzsche Studies* 44 (2013): 329–341.

20 Stephen Jay Gould and Elizabeth Vrba, "Exaptation—a Missing Term in the Science of Form," *Paleobiology* 8 (1982): 4–15. A more recent study by Richard O. Prum, "Development and Evolutionary Origin of Feathers," *Journal of Experimental Zoology* 285 (1999): 291–306, shows that feathers are aerodynamic only in later evolutionary stages, and therefore must have originated in response to different selection pressures. I will return to this point later.

uses are merely fortuitous effects jury-rigged by evolution, or perhaps only recent history should determine what counts as a function.[21]

This move, to invoke evolutionary history to ground the notion of biological function, is one promising way to naturalize teleology. It is not the only option. Another approach focuses on the ahistorical version of function, the one Darwin himself used, based on the role a trait or structure currently plays. These two competing accounts of function have structured contemporary efforts to analyze teleology in biology. The following section will look at the proposed accounts of function in more detail with the goal of assessing how they attempt to naturalize the concept and whether they succeed in doing so.

9.3. Etiology versus Causal Role

The two primary contemporary approaches to biological function are the etiological account proposed by Larry Wright and the causal role account proposed by Robert Cummins. These were not the first attempts at analyzing the notion of function, but they have become the most successful, in part due to the explicit connection made between functional ascription and explanation. They each have enjoyed considerable elaboration. Consider their original definitions:

(1) Etiological: "The function of X is Z ***means*** (a) X is there because it does Z, (b) Z is a consequence (or result) of X's being there."[22]

(2) Causal role: "X functions as Z in S (or: the function of X in S is to Z) relative to an analytical account A of S's capacity to C

---

[21] For instance, Elisabeth Lloyd and Stephen Jay Gould, "Exaptation Revisited: Changes Imposed by Evolutionary Psychologists and Behavioral Biologists," *Biological Theory* 12 (2017): 50–65, defend the former, whereas Paul G. Griffiths, "Functional Analysis and Proper Functions," *British Journal for the Philosophy of Science* 44 (1993): 409–422, and Peter Godfrey-Smith, "A Modern History Theory of Functions," *Noûs* 28 (1994): 344–362, defend the latter.

[22] Larry Wright, "Functions," *Philosophical Review* 82 (1973): 161.

just in case *X* is capable of *Z*-ing in *S* and *A* appropriately and adequately accounts for *S*'s capacity to *C* by, in part, appealing to the capacity of *X* to *Z* in *S*."[23]

Both Wright and Cummins tied their accounts to a broadly pragmatic account of explanation. While (1) does not explicitly mention explanation, Wright elaborates that "'[b]ecause' is of course to be understood in its explanatory sense."[24] Cummins built explanation explicitly into (2) by referencing the "analytical account *A*." These connections to explanation represent a conceptual step forward. Wright and Cummins each proposed powerful analyses of function that aimed to unify the uses of the concept found across the sciences. Although neither analysis managed to achieve consensus, their lasting importance is due to the close ties made between functional ascriptions and explanations.[25] Yet these links created vulnerabilities as well. Let me examine some of the standard strengths and weaknesses associated with the etiological and causal role analyses to help clarify how, exactly, the vulnerabilities manifest, and to diagnose a shared cause for them.

Wright's original account aimed at unifying functional ascriptions in biology and artifacts by appealing to the reasons for "being there." The immediate trouble is that, despite the connection to explanation, the conditions are perhaps too easy to satisfy, identifying functions that clash with our intuitions. For instance, obesity prevents strenuous exercise and the prevention of exercise is a consequence of obesity, but it's a mistake to conclude that the function of obesity is exercise

---

23 R. Cummins, "Functional Analysis," *Journal of Philosophy* 72 (1975): 762; notation changed slightly for consistency.
24 Wright, "Functions," 157.
25 Peter Godfrey-Smith, "Functions: Consensus without Unity," *Pacific Philosophical Quarterly* 74 (1993): 196–208, embraces this point and argues for pluralism with respect to accounts of function.

prevention.[26] Many counterexamples can be handled by putting constraints on what counts as an acceptable etiology, and the obvious solution, for biology at least, is to appeal to evolutionary history. The function of some structure or trait is what that trait was selected *for*. The function of a human heart is to pump blood because there is a history of evolution by natural selection for blood pumping. Hearts also make noise, but this is merely a side effect, no matter how useful that effect may prove to medical practice.

Relying on evolutionary histories of selection to naturalize functional ascriptions is striking in its power and simplicity. To say that the function of the squid's light organ is to cultivate bioluminescent symbionts that provide camouflage against the night sky is just to say that there is a history of natural selection for this. Facts about squid evolution ground the functional ascription. We can identify when the light organ malfunctions: if squid are not able to recruit *V. fisherii* at the right time, the organ does not develop in the right way and they never are able to acquire symbionts. The organ still has the same function even though it cannot perform it in some cases. We can also distinguish between function and side effect: the light organ may also signal a squid's presence to conspecifics or potential mates, but this would not be the organ's function given the (presumed) evolutionary history, just a side effect co-opted for another use.[27] The same sort of analysis would apply to behaviors, too. To say that the function of the peregrine falcon's high-speed stoop is to maximize the chances of catching agile aerial prey is just to say that there is a corresponding history of selection in the falcon lineage.

As appealing as the account may be, there are some enduring problems. Reconstructing the deep past is notoriously difficult, and our

---

26 Christopher Boorse, "Wright on Functions," *Philosophical Review* 85 (1976): 70–86. Mark Bedau, "Can Biological Teleology Be Naturalized?," *Journal of Philosophy* 88 (1991): 647–655, provides a counterexample involving nonliving systems.

27 Of course, if there were selection for signaling, this, too, would count as a function of the light organ. Biological traits can have multiple functions.

tendency to ascribe functions to all sorts of biological structures and behaviors far outstrips the current capacity of evolutionary biologists to provide accurate histories to underwrite these ascriptions. Some argue that the challenge of epistemic access undermines any etiological account of functions, but this objection is not decisive.[28] The difficulty of a task should not count against its necessity. However, the problem of access acts as an enabling condition for two more serious problems with etiological accounts. The first concerns the prevalence of natural selection across the tree of life, and the connected controversy over adaptationism; the second concerns how to handle changes in function over evolutionary time.

The first problem involves a potential mismatch between the prevalence of functional ascriptions and the prevalence of histories of selection. We ascribe biological functions with ease and abundance, often presuming these ascriptions will be borne out by investigations into evolutionary history. This is an empirical bet about the history of biological evolution, yet the prospects of this bet are hotly contested. To put it simply, adaptationists find the bet not only sensible but settled in their favor based on a suite of arguments about the power of natural selection and the complexity of biological design.[29] Opponents stress the epistemic challenge, that current utility and evolutionary origins often come apart, and point toward increasingly sophisticated alternatives that invoke developmental constraints or neutral evolution. While we cannot settle this bet here, it does have some relevance for assessing the

---

28 Ron Amundson and G. V. Lauder, "Function without Purpose: The Uses of Causal Role Function in Evolutionary Biology," *Biology and Philosophy* 9 (1994): 443–469, push this sort of objection against etiological accounts in support of their preferred causal role account, arguing that the evidential demands of the etiological account are simply too high to be met in most cases. This general argument is elaborated in more detail by Paul S. Davies, *Norms of Nature: Naturalism and the Nature of Functions* (Cambridge, MA: MIT Press, 2001), chapter 5.

29 Dawkins, *Blind Watchmaker* and Daniel C. Dennett, *Dangerous Idea: Evolution and the Meanings of Life* (New York: Simon & Schuster, 1995), are considered canonical defenses of adaptationism. For discussion see Peter Godfrey-Smith, "Three Kinds of Adaptationism," in *Adaptationism and Optimality*, ed. Stephen H. Orzack and Elliott Sober (Cambridge: Cambridge University Press, 2001), 335–357, or Tim Lewens, "Seven Types of Adaptationism," *Biology and Philosophy* 24 (2009): 161–182.

etiological strategy for naturalizing teleology. To be clear, the etiological account of function is logically independent of any theses associated with adaptationism, but there are relations of support. If it turns out to be the case that the bet is settled in favor of adaptationists, this would alleviate the mismatch concern. On the other hand, if the bet goes the other way, the mismatch causes a problem for the etiological account: either there is much less teleological organization in the biological realm than we presumed, or the account fails to naturalize all functional ascriptions.

The second problem involves potential changes in the function(s) of some biological structure over evolutionary history, and how the etiological account of function should handle these changes. Evolutionary origins are not discrete events; complex biological structures or behaviors, such as the light organs of bobtail squid or the stooping hunting strategy of peregrine falcons, emerge gradually over time and involve the integration of numerous traits. Furthermore, selection pressures can change, sometimes dramatically, co-opting existing adaptations to serve new roles. These concerns motivated a controversial proposal, put forth by Stephen Jay Gould and Elisabeth Vrba, about how to think about function in these complex cases: the function of a trait, structure, or behavior, is determined by the original, ancestral history of selection.[30] On this proposal, subsequent evolutionary history, changes in selection pressures, or transitions to vestiges do not change the function of a trait. Consider the classic case of feathers. According to the evolutionary history described by Gould and Vrba, feathers originated as an adaptation for thermoregulation.[31] This history of selection determines their function in the ancestral lineage leading to Aves.

---

[30] Gould and Vrba, "Exaptation." Lloyd and Gould, "Exaptation Revisited," provide clarifications and further defense of this proposal about functions. Interestingly, given Gould's commitment to Darwin's original views, this proposal involves a striking departure from Darwin's use of biological function, as illustrated in the quotation.

[31] Of course, the analysis can change if new evidence regarding the evolutionary origins of feathers comes to light. That said, contemporary work bears out the claim that feathers originated much earlier than their use in flight; see Prum, "Origin of Feathers."

Much later feathers became co-opted for flight, undergoing significant structural change in response to new selection pressures. However, on Gould and Vrba's proposal, they retain the function of thermoregulation (even in cases where there is no continuing selection pressure for this, say in the tropics) despite subsequent evolution. Their role in flight is a useful side effect co-opted by evolution, not their function. To use their terminology: feathers are an *adaptation* for thermoregulation and an *exaptation* for flight.

This proposal, to naturalize function by appealing to original, potentially ancient histories of selection, strikes many as odd at best and crippling at worst. The claim that the finely tuned wing feathers of the peregrine falcon do not have the function to provide aerodynamic control over their high-speed dives conflicts with both biological usage and philosophical intuition. Furthermore, reconstructing *ancient* evolutionary history compounds epistemic challenges, and this creates leverage against the etiological account. The mismatch argument—that the frequency of legitimate functional ascriptions outstrips our ability to provide evolutionary histories of direct selection—gains further traction as the difficulty of access increases. However, it would be premature to reject any etiological account on these grounds, for there is an insightful revision available. Rather than fix functional ascriptions by appeal to ancient history, we can do so by appeal to the most recent history of selection.[32] This modern history account dispels some of the strangeness associated with the peregrine's feathers. Given the most recent history of selection, the feathers do have an aerodynamic function. They may also have the function for thermoregulation, provided there is still recent selection for this effect of feathers. Yet if that selection pressure were removed, feathers would no longer have the function of thermoregulation. The account also handles vestiges in an appealing way. Vestigial organs, such as the human appendix or the eyes

---

32 Godfrey-Smith, "Modern History," provides a canonical argument for this proposal.

of some cave-dwelling creatures, no longer perform a salient role in the organism; they are vestiges of older traits that, so the intuition goes, once had a function but no longer do. On Gould and Vrba's proposal, these vestiges would still have a function in contemporary organisms even though they are no longer, and cannot be, used for their original function. Relying on more recent histories of selection to determine functional ascriptions allows for loss of function for vestiges.[33]

Regardless of the exact configuration, etiological accounts identify a clear path toward naturalizing biological function. Functions are determined by evolutionary histories of selection. The drawback to these accounts is the difficulty of accessing these historical facts, especially given our propensity to ascribe functions. The alternative is to attempt to naturalize biological function in a different way, one that does not depend on history.

The causal role approach, rather than leaning on evolutionary history, attempts to carry out the project of naturalization by focusing on the way some structure or trait functions in some overarching system. Cummins originally proposed the account to make sense of functional ascriptions in psychology, and the approach has enduring appeal because both biological and technological realms exhibit striking hierarchical organization.[34] While there are diverse elaborations of the original definition, the approach stays true to (2): functional ascriptions are determined by the role parts play in contributing to the capacities or abilities of some organized system. The relations between parts, as well as the contributions parts make to the capacities of wholes, are usually presumed to be causal, and it is this causal structure that provides the grounds for naturalizing biological function.

---

33 Griffiths, "Functional Analysis."
34 This focus on psychology is not incidental to debates over teleology in biology. Identifying histories of selection for human psychological capacities is notoriously difficult and controversial; for discussion see Kevin N. Laland and Gillian R. Brown, *Sense and Nonsense: Evolutionary Perspectives on Human Behavior*, 2nd ed. (Oxford: Oxford University Press, 2011). The contours of the debate over human evolution have probably contributed to the attraction of causal role accounts of biological function for features of human cognition and behavior.

Causal role accounts often return the same or similar verdicts on many functional ascriptions, though they have a general tendency to be more expansive than etiological accounts. In the case of the squid, the light organ has the function of camouflage in virtue of the causal role bioluminescence plays in the current marine ecology that includes the lifeways of the squid and its predators; the light organ contributes to bioluminescence capabilities, and these capabilities permit the squid to remain undetected. If the light organ also facilitated the capacity to signal to conspecifics, then this would count as a function as well. A similar analysis works for the peregrine falcon: feathers have the function of aerodynamic performance in flight and the high-speed stoop hunting strategy since having feathers (of a very specific construction) contributes to the abilities of the falcon to fly and hunt. The primary attraction of the causal role approach is that functional ascriptions are easily identifiable based on current causal structure. There is no need for painstaking reconstruction of evolutionary history. Ecologists, physiologists, and neuroscientists routinely identify functions for animal behaviors, biological organs, or neuron firings in different regions of the brain without any knowledge of evolutionary history. On causal role accounts these ascriptions are easily analyzed without any covert commitment to an evolutionary history. In contrast to the etiological approach, this strategy avoids the mismatch problem and identifies easily satisfiable evidential demands for determining functional ascriptions.

These features of the causal role approach also conspire to create its key flaw: the account is *too* flexible in ascribing functions, identifying legitimate functions in cases that we intuitively find do not merit a functional ascription. For instance, using a heavy book as a way to elevate your monitor a few inches could count as a function on the causal role account. In the current ergonomic economy of my desktop system, the book contributes to the capacity to alleviate neck pain by elevating my monitor to the proper height. Therefore, this counts as a function of the book. However, this attribution seems to get it wrong—it is tempting to insist that the book's function involves recording and packaging information, not ergonomic adjustment, regardless of any jury-rigging on my part.[35] Biological structures evoke even stronger intuitions. The function of the human heart is to pump blood, not to make noise, yet according to the causal role account, noise-making would count as a function in virtue of the role this effect plays in medical diagnosis. Furthermore, the account ascribes functions to malfunctions in some cases as well. Neuronal degradation and cell death contribute to muscle failure and paralysis in a number of degenerative diseases, and the causal role account seems to ascribe the functions of failure and paralysis to these processes. This problem of "overbreadth," ascribing functions to all sorts of features based on their current and perhaps fortuitous causal roles, carries with it the concomitant failure to distinguish between function, side effect, and malfunction. Therefore, if the causal role account cannot be appropriately revised, it fails to meet the desiderata for naturalizing the concept of biological function.

Part of the problem here, and part of the justification for capturing the differences between functions, effects, and malfunctions, is that ascribing biological functions looks to be a *normative* endeavor. That is, any successful naturalization should identify *proper* functions, and thus identify when some structure fails to function or functions improperly. Proponents of the etiological approach argue that only by invoking evolutionary history can we get a suitably normative account of proper functions.[36] In response, proponents of the causal role approach argue that such distinctions can be rescued by restricting the sorts of systems that can legitimately be deployed in (2) to ascribe functions.[37] Once such restrictions are in place, we can restore

---

35 Or perhaps not: a causal role theorist would have no trouble ascribing this function to the particular book.
36 Millikan, "Proper Functions."
37 Davies, *Norms of Nature*, chapter 4, makes the case for normative causal role functions. Philip Kitcher, "Function and Design," *Midwest Studies in Philosophy* 18 (1993): 379–397, proposes a

the normative features of functional ascriptions, or so the argument goes. The trouble is that such restrictions, to hierarchically organized systems or to target systems of some established scientific practice, are insufficiently restrictive to handle all the counterexamples.[38]

One attractive response to the controversy over using etiology versus causal roles to naturalize the concept of biological function is to split the difference. Perhaps each has a place in the final theory. The etiological account can handle evolutionary biology and underwrite the normative force of some functional ascriptions, while the causal role account can make sense of functional ascriptions made in the disciplines of molecular biology, medicine, and neuroscience.[39] There are, however, concerns that the plausibility of pluralism may stem more from argumentative fatigue than principled concerns. Participants in the debate seem unlikely to concede ground. Causal role theorists observe that etiological functions presume the existence of causal role functions in the past, and so are ultimately parasitic.[40] Why burden us with the mismatch problem and unrealistic evidential demands when we can analyze evolved functions as a historical sequence of causal role functions? In contrast, etiological theorists claim that any legitimate causal role functional ascriptions, even in medicine and neuroscience, make covert appeals to evolution, in the form of either empirical commitments about evolutionary history,[41] or forward-looking predictions about how those structures contribute to current fitness.[42] These

---

restriction on causal role functions motivated from broadly evolutionary concerns, forging a near unification of the two approaches to biological function.

38 Garson, *Critical Overview*, 87–89.

39 Godfrey-Smith, "Functions," makes an early case for disciplinary pluralism. However, even if pluralism is the right view, an appropriate application of the etiological and causal role accounts will not map exactly onto disciplinary boundaries. Molecular biology, for instance, will involve a combination of causal role functions (e.g., in metabolic biochemistry) and etiological functions (e.g., in molecular evolution); see Justin Garson, "How to Be a Function Pluralist," *British Journal for the Philosophy of Science* 69, no. 4 (2018): 1101–1122.

40 Amundson and Lauder, "Function without Purpose."

41 Karen Neander, "Functional Analysis and the Species Design," *Synthese* 194 (2017): 1147–1168.

42 Paul G. Griffiths, "In What Sense Does 'Nothing Make Sense Except in the Light of Evolution'?," *Acta Biotheoretica* 57 (2008): 11–32.

moves amount to a claim that only evolutionary histories, in some fashion or other, provide the right restriction on permissible systems for (2)—historical facts are the solution to the flexibility problem.

I suspect some version of pluralism is right. This is, in part, due to the respective strengths of etiological and causal role approaches. Yet the primary reason for my suspicion has to do with the connection both approaches make to explanation. The contemporary debates have revealed that this connection, while an important conceptual advance, compromises the ability of both approaches to succeed in the project of naturalization. Let me explain.

9.4. A Devil's Bargain

Contemporary approaches to teleology aim to naturalize biological function as the key to demonstrating the utility and respectability of teleological organization after Darwin. A central goal for this project of naturalization is that the account should show how functional ascriptions are determined by biological facts, and do not make constitutive appeal to investigator perspective, interests, or explanatory queries. If our individual perspectives or interests matter for the correct ascription of functions, then teleological organization would, in part, be projected onto the biological world by us. By forging a connection between function ascriptions and explanation both approaches to function often, though not always, make such constitutive appeals. To unpack this, we need to take a closer look at a general feature of scientific explanation, and how this feature connects to the etiological and causal role accounts.

Evolutionary histories and causal structures include a dizzying array of events, factors, and relations that extend beyond the scope of any single explanation. A complete and accurate accounting of all the factors responsible for, say, the evolution of the squid's light organ, or the role of the falcon's high-speed hunting strategy in its ecology, would involve producing something that would not be recognizable as an explanation. By their nature and design, explanations are for consumption *by us*, and we routinely discriminate between trivial details and the factors that make a difference. This contrast, between the trivial and the difference makers, is notoriously hard to make in a principled and general manner. This is because there is a trade-off of sorts between accuracy, detail, and completeness, on the one hand, and clarity, generality, and usefulness, on the other.[43] Good explanations tend to be clear, general, and useful to us, but this requires compromising on the accuracy, detail, and completeness of the array of facts marshaled in such an explanation.

Consider our candidate sources of facts for grounding functional ascriptions: evolutionary history and causal structure. In evolution, natural selection never operates in isolation—the process is inherently connected to constraints, random mutations, and neutral evolution. Identifying adaptations involves finding evidence that selection acted in a way that overcame the interference and interaction of other evolutionary factors.[44] To claim there is a history of selection for the squid's light organ to provide camouflage from nocturnal predators does not, and should not, require the complete denial of a role for structural constraints imposed by the marine environment, or by the squid developmental toolkit. Rather, it requires that natural selection make the right difference in the ancestral lineage of bobtail squid, where "make the right difference" needs to be explicated by our theories concerning evolutionary explanation. Regarding causal structure, especially in complex, hierarchical biological systems, there are far too many causal relations to track. To understand the functional role of the peregrine's hunting strategy, we do not want to include molecular interactions of the air, or track the distribution of photons of light, even though these causal features are part of the system (the falcon navigates through the

---

[43] See, for example, Michael Strevens, *Depth: An Account of Scientific Explanation* (Cambridge, MA: Harvard University Press, 2008).
[44] Sober, *Evidence and Evolution*.

air using its sharp eyesight). Again, when we seek to explain how the hunting strategy works, we aim to identify the relevant causal factors responsible for the impressive aerial behavior of falcons, where "relevant difference maker" is unpacked by our theories of mechanistic or causal explanation.[45] Instead of an inundation of causal detail, requests for explanation help us focus on a subset of these factors that we judge salient.[46]

Further, idealizations—false, simplifying assumptions—play an ineliminable role in many explanations. Frictionless planes, infinite populations, point masses, and so on are crucial elements of formal modeling across the sciences, and this is especially true in biology.[47] These idealizations cannot be factored out or quarantined; they are woven into the fabric of the models we deploy in our explanations.[48] The work on falcon aerodynamics is a case in point. Without relying on idealizations there is no way to abbreviate the complicated physics to provide the explanation for the peregrine falcon's hunting strategy, which involves layers of simulation.[49] These idealizations permit the packaging and processing of information in ways that allow us to understand the explanation. They are part of a strategy needed to focus an explanation on the relevant subset of historical or causal factors, and in the process of this focusing some distortion is inevitable.

---

[45] For instance, see Stuart Glennan, *The New Mechanical Philosophy* (Oxford: Oxford University Press, 2017), for mechanisms, and James C. Woodward, *Making Things Happen: A Theory of Causal Explanation* (Oxford: Oxford University Press, 2003), for causes.

[46] Carl F. Craver, "Role Functions, Mechanisms, and Hierarchy," *Philosophy of Science* 68 (2001): 31–55; Arnon Levy and William Bechtel, "Abstraction and the Organization of Mechanisms," *Philosophy of Science* 80 (2012): 241–261.

[47] William Wimsatt, *Re-engineering Philosophy for Limited Beings: Piecewise Approximations of Reality* (Cambridge, MA: Harvard University Press, 2007).

[48] Collin Rice, "Models Don't Decompose That Way: A Holistic View of Idealized Models," *British Journal for the Philosophy of Science* 70, no. 1 (March 20, 2019): 179–208, https://doi.org/10.1093/bjps/axx045.

[49] Mills et al., "Aerial Attacks by Peregrine Falcons," 13.

Thus, the connection to explanation made by both etiological and causal role accounts, while potent and important, may ultimately compromise the project of naturalization. This is not intended as a damning critique of the contemporary approaches—the connection to explanation has paid off, enabling genuine philosophical progress. Rather, by recognizing that functional ascriptions are explanations, crafted by us for us, we can evaluate when and where etiological versus causal role accounts are more appropriate for the questions at hand, that is, whether it makes more sense to organize biological facts for our consumption using etiological versus causal role functional ascriptions.

On a more positive note, not all is lost. While I am doubtful that either contemporary account can provide a general, unified, and naturalized account of biological functions, both offer resources for naturalizing some functional ascriptions in specific cases. Work in evolutionary biology has produced high-quality evidence for histories of natural selection for numerous traits and structures. In cases where we have met the evidential demands for ascribing an etiological function, we have succeeded in naturalizing a teleological element of a biological system. If the work done on bobtail squid and their symbiosis with *V. fisherii* stands, then we have identified what the bioluminescence is *for*. The trouble is we cannot generalize—empirical bets about adaptationism are not yet settled and, at the end of inquiry, I suspect our tendency to ascribe etiological functions will still outstrip the prevalence of histories of direct natural selection. Work on closed causal systems will exhibit similar features. When there is consensus about the scope of the system and the theoretical resources available for analysis, the causal role account can naturalize teleological elements of these systems. But again, we cannot generalize—most causal systems are not sufficiently isolated, and on the frontiers of science consensus regarding the right way to analyze a system is rare.

The recognition that teleological organization is often projected onto the biological world allows us to evaluate a source other than evolutionary history or causal structure: the use of agential language for organizing and understanding biological systems. We often talk about genes deploying strategies, being selfish, having interests.[50] We talk of animals as having agendas, intentions, and plans.[51] This involves, as Kant suggested, imposing a kind of teleological order onto the world, and we should investigate whether and when this sort of language is appropriate.[52] Agential language, in particular, and teleological thinking, in general, are very powerful ways for us to organize the world. They are powerful because they are so well integrated into our cognition. There is even a good evolutionary rationale for this. Perhaps the key innovation in human evolution may be our ability to understand and predict the behavior, motivation, and interests of fellow human agents to facilitate cooperative social interactions.[53] I suspect we have co-opted this powerful way of thinking to organize our understanding of the wider biological world. And is it really so surprising that the world may not always fit the organizing principles we bring to bear?

---

50 Dawkins, *Blind Watchmaker*; Dennett, *Bacteria to Bach*.
51 Frans de Waal, *Are We Smart Enough to Know How Smart Animals Are?* (New York: Norton, 2017).
52 Samir Okasha, *Agents and Goals in Evolution* (Oxford: Oxford University Press, 2018), undertakes just this sort of investigation for contemporary biological science by making a thorough comparison between evolutionary modeling and formal models of rational choice in economics. For discussion of Kant's views on teleology, see Guyer, this volume.
53 Kim Sterelny, *The Evolved Apprentice: How Evolution Made Humans Unique* (Cambridge, MA: MIT Press, 2012).

Bibliography

Primary Sources

Albert the Great. *Opera Omnia*. Edited by P. Jammy. Lyon, 1651.
Alexander, Gavin, ed. *Sidney's "The Defence of Poesy" and Selected Renaissance Literary Criticism*. London: Penguin, 2004.
Anselm. *Basic Writings*. Translated by T. Williams. Indianapolis: Hackett, 2007.
Aristotle. *The Complete Works of Aristotle: The Revised Oxford Translation*. 2 vols. Edited by J. Barnes. Princeton, NJ: Princeton University Press, 1984.
Aristotle. *Opera Omnia*. In *Thesaurus Lingua Graecae: Canon of Greek Authors and Works*, 3rd ed. Oxford: Oxford University Press, 1990.
Aristotle. *Physics*. In *The Complete Works of Aristotle: The Revised Oxford Translation*, ed. Jonathan Barnes, vol. 1., 315–446. Princeton, NJ: Princeton University Press, 1984.
Aristotle. *Poetics*. Translated by Anthony Kenny. Oxford: Oxford University Press, 2013.
Augustine. *The Works of Saint Augustine: A Translation for the 21st Century*. Edited by J. E. Rotelle. New York: New City Press, 1990–.
Averroës. *Aristotelis opera cum Averrois commentariis*. Venice: apud Junctas, 1562; reprint, Frankfurt am Main: Minerva, 1962.
Averroës. *Tafsīr mā baʿd al-ṭabīʿa* [Long Commentary on the *Metaphysics*]. Edited by M. Bouyges. 3rd ed. 3 vols. Beirut: Dar el-Machreq, 1990.
Avicenna. *Al-Shifāʾ: Al-Samāʿ Al-Ṭabīʿī*. Edited by M. Qasim. Cairo: Organisation Générale des Imprimeries Gouvernementales, 1983.
Avicenna. *Al-Shifāʾ: Al-Ilāhiyyāt*. Vol. 1. Edited by G. C. Anawati and S. Zayed. Cairo: Organisation Générale des Imprimeries Gouvernementales, 1960.

Avicenna. *Al-Shifāʾ: Al-Ilāhiyyāt. Vol. 2*. Edited by M. Y. Moussa, S. Dunya, and S. Zayed. Cairo: Organisation Générale des Imprimeries Gouvernementales, 1960.

Avicenna. *Kitāb al-Nafs*. Edited by Fazlur Rahman. London: Oxford University Press, 1959.

Avicenna. *The Metaphysics of the Healing*. Translated by M. Marmura. Provo, UT: Brigham Young University Press, 2005.

Avicenna. *The Physics of the Healing*. Translated by J. McGinnis. Provo, UT: Brigham Young University Press, 2009.

Babylonian Talmud. Ed. I. Epstein. London: Soncino Press, 1952.

Bacon, Francis. "De augmentis scientiarum." In *Works, vol. 1*, edited by James Spedding, Robert Leslie Ellis, and Douglas Denon Heath. London: Longman, 1858; facsc. repr. Stuttgart-Bad Cannstatt: Friedrich Frommann, 1963.

Bacon, Francis. *The Two Bookes of Francis Bacon. Of the proficience and aduancement of Learning*. Edited by Michael Kiernan. Oxford: Clarendon Press, 2000.

Berkowitz, Luci, and William Allen Johnson, eds. *Thesaurus Linguae Graecae: Canon of Greek Authors and Works*. Oxford: Oxford University Press, 1990.

Bernard of Clairvaux. *On Loving God*. Translated by M. S. Burrows. In *Christian Spirituality: The Classics*, 86–97. London: Routledge, 2009.

Bonaventure of Bagnoregio. *Breviloquium*. Translated and edited by Dominic Monti. St Bonaventure, NY: Franciscan Institute, 2005.

Bonaventure of Bagnoregio. *Legenda maior Prologue 1*. Translated and edited by Regis J. Armstrong, William J. Short, and J. A. Wayne Hellman. In *Francis of Assisi: Early Documents, vol. 2*. St Bonaventure, New York, 2000.

Boyle, Robert. *The Works of the Honorable Robert Boyle*. Edited by Thomas Birch. New ed. 6 vols. London, 1772; reprint Hildesheim: Georg Olms, 1966.

Cicero. *De officiis*. Translated by W. Miller. Cambridge, MA: Harvard University Press, 1913.

Crescas, Hasdai. *Or ha-Shem*. Edited by Shlomo Fisher. Jerusalem: Ramot, 1990.

Darwin, Charles. *The Origin of Species*. 2nd ed. Oxford: Oxford University Press, [1859] 1998.

Darwin, Charles, and Alfred Russell Wallace. "On the Tendency of Species to Form Varieties; and on the Perpetuation of Varieties and Species by Natural Means of Selection." *Journal of the Proceedings of the Linnean Society* 3 (1858): 45–62.

De Lacy, P. *Galeni De placitis Hippocratis et Platonis*. 3 vols. *Corpus Medicorum Graecorum 5.4.1.2*. Berlin: Akademie-Verlag, 1978–84.

Descartes, René. *Oeuvres de Descartes*. Edited by Charles Adam and Paul Tannery. Paris: Vrin, 1978.

Descartes, René. *The Philosophical Writings of Descartes*. Translated by John Cottingham, Robert Stoothoff, and Dugald Murdoch. 2 vols. Cambridge: Cambridge University Press, 1985.

Duns Scotus, John. *Questions on the Metaphysics of Aristotle*. Edited by G. J Etzkorn and A. B. Wolter. St. Bonaventure, NY: Franciscan Institute, 1997–98.

Duns Scotus, John. *Selected Writings on Ethics*. Translated by T. Williams. Oxford: Oxford University Press, 2017.

Ergas, Yosef. *Shomer Emunim*. Jerusalem: Be-Ferush uve-Remez Press, 1965.

Frugoni, Chiara. *Quale Francesco? Il messaggio nascosto negli affreschi della Basilica Superiore ad Assisi*. Turin: Einaudi, 2015.

Galen. *Galen on the Usefulness of the Parts of the Body. Peri chreias moriōn. De usu partium*. 2 vols. Translated by Margaret Tallmadge May. Ithaca, NY: Cornell University Press, 1968.

Galen. *On anatomical procedures: De anatomicis administrationibus*. Edited by Charles Singer. New York: Published for the Wellcome Historical Medical Museum by Oxford University Press, 1956.

Gaon, Saadia. *The Book of Beliefs & Opinions*. Translated by Samuel Rosenblatt. New Haven: Yale University Press, 1948.

Gaon, Saadia. *Emunot ve-Deot*. Translated by Judah Ibn Tibbon. Constantinople, 1562.

Halevi, Judah. *The Kuzari*. Translated by Hartwig Hirschfeld, revised by Lisa Greenwald. Jerusalem: Sefer ve-Sefel Publishing, 2003.

Harvey, William. *An Anatomical Disputation Concerning the Movement of the Heart and Blood in Living Creatures*. Translated by Gweneth Witteridge. London: Blackwell Scientific Publications, 1976.

Harvey, William. *Exercitatio Anatomica de motu cordis et sanguines in animalibus*. Frankfurt am Main, 1628.

Hegel, Georg W. F. *Aesthetics: Lectures on Fine Art*. 3 vols. Translated by T. M. Knox. Oxford: Clarendon Press, 1975.

Hegel, Georg W. F. *Critique of the Power of Judgment*. Translated by Paul Guyer and Eric Mathews. Cambridge: Cambridge University Press, 2000.

Hegel, Georg W. F. *The Encyclopedia Logic*. Translated by T. F. Geraets, H. S. Harris, and W. A. Suchting. Indianapolis: Hackett, 1991.

Hegel, Georg W. F. *Gesammelte Werke*. Meiner, 1968–.

Hegel, Georg W. F. *Hegel's Philosophy of Nature*. Translated by W. Wallace and A. V. Miller. New York: Oxford University Press, 1970.

Hegel, Georg W. F. *Hegel's Science of Logic*. Translated by A. V. Miller. London: George Allen & Unwin, 1969.

Hegel, Georg W. F. *Lectures on the History of Philosophy.* 3 vols. Translated by E. S. Haldane and Frances H. Simson. Lincoln: University of Nebraska Press, 1995.
Hegel, Georg W. F. *Phenomenology of Spirit.* Translated by A. V. Miller. Oxford: Oxford University Press, 1977.
Hegel, Georg W. F. *The Philosophical Propaedeutic.* Translated by M. George and A. Vincent and edited by A. V. Miller. Oxford: Blackwell, 1986.
Hegel, Georg W. F. *Werke in zwanzig Bände.* Edited by E. Moldenhauer und K. Michel. Frankfurt am Main: Suhrkamp, 1970–71.
Helmreich, G. *Galeni. De usu partium Libri XVII.* 2 vols. In *Claudii Galeni Pergameni scripta minora,* vol. 3. Leipzig: Teubner, [1884–93], 1907–9.
Henry of Ghent. *Quodlibetal Questions on Moral Problems.* Translated by R. J. Teske. Milwaukee: Marquette University Press, 2005.
Hume, David. *Dialogues Concerning Natural Religion.* Indianapolis: Hackett, [1776] 1980.
Hume, David. *An Enquiry Concerning Human Understanding.* Edited by Tom L. Beauchamp. Oxford: Clarendon Press, 2000.
Hume, David. *The Natural History of Religion and Dialogues concerning Natural Religion.* Edited by A. Wayne Colver and John Valdimir Price. Oxford: Clarendon Press, 1976.
Ibn Gabbai, Meir. *Avodat ha-Qodesh.* Jerusalem, 2010.
Jablonka, Eva, and Marion J. Lamb. *Evolution in Four Dimensions: Genetic, Epigenetic, Behavioral, and Symbolic Variation in the History of Life.* Cambridge, MA: MIT Press, [2005] 2014.
Kant, Immanuel. *Anthropology, History, and Education.* Translated and edited by Günter Zöller and Robert B. Louden. Cambridge: Cambridge University Press, 2006.
Kant, Immanuel. *Correspondence.* Translated and edited by Arnulf Zweig. Cambridge: Cambridge University Press, 1999.
Kant, Immanuel. *Critique of Pure Reason.* Translated and edited by Paul Guyer and Allen W. Wood. Cambridge: Cambridge University Press, 1998.
Kant, Immanuel. *Critique of the Power of Judgment.* Translated and edited by Paul Guyer. Cambridge: Cambridge University Press, 2000.
Kant, Immanuel. *Gesammelte Schriften.* Edited by the Royal Prussian (later German, then Berlin-Brandenburg) Academy of Sciences. 29 vols. Berlin: Georg Reimer (later Walter de Gruyter & Co.), 1900–.
Kant, Immanuel. *Practical Philosophy.* Translated and edited by Mary J. Gregor. Cambridge: Cambridge University Press, 1996.
Kant, Immanuel. *Religion and Rational Theology.* Translated and edited by Allen Wood and George di Giovanni. Cambridge: Cambridge University Press, 1996.

Kant, Immanuel. *Theoretical Philosophy, 1755–1770*. Edited by David E. Walford. Cambridge: Cambridge University Press, 1992.

Kühn, C. G. *Claudii Galeni Opera Omnia*. 20 vols. Leipzig: Knobloch, 1821–33; reprint Hildesheim: Georg Olms, 1965.

Lamarck, Jean-Baptiste. *Zoological Philosophy*. Translated by Hugh Elliot. New York: Hafner, [1809] 1963.

Maimonides, Moses. *Guide of the Perplexed*. Translated by Shlomo Pines. 2 vols. Chicago: University of Chicago Press, 1963.

Maimonides, Moses. *Haqdamot le-Perush ha-Mishnah*. Jerusalem: Mossad ha-Rav Kuk, 1961.

Maimonides, Moses. *Moreh Newokhim*. Translated by Shmuel Ibn Tibbon with commentaries by Efodi, Shem Tov, Asher Crescas, and Yitzhak Abravanel. Jerusalem 1960.

Maupertuis, Pierre. "Les loix du movement et du repos, déduites d'un principe de métaphysique." In *Histoire de l'Académie Royale des Sciences et Belles-Lettres*. Berlin, 1746.

McGrade, A. S., John Kilcullen, and Matthew Kempshall. *The Cambridge Translations of Medieval Philosophical Texts*. Vol. 2: *Ethics and Political Philosophy*. Cambridge: Cambridge University Press, 2000.

Midrash Rabbah im kol ha-Mefarshim. 2 vols. Jerusalem, n.d.

Midrash Tanhuma. Warsaw: Y.G. Munk Press, 1873.

Nahman of Bratslav. *Likutei Muharan*. Jerusalem: Makhon Torat ha-Netzah, 1992.

Newton, Isaac. *Opticks, or A Treatise on the Reflections, Refractions, Inflections and Colours of Light*. Based on the 4th ed., London, 1730. New York: Dover, 1952.

Nietzsche, Friedrich. *The Genealogy of Morals*. Translated by Walter Kaufmann. New York: Vintage, [1887] 1989.

Paley, William. *Natural Theology, or Evidences of the Existence and Attributes of the Deity, Collected from the Appearances of Nature*. 12th ed. London: Rivington, [1802] 1809.

Plato. *Cratylus*. In *Complete Works*, edited by John Cooper, 101–156. Indianapolis: Hackett, 1997.

Plato. *Phaedo*. In *Euthyphro. Apology. Crito. Phaedo. Phaedrus*, translated by Harold North Fowler, 200–406. Loeb Classical Library 36. Cambridge, MA: Harvard University Press, 1914.

Plato. *Republic*. In *Complete Works*, edited by John Cooper, 971–1223. Indianapolis: Hackett, 1997.

Plato. *Statesman*. Translated by C. J. Rowe. Warminster: Aris and Phillips, 1995.

Plato. *Timaeus*. In *Timaeus and Critias*, translated by Desmond Lee, revised by Thomas K. Johansen. New York: Penguin, 2008.

Sidney, Philip. *The Major Works*. Edited by Katherine Duncan Jones. Rev. ed. Oxford: Oxford University Press, 2008.

Spinoza, Baruch. *The Collected Works of Spinoza*. Translated by Edwin Curley. 2 vols. Princeton, NJ: Princeton University Press, 1985–2016.

Spinoza, Benedict. *Opera*. Edited by Carl Gebhardt. 4 vols. Heidelberg: Carl Winter, 1925.

Suárez, Francisco. *Disputationes Metaphysicae*. 2 vols. Reprint, Hildesheim: Georg Olms, 2009.

Thomas Aquinas. *Opera omnia*. Edited by the Leonine Commission. Rome: Commissio Leonina, 1882–.

Ulanov, Barry. "Are We Cantankerous? An Examination of Some Criticism of Criticism Explaining Some Changes of Mind and Declaring Some Principles." *Metronome* 65, no. 4 (April 1949): 15–28.

Ulanov, Barry. "The Function of the Critic in Jazz: He Must Match the Musician, Intuition for Intuition, Tension for Tension, Inspiring Some and Guiding Others." *Metronome* 65, no. 8 (August 1949): 16–17.

Ulanov, Barry. "The Function of the Musician: The What, How, Where and When of the Modern Jazzman, Properly Answered, Point to Maturity, Dignity and Great Resources." *Metronome* 65, no. 10 (October 1949): 16, 26.

Ulanov, Barry. "What's Hot and What's Not: How to Tell Good from Bad in Jazz." *Metronome* 65, no. 7 (July 1949): 18, 30–31.

Vesalius, A. *De humani corporis fabrica libri septem*. Basel: Ex officina Joannis Oporini, 1543, 1555.

William of Ockham. *Opera philosophica et theologica*. St. Bonaventure, NY: Franciscan Institute, 1967–89.

William of Ockham. *Quodlibetal Questions*. Translated by A. Freddoso and F. Kelley. New Haven: Yale University Press, 1991.

Wolff, Christian. *Vernünfftige Gedancken von den Absichten der natürlichen Dinge, andere Auflage*. Frankfurt am Main: Renger, 1726.

Zohar. Vilnius: Widow and Brothers Romm Print, 1882.

Secondary Sources

Adams, Marilyn McCord. "Ockham on Final Causality: Muddying the Waters." *Franciscan Studies* 56 (1998): 1–46.

Adams, Marilyn McCord. "The Structure of Ockham's Moral Theory." *Franciscan Studies* 46 (1986): 1–35.

Adams, Marilyn McCord. *William Ockham*. 2 vols. Notre Dame, IN: University of Notre Dame Press, 1987.

Amundson, Ron, and G. V. Lauder. "Function without Purpose: The Uses of Causal Role Function in Evolutionary Biology." *Biology and Philosophy* 9 (1994): 443–469.

Annas, Julia. *The Morality of Happiness*. New York: Oxford University Press, 1993.

Bateson, Patrick, and Kevin N. Laland. "Tinbergen's Four Questions: An Appreciation and an Update." *Trends in Ecology and Evolution* 28 (2013): 712–718.

Beck, Lewis White. *Early German Philosophy: Kant and His Predecessors*. Cambridge, MA: Harvard University Press, 1969.

Bedau, Mark. "Can Biological Teleology Be Naturalized?" *Journal of Philosophy* 88 (1991): 647–655.

Beiser, F. C. *Hegel*. New York: Routledge, 2005.

Boorse, Christopher. "Wright on Functions." *Philosophical Review* 85 (1976): 70–86.

Boudri, J. Christiaan. *What Was Mechanical about Mechanics? The Concept of Force between Metaphysics and Mechanics from Newton to Lagrange*. Dordrecht: Kluwer, 2002.

Bowler, Peter J. *Evolution: The History of an Idea*. Berkeley: University of California Press, [1983] 2009.

Broadie, Sarah. "Nature and Craft in Aristotelian Teleology." In *Biologie, logique et métaphysique chez Aristote*, edited by Daniel Devereux and Pierre Pellegrin, 389–403. Paris: Editions du Centre National de la Recherche Scientifique, 1990.

Broadie, Sarah. *Nature and Divinity in Plato's "Timaeus"*. Cambridge: Cambridge University Press, 2012.

Broadie, Sarah. "Nature, Craft and Phronesis in Aristotle." *Philosophical Topics* 15 (1987): 35–50.

Buller, David. "Etiological Theories of Function: A Geographical Survey." *Biology and Philosophy* 13 (1998): 505–527.

Buller, David, ed. *Function, Selection, and Design*. Albany: State University of New York Press, 1999.

Burr, David. "Franciscan Exegesis and Francis as Apocalyptic Figure." *Sewanee Medieval Studies* 4 (1989): 51–62.

Cameron, Rich. "Aristotle's Teleology." *Philosophy Compass* 5, no. 12 (2010): 1096–1106.

Carlin, Laurence. "The Importance of Teleology to Boyle's Natural Philosophy." *British Journal for the History of Philosophy* 19, no. 4 (2011): 665–682.

Carraud, Vicent. *Causa sive ratio: La raison de la cause, de Suarez à Leibniz*. Paris: Presses Universitaires de France, 2002.

Carriero, John. "Spinoza on Final Causality." *Oxford Studies in Early Modern Philosophy* 2 (2005): 105–147.
Charles, David. "Teleological Causation." In *The Oxford Handbook of Aristotle*, edited by Christopher Shields, 226–266. Oxford: Oxford University Press, 2012.
Charles, David. "Teleological Causation in the *Physics*." In *Aristotle's Physics: A Collection of Essays*, edited by L. Judson, 101–128. Oxford: Oxford University Press, 1991.
Cooper, J. M. "Aristotle on Natural Teleology." In *Language and Logos*, edited by M. Schofield and M. Nussbaum, 187–222. Cambridge: Cambridge University Press, 1986.
Cornford, F. M. *Plato's Cosmology*. London: Routledge, 1937.
Craver, Carl F. "Role Functions, Mechanisms, and Hierarchy." *Philosophy of Science* 68 (2001): 31–55.
Davidson, Donald. "Actions, Reasons, and Causes." *Journal of Philosophy* 60 (1963): 685–700.
Cummins, R. "Functional Analysis." *Journal of Philosophy* 72 (1975): 741–765.
Davies, Paul S. *Norms of Nature: Naturalism and the Nature of Functions*. Cambridge, MA: MIT Press, 2001.
Dawkins, Richard. *The Blind Watchmaker: Why the Evidence of Evolution Reveals a Universe without Design*. New York: Norton, [1986] 1996.
Dennett, Daniel C. *Darwin's Dangerous Idea: Evolution and the Meanings of Life*. New York: Simon & Schuster, 1995.
Dennett, Daniel C. *From Bacteria to Bach and Back: The Evolution of Minds*. New York: Norton, 2017.
Denyer, Nicholas. "Sun and Line: The Role of the Good." In *The Cambridge Companion to Plato's Republic*, edited by G. R. F. Ferrari, 284–309. Cambridge: Cambridge University Press, 2007.
Des Chene, Dennis. *Physiologia: Natural Philosophy in Late Aristotelianism and Cartesian Thought*. Ithaca, NY: Cornell University Press, 1996.
DeVries, W. "The Dialectic of Teleology." *Philosophical Topics* 19 (1991): 51–70.
Distelzweig, Peter. "'*Meam de motu & usu cordis, & circuitu sanguinis sententiam*': Teleology in William Harvey's *De motu cordis*." *Gesnerus: Swiss Journal of the History of Medicine and Sciences* 71, no. 2 (2014): 258–270.
Düsing, K. "Die Idee des Lebens in Hegels Logik." In *Hegels Philosophie der Natur*, edited by R. P. Horstmann and M. J. Petry. Stuttgart: Klett-Cotta, 1986.
Emilsson, Eyjólfur. *Plotinus*. London: Routledge, 2017.
Forber, Patrick. "Biological Inheritance and Cultural Evolution in Nietzsche's Genealogy." *Journal of Nietzsche Studies* 44 (2013): 329–341.

Forber, Patrick. "Debating the Power and Scope of Adaptation." In *The Philosophy of Biology: A Companion for Educators*, edited by Kostas Kampourakis, 145–160. Dordrecht: Springer, 2013.

Frede, Michael. "The Original Notion of Cause." In *Essays in Ancient Philosophy*, 125–150. Minneapolis: University of Minnesota Press, 1987.

Fugate, Courtney D. *The Teleology of Reason: A Study of the Structure of Kant's Critical Philosophy*. Boston: Walter de Gruyter, 2014.

Gallagher, David. "Thomas Aquinas on Self-Love as the Basis for Love of Others." *Acta Philosophica* 8 (1999): 23–44.

Garber, Daniel. *Descartes Embodied: Reading Cartesian Philosophy through Cartesian Science*. Cambridge: Cambridge University Press, 2001.

Garrett, Don. "Teleology in Spinoza and Early Modern Rationalism." In *New Essays on the Rationalists*, edited by Rocco J. Gennaro and Charles Huenemann, 310–335. Oxford: Oxford University Press, 1999.

Garson, Justin. *A Critical Overview of Biological Functions*. Dordrecht: Springer, 2016.

Garson, Justin. "How to Be a Function Pluralist." *British Journal for the Philosophy of Science* 69, no. 4 (2018): 1101–1122.

Glennan, Stuart. *The New Mechanical Philosophy*. Oxford: Oxford University Press, 2017.

Godfrey-Smith, Peter. "Functions: Consensus without Unity." *Pacific Philosophical Quarterly* 74 (1993): 196–208.

Godfrey-Smith, Peter. "A Modern History Theory of Functions." *Noûs* 28 (1994): 344–362.

Godfrey-Smith, Peter. "Three Kinds of Adaptationism." In *Adaptationism and Optimality*, edited by Stephen H. Orzack and Elliott Sober, 335–357. Cambridge: Cambridge University Press, 2001.

Goldberg, Benjamin. "William Harvey on Anatomy and Experience." *Perspectives on Science* 24, no. 3 (2016): 305–323.

Goodman, Lenn E. "Maimonides and Leibniz." *Journal of Jewish Studies* 31 (1980): 214–236.

Gotthelf, Allan. "Aristotle's Conception of Final Causality." *Review of Metaphysics* 30 (1976–77): 226–254. Reprinted with additional notes and a postscript in *Philosophical Issues in Aristotle's Biology*, edited by Allan Gotthelf and James G. Lennox, 204–242. Cambridge: Cambridge University Press, 1987.

Gotthelf, Allan. "The Elephant's Nose: Further Reflections on the Axiomatic Structure of Biological Explanations in Aristotle." In *Aristotelische Biologie: Intentionen, Methoden, Ergebnisse*, edited by Wolfgang Kullmann and Sabine Föllinger, 85–95. Stuttgart: Franz Steiner, 1997.

Gotthelf, Allan. "The Place of the Good in Aristotle's Teleology." *Proceedings of the Boston Colloquium in Ancient Philosophy* 4 (1988): 13–39.

Gould, Stephen Jay, and Richard C. Lewontin. "The Spandrels of San Marco and the Panglossian Paradigm: A Critique of the Adaptationist Programme." *Proceedings of the Royal Society B, Biological Sciences* 205 (1979): 581–598.

Gould, Stephen Jay, and Elizabeth Vrba. "Exaptation—a Missing Term in the Science of Form." *Paleobiology* 8 (1982): 4–15.

Griffiths, Paul G. "Functional Analysis and Proper Functions." *British Journal for the Philosophy of Science* 44 (1993): 409–422.

Griffiths, Paul G. "In What Sense Does 'Nothing Make Sense Except in the Light of Evolution'?" *Acta Biotheoretica* 57 (2008): 11–32.

Guyer, Paul. "The Harmony of the Faculties Revisited." In *Values of Beauty: Historical Essays in Aesthetics*, 77–109. Cambridge: Cambridge University Press, 2005.

Guyer, Paul. *Kant*. 2nd ed. London: Routledge, 2014.

Guyer, Paul. "Kant on the Systematicity of Nature: Two Puzzles." *History of Philosophy Quarterly* 20 (2003): 277–295. Reprinted in *Kant's System of Nature and Freedom: Selected Essays*, 56–73. Oxford: Clarendon Press, 2005.

Guyer, Paul. "Kant's Ether Deduction and the Possibility of Experience." In *Akten des Siebenten Internationalen Kant Kongresses*, vol. 2, pt. 1, edited by Gerhard Funke, 119–132. Bonn: Bouvier Verlag, 1991. Reprinted in *Kant's System of Nature and Freedom: Selected Essays*, 74–85. Oxford: Clarendon Press, 2005.

Guyer, Paul. "Kant's Principles of Reflecting Judgment." In *Kant's Critique of the Power of Judgment: Critical Essays*, 1–61. Lanham, MD: Rowman & Littlefield, 2003.

Guyer, Paul. *Kant's System of Nature and Freedom: Selected Essays*. Oxford: Clarendon Press, 2005.

Guyer, Paul. "Kant's Teleological Conception of Philosophy and Its Development." *Kant Yearbook* 1 (2009): 57–97.

Guyer, Paul. "Organisms and the Unity of Science." In *Kant and the Sciences*, edited by Eric Watkins, 259–281. Oxford: Oxford University Press, 2001.

Harvey, Warren Zev. "Spinoza and Maimonides on Teleology and Anthropocentrism." In *Spinoza's Ethics: A Critical Guide*, edited by Yitzhak Y. Melamed, 43–55. Cambridge: Cambridge University Press, 2017.

Henry, Devin. "The Cosmological Significance of Animal Generation." In *Theory and Practice in Aristotle's Natural Science*, edited by David Ebrey, 100–118. Cambridge: Cambridge University Press, 2015.

Henry, Devin. "How Sexist Is Aristotle's Developmental Biology?" *Phronesis* 52 (2007): 251–269.

Horstmann, R. P. *Die Grenzen der Vernunft: Eine Untersuchung zu Zielen und Motiven des Deutschen Idealismus.* Frankfurt am Main: Anton Hain, 1991.
Insole, Christopher J. *Kant and the Creation of Freedom: A Theological Problem.* Oxford: Oxford University Press, 2013.
Irwin, Terence. *The Development of Ethics: A Historical and Critical Study.* 3 vols. Oxford: Oxford University Press, 2007–9.
Johansen, Thomas K. "The Origins of Teleology." In *The Cambridge Companion to Ancient Greek and Roman Science,* edited by L. Taub. Cambridge: Cambridge University Press, forthcoming.
Johansen, Thomas K. *Plato's Natural Philosophy.* Cambridge: Cambridge University Press, 2004.
Johansen, Thomas K. "The Two Kinds of End in Aristotle: The View from the *De Anima.*" In *Theory and Practice in Aristotle's Natural Science,* edited by David Ebrey, 119–136. Cambridge: Cambridge University Press, 2015.
Johansen, Thomas K. "*Timaeus* and the Principles of Cosmology." In *The Oxford Handbook of Plato,* edited by Gail Fine, 463–483. Oxford: Oxford University Press, 2011.
Johansen, Thomas K. "Why the Cosmos Needs a Craftsman: Plato's *Timaeus* 27d5–29b." *Phronesis* 59 (2014): 297–320.
Johnson, Monte R. *Aristotle on Teleology.* Oxford: Oxford University Press, 2005.
Jouanna, J., P. Van der Eijk, and N. Allies. *Greek Medicine from Hippocrates to Galen: Selected Papers.* Vol. 40. Leiden: Studies in Ancient Medicine, 2012.
Judson, Lindsay. "Aristotelian Teleology." *Oxford Studies in Ancient Philosophy* 29 (2005): 341–366.
Keleman, Deborah. "The Scope of Teleological Thinking in Preschool Children." *Cognition* 70 (1999): 241–272.
Keleman, Deborah, and E. Rosset. "The Human Function Compunction: Teleological Explanation in Adults." *Cognition* 111 (2009): 138–143.
Kent, Bonnie. "Augustine's Ethics." In *The Cambridge Companion to Augustine,* edited by N. Kretzmann and E. Stump, 205–233. Cambridge: Cambridge University Press, 2001.
Kim, J. "Explanatory Knowledge and Metaphysical Dependence." *Philosophical Issues* 5 (1994): 51–69.
King, Peter. "Scotus's Rejection of Anselm: The Two-Wills Theory." In *John Duns Scotus, 1308–2008: Investigations into His Philosophy,* edited by L. Honnefelder et al., 359–378. Münster: Aschendorff, 2011.
Kitcher, Philip. "Function and Design." *Midwest Studies in Philosophy* 18 (1993): 379–397.

Kreines, James. "Hegel's Critique of Pure Mechanism and the Philosophical Appeal of the Logic Project." *European Journal of Philosophy* 12, no. 1 (2004): 38–74.

Kreines, James. "The Inexplicability of Kant's *Naturzweck*: Kant on Teleology, Explanation and Biology." *Archiv für Geschichte der Philosophie* 87, no. 3 (2005): 270–311.

Kreines, James. "Kant and Hegel on Teleology and Life from the Perspective of Debates about Free Will." In *The Freedom of Life*, edited by T. Khurana, 111–153. Cologne: Walther König, 2013.

Kreines, James. "Kant on the Laws of Nature: Restrictive Inflationism and Its Philosophical Advantages." *The Monist* 100, no. 3 (2017): 326–341.

Kreines, James. "Kant on the Laws of Nature and the Limitation of Our Knowledge." *European Journal of Philosophy* 17 (2009): 527–558.

Kreines, James. *Reason in the World: Hegel's Metaphysics and Its Philosophical Appeal*. Oxford: Oxford University Press, 2015.

Krohs, Ulrich, and Peter Kroes, eds. *Functions in Biological and Artificial Worlds*. Cambridge, MA: MIT Press, 2009.

Lagerlund, Henrik. "The Unity of Efficient and Final Causality: The Mind/Body Problem Reconsidered." *British Journal for the History of Philosophy* 19 (2011): 587–603.

Laland, Kevin N., and Gillian R. Brown. *Sense and Nonsense: Evolutionary Perspectives on Human Behavior*. 2nd ed. Oxford: Oxford University Press, 2011.

Lammer, Andreas. "Defining Nature: From Aristotle to Philoponus to Avicenna." In *Aristotle and the Arabic Tradition*, edited by Ahmed Alwishah and Josh Hayes, 121–142. Cambridge: Cambridge University Press, 2015.

Lennox, James G. *Aristotle's Philosophy of Biology: Studies in the Origins of Life Science*. Cambridge: Cambridge University Press, 2001.

Lennox, James G. "The Comparative Study of Animal Development: William Harvey's Aristotelianism." In *The Problem of Animal Generation in Early Modern Philosophy*, edited by Justin E. H. Smith, 21–46. New York: Cambridge University Press, 2006.

Lennox, James G. "Plato's Unnatural Teleology." In *Aristotle's Philosophy of Biology*, 195–218. Cambridge: Cambridge University Press, 2000.

Lennox, James G. "Robert Boyle's Defense of Teleological Inference in Experimental Science." *Isis* 74, no. 1 (1983): 38–52.

Leunissen, Mariska. *Explanation and Teleology in Aristotle's Science of Nature*. Cambridge: Cambridge University Press, 2010.

Leunissen, Mariska, and Allan Gotthelf. "What's Teleology Got to Do with It? A Reinterpretation of Aristotle's Generation of Animals V." *Phronesis* 55, no. 4 (2010): 325–356. Reprinted (with slight modifications) in *Teleology, First Principles, and Scientific Method in Aristotle's Biology*, edited by Allan Gotthelf, 108–130. Oxford: Oxford University Press, 2012.

Levy, Arnon, and William Bechtel. "Abstraction and the Organization of Mechanisms." *Philosophy of Science* 80 (2012): 241–261.

Lewens, Tim. *Organisms and Artifacts*. Cambridge, MA: MIT Press, 2004.

Lewens, Tim. "Seven Types of Adaptationism." *Biology and Philosophy* 24 (2009): 161–182.

Lin, Martin. "Teleology and Human Action in Spinoza." *Philosophical Review* 115 (2006): 317–354.

Lloyd, Elisabeth, and Stephen Jay Gould. "Exaptation Revisited: Changes Imposed by Evolutionary Psychologists and Behavioral Biologists." *Biological Theory* 12 (2017): 50–65.

Lyssy, Ansgar. "L'économie de la nature—Maupertuis et Euler sur le principe de moindre action." *Philosophiques* 42, no. 1 (2015): 31–51.

MacDonald, Scott. "Egoistic Rationalism: Aquinas's Basis for Christian Morality." In *Christian Theism and the Problems of Philosophy*, edited by M. Beaty, 327–354. Notre Dame, IN: University of Notre Dame Press, 1990.

MacFarland, J. D. *Kant's Concept of Teleology*. Edinburgh: University Press, 1970.

Maier, Anneliese. *Metaphysische Hintergründe der spätscholastischen Naturphilosophie*. Rome: Edizioni di Storia e Letteratura, 1955.

Manson, Neil. *God and Design: The Teleological Argument and Modern Science*. New York: Routledge, 2003.

Marx, Karl. 1975. *Economic and Philosophic Manuscripts of 1844*. In *Marx-Engels Collected Works*, vol. 3, 229–346. New York: International Publishers, 1975.

Massimi, Michela, and Angela Breitenbach, eds. *Kant and the Laws of Nature*. Cambridge: Cambridge University Press, 2017.

Matthen, M. "Evolution, Wisconsin Style: Selection and the Explanation of Individual Traits." *British Journal for the Philosophy of Science* 50 (1999): 143–150.

McDonough, Jeffrey K. "The Heyday of Teleology and Early Modern Philosophy." *Midwest Studies in Philosophy* 35 (2011): 179–204.

McFall-Ngai, Margaret. "Divining the Essence of Symbiosis: Insights from the Squid-Vibrio Model." *PLoS Biology* 12 (2014): e1001783.

McGinnis, Jon, and Anthony Ruffus. "Willful Understanding: Avicenna's Philosophy of Action and Theory of the Will." *Archiv für Geschichte der Philosophie* 97, no. 2 (2015): 160–195.

McLaughlin, Peter. *Kant's Critique of Teleology in Biological Explanation: Antinomy and Teleology*. Lewiston, ME: Edwin Mellen Press, 1990.

McLaughlin, Peter. "Mechanical Explanation in the 'Critique of the Teleological Power of Judgment.'" In *Kant's Theory of Biology*, edited by Ina Goy and Eric Watkins, 149–165. Boston: Walter de Gruyter, 2014.

McTaggart, J. A. *Commentary on Hegel's Logic*. Cambridge: Cambridge University Press, 1910.

Melamed, Yitzhak Y. "The Causes of Our Belief in Free Will: Spinoza on Necessary, Innate, yet False Cognitions." In *Spinoza's Ethics: A Critical Guide*, edited by Yitzhak Y. Melamed, 121–141. Cambridge: Cambridge University Press, 2017.

Melamed, Yitzhak Y. "Spinoza's Deification of Existence." *Oxford Studies in Early Modern Philosophy* 6 (2012): 75–104.

Melamed, Yitzhak Y. "Spinoza's Monster Cause." Manuscript.

Menn, Steven. "Aristotle and Plato on God as Nous and as the Good." *Review of Metaphysics* 45 (1992): 543–573.

Messina, James. "Kant's Necessitation Account of Laws and the Nature of Natures." In *Kant and the Laws of Nature*, edited by Michela Massimi and Angela Breitenbach, 131–149. Cambridge: Cambridge University Press, 2017.

Millikan, Ruth G. "In Defense of Proper Functions." *Philosophy of Science* 56 (1989): 288–302.

Millikan, Ruth G. *Language, Thought, and Other Biological Categories*. Cambridge, MA: MIT Press, 1984.

Millikan, Ruth. G. *White Queen Psychology and Other Essays for Alice*. Cambridge, MA: MIT Press, 1993.

Mills, Robin, Hanno Hildenbrandt, Graham K. Taylor, and Charlotte K. Hemelrijk. "Physics-Based Simulations of Aerial Attacks by Peregrine Falcons Reveal That Stooping at High Speed Maximizes Catch Success against Agile Prey." *PLOS Computational Biology* (2018): 10.1371.

Neander, Karen. "Functional Analysis and the Species Design." *Synthese* 194 (2017): 1147–1168.

Neander, Karen. "Functions as Selected Effects: The Conceptual Analyst's Defense." *Philosophy of Science* 58 (1991): 168–184.

Neander, Karen. "The Teleological Notion of 'Function.'" *Australasian Journal of Philosophy* 69, no. 4 (1991): 454–468.

Neander, Karen. "Teleological Theories of Mental Content." Last edited Spring 2018. In *The Stanford Encyclopedia of Philosophy*, edited by Edward N. Zalta. https://plato.stanford.edu/archives/spr2018/entries/content-teleological.

Nielsen, Karen. "The Private Parts of Animals: Aristotle on the Teleology of Sexual Difference." *Phronesis* 53 (2008): 373–405.

Noble, Chris, and Nathan M. Powers, "Creation and Divine Providence in Plotinus." In *Causation and Creation in Late Antiquity*, edited by A. Marmodoro and B. Prince, 51–70. Cambridge: Cambridge University Press, 2015.

Normore, Calvin G. "Picking and Choosing: Anselm and Ockham on Choice." *Vivarium* 36 (1998): 23–39.

Nutton, V. "Logic, Learning, and Experimental Medicine." *Science* 295, no. 5556 (2002): 800–801.

Okasha, Samir. *Agents and Goals in Evolution*. Oxford: Oxford University Press, 2018.

Osborne, Thomas M., Jr. *Love of Self and Love of God in Thirteenth-Century Ethics*. Notre Dame, IN: University of Notre Dame Press, 2005.

Pasnau, Robert. "Intentionality and Final Causes." In *Ancient and Medieval Theories of Intentionality*, edited by D. Perler, 301–323. Leiden: Brill, 2001.

Pasnau, Robert. *Metaphysical Themes, 1274–1671*. Oxford: Clarendon Press, 2011.

Prum, Richard O. "Development and Evolutionary Origin of Feathers." *Journal of Experimental Zoology* 285 (1999): 291–306.

Pulte, Helmute. *Das Prinzip der kleinsten Wirkung und die Kraftkonzeptionen der rationale Meckanik: Eine Untersuchung zur Grudlegungsproblematik bei Leonhard Euler, Pierre Louis Moreau de Maupertuis und Joseph Louis Lagrange*. Stuttgart: Franz Steiner Verlag, 1989.

Quarantotto, Diana. *Causa finale, sostanza, essenza in Aristotele: Saggi sulla struttura dei processi teleologici naturali e sulla funzione dei telos*. Naples: Bibliopolis, 2005.

Rice, Collin. "Models Don't Decompose That Way: A Holistic View of Idealized Models." *British Journal for the Philosophy of Science* 70, no. 1 (March 20, 2019): 179–208, https://doi.org/10.1093/bjps/axx045.

Richardson, John. "Aristotle's Teleologies." Manuscript.

Richardson, Kara. "Avicenna and the Principle of Sufficient Reason." *Review of Metaphysics* 67 (2014): 743–768.

Richardson, Kara. "Two Arguments for Natural Teleology from Avicenna's Shifā'." *History of Philosophy Quarterly* 32 (2015): 123–140.

Roth, Leon. "Fundamentalism and Judaism." *L'Eylah* 25 (April 1988): 9.

Saperstein, Marc. *Exile in Amsterdam: Saul Levi Mortera's Sermons to a Congregation of "New Jews"*. Cincinnati: Hebrew Union College Press, 2005.

Scharle, Margaret. "Elemental Teleology in Aristotle's Physics II.8." *Oxford Studies in Ancient Philosophy* 34 (2008): 147–183.

Schiefsky, M. J. "Galen's Teleology and Functional Explanation." *Oxford Studies in Ancient Philosophy* 33 (2007): 369–400.

Schmid, Stephan. "Finality without Final Causes? Suárez's Account of Natural Teleology." *Ergo* 2 (2015): 393–425.

Schmid, Stephan. *Finalursachen in der Frühen Neuzeit* (New York: de Gruyter, 2011).

Schmid, Stephan. "Teleology and the Dispositional Theory of Causation in Thomas Aquinas." *Logical Analysis and History of Philosophy* 14 (2011): 21–39.

Sedley, David. "Is Aristotle's Teleology Anthropocentric?" *Phronesis* 36 (1991): 179–197.

Sedley, David. "Platonic Causes." *Phronesis* 43 (1998): 114–132.

Sedley, David. "Teleology and Myth in the *Phaedo*." *Proceedings of the Boston Area Colloquium in Ancient Philosophy* 5 (1989): 359–383.

Shanahan, Timothy. "Teleological Reasoning in Boyle's Disquisition about Final Causes." In *Robert Boyle Reconsidered*, edited by Michael Hunter, 177–192. New York: Cambridge University Press, 1994.

Siraisi, N. G. "Vesalius and the Reading of Galen's Teleology." *Renaissance Quarterly* 50 (1997): 1–34.

Sober, Elliott. "The Design Argument." In *The Blackwell Guide to the Philosophy of Religion*, edited by William E. Mann, 117–147. Hoboken, NJ: Wiley-Blackwell, 2004.

Sober, Elliott. *Evidence and Evolution: The Logic behind the Science*. Cambridge: Cambridge University Press, 2008.

Sober, Elliott. "Evolution, Population Thinking, and Essentialism." *Philosophy of Science* 47 (1980): 350–383.

Steel, Carlos. "Avicenna and Thomas Aquinas on Evil." In *Avicenna and His Heritage: Acts of the International Colloquium, Leuven, September 8–11, 1999*, edited by Jules Janssens and Daniel De Smet, 171–196. Leuven: Leuven University Press, 2002.

Sterelny, Kim. *The Evolved Apprentice: How Evolution Made Humans Unique*. Cambridge, MA: MIT Press, 2012.

Strevens, Michael. *Depth: An Account of Scientific Explanation*. Cambridge, MA: Harvard University Press, 2008.

Terrall, Mary. *The Man Who Flattened the Earth*. Chicago: University of Chicago Press, 2002.

Tinbergen, Niko. "On the Aims and Methods in Ethology." *Zeitschrift für Tierpsychologie* 20 (1963): 410–433.

Van Fraasen, Bas. *The Scientific Image*. Oxford: Clarendon Press, 1980.

Vlastos, Gregory. "Reasons and Causes in the *Phaedo*." *Philosophical Review* 78 (1969): 291–325.

Waal, Frans de. *Are We Smart Enough to Know How Smart Animals Are?* New York: Norton, 2017.

Walsh, James J. "Teleology in the Ethics of Buridan." *Journal of the History of Philosophy* 18 (1980): 265–286.

Wattles, Jeffrey. *The Golden Rule*. New York: Oxford University Press, 1996.

Williams, Thomas. "From Metaethics to Action Theory." In *The Cambridge Companion to Duns Scotus*, edited by T. Williams, 332–351. Cambridge: Cambridge University Press, 2003.

Wilson, Catherine. "The Building Forces of Nature and Kant's Teleology of the Living." In *Kant and the Law of Nature*, edited by Michela Massimi and Angela Breitenbach, 256–274. Cambridge: Cambridge University Press, 2017.

Wimsatt, William. *Re-engineering Philosophy for Limited Beings: Piecewise Approximations of Reality*. Cambridge, MA: Harvard University Press, 2007.

Wisnovsky, Robert. "Avicenna on Final Causality." PhD dissertation, Yale University, 1994.

Wisnovsky, Robert. *Avicenna's Metaphysics in Context*. London: Duckworth, 2003.

Wolfson, Harry Austryn. *The Philosophy of Spinoza: Unfolding the Latent Process of Reasoning*. 2 vols. Cambridge, MA: Harvard University Press, 1934.

Woodward, James C. *Making Things Happen: A Theory of Causal Explanation*. Oxford: Oxford University Press, 2003.

Wright, Larry. "Functions." *Philosophical Review* 82 (1973): 139–168.

Zuckert, R. "Purposiveness, Time, and Unity: A Reading of the *Critique of Judgment*." PhD dissertation, University of Chicago, 2000.

Index

aesthetics, 10, 200, 205–207, 249–254
agency, 7–8, 16, 21, 48, 50, 72–100, 112–115, 130–131, 138–139, 145, 206, 220, 236, 277–278
aitia, 15, 16n5, 21, 27, 28
Albert the Great, 105, 107, 112–113
anatomy, 10, 13, 64–70, 152–154, 165
Anaxagoras, 5, 15–17, 21, 29–30
animals, 3, 11, 36, 94, 100n23, 112, 128, 256–278
    Aristotle and, 7, 39–45, 48–63, 132, 148n68
    Avicenna and, 74n13, 75–77, 80, 82, 85–87
    Boyle and, 163, 166–168
    Galen and, 64–66
    Harvey and, 153–154, 157–158, 160–161, 168, 177
    Kant and, 195, 198–199, 221–222
    Maupertuis and, 170, 172, 174, 176

Anselm, 105, 111–113
anthropocentrism, 35–37, 48n14, 124, 128–129, 134, 135n41, 141, 148, 194.
    See also teleology: anthropocentric
anthropomorphism, 9, 139, 141, 145, 187, 196–198
Apocalypse, 116–117
Aquinas, Thomas, 79n25, 91, 93–94, 97, 100n23, 106–113, 127n10, 132n25
Aristotle, 6–8, 11, 13–16, 23–25, 31, 35–63, 71–75, 85, 88, 90–97, 100, 106, 109n36, 110–113, 123, 127, 130, 132–133, 141, 148–149, 170, 176, 181–185, 220–221, 228–235, 237n35, 242, 245–246
    and animals, 39–45, 48–63
    and chance, 40–41, 45, 47
    and cosmology, 39–40
    and craft, 23–24
    and embryogenesis, 51, 56
    and forms, 42–45, 95, 235, 242

Aristotle (*cont.*)
  and natural teleology, 24, 37–38, 40–50, 63, 75–76, 90, 94, 100, 106, 132–133, 141, 223, 225, 233, 238, 240, 248–249
  (*see also* teleology: natural)
  Nicomachean Ethics, 20n36, 23n21, 109n36, 181
  Parts of Animals, 39–44, 48–50, 56–60, 65
  Physics, 23–25, 37–38, 41n, 45–48, 92, 176
  and Plato, 6–7, 13–16, 23–25, 37–38, 42, 65–66
  Poetics, 181–183
  and reproduction, 50–56
  and Unmoved Mover, 43
art, 39n1, 40–41, 48, 56, 93, 181–182, 249, 253
artifacts, 3–4, 20, 41n3, 65, 220, 223n9, 225–230, 237, 265
Augustine, 104n27, 105
Averroës (Ibn Rushd), 86n40, 91–92, 97–98, 127n10
Avicenna (Ibn Sina), 7–8, 71–91, 96–98, 127n10
  on God, 74, 85–88
  Metaphysics, 72–73
  Physics, 72–73, 75–76
  and voluntary action, 74, 77, 80–84

Bacon, Francis, 150, 152, 158–159, 161, 177, 181
Baumgarten, Alexander Gottlieb, 188, 194
Bernard of Clairvaux, 105
Bible, 103, 116, 123, 162
biology, 152, 156, 177, 238–240, 255–278
  in Aristotle, 39–45, 48–63
  evolutionary, 260, 256–278
  modern, 12, 95, 210, 256–278
  philosophy of, 218, 238
Bonaventure, 119–120
Boyle, Robert, 10–11, 128n14, 152, 161, 170, 173, 175–178, 188, 195, 201
  and defense of teleology, 162–169
Buffon, Georges Louis Leclerc, 207

causation, 4–9, 12, 14–34, 38–39, 45, 53–54, 58–62, 142–148, 171, 184, 197, 201–203, 208, 210, 213, 222–226, 241–242

  in biology, 264–273
  efficient, 4–5, 9, 41, 45, 54–55, 65, 72, 73–78, 82–83, 87–88, 95–101, 117, 122, 141, 144, 146–148, 151, 175, 187, 223–226
  final, 1, 7, 23–24, 41, 43, 54, 57, 65–66, 71–84, 88–101, 127, 131–136, 140, 146, 150–153, 158–163, 168–170, 175–177, 186–187, 209, 226
  formal, 41, 49–54, 57, 61, 73, 92, 101
  material, 15, 17–18, 26–31, 45–50, 55–59, 65–67, 73–75, 92, 101, 209, 235, 237
Celenza, Anna Harwell, 13
chance, 40–41, 45, 47, 69, 162–163, 171, 237. *See also* Aristotle: and chance
Christ, Jesus, 103, 116–122, 217
Christian, Charlie, 254
Christianity, 13, 85, 103–107, 110, 116–118, 120, 123, 162. *See also* teleology: Christian
Cicero, 102, 104, 170
Cimabue, 13, 116–122
  Adoration of the Lamb, 117–118
  Christ in Glory with Seven Angels, 120–121
  Fall of Babylon, 121–122
Clemens, James Ross, 150, 152
Clemens, Samuel (Mark Twain), 150
cosmogony, 23
cosmology, 6, 23, 37, 40
craft, 6, 29–32, 34–35, 37
creation, 22, 126–127
  in Aristotle, 42, 65
  in Boyle, 165–166
  of humans, 20, 26n30, 134, 212–213
  in Kant, 196, 212–213
  in medieval Jewish philosophy, 127–129, 134–139
  in Plato, 22–26, 32–37, 65
Crescas, Hasdai, 125n3, 127n10, 128n13, 129n16, 135
Cummins, Robert, 264–265, 270

Darwin, Charles, 12–13, 172, 194, 210, 256–264, 268n30, 274

INDEX

demiurge. *See* Plato: and the divine craftsman
Descartes, René, 151–152, 158–159, 161–162, 171, 174, 177, 186–188, 235, 236n33
design, 3, 60–67, 132, 148, 162–176, 212–214, 217, 220, 224, 227–230, 255–259, 267, 275
　divine, 65–67, 168, 173–176, 198, 204, 228
　intelligent, 3, 61, 65–67, 132, 148, 168, 171–176, 187–189, 210, 217, 220, 230–238, 258–259
determinism, 147, 213
dissection, 13, 60, 64, 66–70, 154, 156, 177

efficient cause. *See* causation: efficient
Ein-Sof, 137–139
Eldridge, Roy, 254
Ellington, Duke, 252, 254
Empedocles, 44–46, 75
Epicureans, 162, 177
Ergas, Joseph, 137–139
ergon, 40, 65, 68
eschatology, 116
eternity, 22, 51, 113
　of species, 25, 51, 85n35, 133
　of the world, 9, 130, 132
ethics, 8, 90, 99, 101, 200
　ancient, 24n22, 102, 104, 112
　Christian, 104, 107, 109n36, 112
　medieval, 103–115
etiology, 18, 266
　in biology, 12, 264–273
eudaimonism, 104, 106–108, 110–114. *See also* teleology: eudaimonistic
Euler, Leonard, 169–170, 175, 177
evolution. *See* natural selection
explanation, 4–8, 11–12, 19, 21, 29, 33–34, 37, 65–66, 92–96, 100, 198, 222–223, 241–246, 260–261, 264–265
　causal, 197, 276
　mechanical, 199, 207n13, 209, 211
　scientific, 12, 274–278
　teleological, 7, 9–11, 20, 57, 90–91, 146, 151, 178
extrinsic teleology. *See* teleology: extrinsic

Fabricius, Hieronymus, 152
Feuerbach, Ludwig Andreas, 243
figure, rhetorical, 184
Flora, Holly, 13
Forber, Patrick, 12, 161n14, 222n7, 240, 263n19
Francis of Assisi, 116–122
free will, 105
　Spinoza and, 141–149
function, 1–4, 10–13, 20, 32, 40, 65–70, 187–191, 201, 255
　anatomical, 65–70, 153–161, 163–168, 176–177
　biological, 12, 239–240, 257–277
　teleological, 1–4, 10–12, 154, 194, 208, 222

Galen of Pergamon, 13, 64–70, 153–156
Galileo, 174
Gaon, Saadia, 127–128, 129n16
God, 8–9, 67, 74, 91, 93–95, 99, 103–113, 117–120, 158
　arguments for the existence of, 171, 176, 195, 258–259
　in Avicenna, 74, 85–88
　in Boyle, 163–168, 188
　in Hegel, 228, 244–245
　in Jewish philosophy, 127–142
　in Kant, 189, 191, 195–208, 213–216
　in Maupertuis, 170–173
　in Plato, 21–36
　in Spinoza, 151, 187, 226n16
　the good, 6–9, 15–18, 126–127, 247–248. *See also* teleology: and goodness
　as a cause, 16–21, 71–89
　Form of, 20
Goodman, Benny, 254
Gospels, 103–107
Gould, Stephen Jay, 263n19–20, 264n21, 268–270
Guyer, Paul, 10–11, 224n11–12, 278n52

Halevi, Judah, 127n9, 128
Harvey, Warren Zev, 149
Harvey, William, 10–11, 152–161, 164–169, 176–178, 187, 201

INDEX

Hawkins, Coleman, 254
Hegel, Georg Wilhelm, 11–12, 217, 219–248
Heraclitus, 39n1
holism, causal, 18–20, 32–35
Hooke, Robert, 161
Hume, David, 108, 186–188, 258n9

Ibn Sina. *See* Avicenna
immanent teleology. *See* teleology: immanent
intentionality. *See* teleology: and intentionality
intrinsic teleology. *See* teleology: intrinsic

Jacobi, Carl Gustav Jacob, 226–228
jazz, 13, 249–254
Jewish philosophy, 9, 123–149
Joachim of Fiore, 116
Johansen, Thomas Kjeller, 6, 42n5, 65n3
John the Evangelist, 116–117

Kabbala, 9, 124, 135n41, 136–139
Kant, Immanuel, 10–13, 179, 186–218, 221–226, 229–239, 248, 249–250, 278
   Critique of Pure Reason, 10, 191–192, 197, 199–201
   and subjectivism about teleology 11–13, 221–224 (*see also* teleology: subjectivism about)
kosmos, 19–21
Kreines, James, 11–12, 202n9, 217

Lamarck, Jean-Baptiste, 259–260
law, 103, 203, 213
   moral, 111–112, 212–213, 215–217
   of nature, 174, 189, 195–196, 200–204, 206–207, 241
   scientific, 10, 28, 162, 196, 201
Leibniz, Gottfried Wilhelm, 136, 146, 151n4, 174, 179, 188, 194–195
Leon, Moshe de, 136
Leunissen, Mariska, 6–7, 31n33, 42n6, 66n4, 93n8, 132n24, 148n68, 176n64
Luria, Issac, 124, 136–138

Maimonides, Moses ben, 9, 124–136, 141–142, 149
   Commentary on the Mishnah, 128
   Guide of the Perplexed, 129–130
Marechal, Patricia, 13, 153n6
Marx, Karl, 243
Maupertuis, Pierre, 10–11, 152, 169–178, 197n7
McDonough, Jeff, 9–10, 70n25, 85n36, 128n14, 135n37, 146n63, 151n4, 187–188, 197n7, 226n15
mechanical philosophy, 95, 162, 167–169, 198–199, 207–211, 228, 234, 236, 242, 276
medicine, 24, 64, 67, 156–157, 181, 266, 272–273
Melamed, Yitzhak, 9, 85n36, 92n4, 144n60, 151n3, 220n3
metaphysics, 95, 110, 179, 188, 214, 219–223, 228–232, 239–245, 248
method, philosophical, 10, 18, 190–191, 194
Midrashim, 123, 127
morality, 101–103, 115, 189–190, 200, 212–217
Murphy, Kathryn, 13
music, 182, 249–254. *See also* jazz

natural selection, 12, 25, 176, 194, 240, 256, 257n7, 259, 262–263, 266–267, 275, 277
naturalism, 5, 8, 15, 23, 95, 97, 151, 163, 177–178
Neander, Karen, 239–240, 255n1
necessity, 26–32, 42–62, 100, 133, 140–143, 156, 187, 194, 203, 206, 211, 241
Neoplatonism, 22
Newton, Isaac, 156–157, 169–171, 174, 178, 211
nous, 16, 21, 26

Ockham, William, 8, 98–101, 111n42, 113–115
organisms, 3, 10, 45, 64–67, 75, 85, 176, 189–190, 195, 198–200, 206–212, 217–218, 231–234, 237–241, 257, 259, 262, 270. *See also* animals

organs, 3–4, 59, 53, 55, 58n32, 69, 163, 165, 168, 172, 177, 189, 190, 195, 199, 208, 239, 256–263, 266, 268–271, 274–275
original sin, 105–106

Paley, William, 258
Parker, Charlie, 252, 254
Pasnau, Robert, 8–9, 72n6, 76n17, 95n11, 127n10, 132n25, 220n3, 226n15
Philoponus, John, 75
physico-theology. *See* teleology: in Kant
physics, 10, 91, 150–152, 173–178, 211, 234
Plato, 5–8, 12–13, 14–38, 183, 247
  and cosmology, 6, 23, 35–37
  Cratylus, 32
  and the divine craftsman, 20–26, 31–32, 34, 36, 42, 65
  and Forms, 18, 22–23, 42
  Phaedo, 5–6, 14–16, 19–21, 27–30, 33–35
  Republic, 19–21, 33, 34, 247
  teleological theory of causation, 14–38
  Timaeus, 6, 14–15, 20–38, 42, 65
Platonism, 137, 242
Plotinus, 86n40, 137
principle of least action, 173–176. *See also* Maupertuis
principle of sufficient reason, 78, 188
profundity, 249–254
providence, divine, 76, 85–87, 106
pseudo-Aristotle, 123
Puttenham, George, 184–185

reasoning, 10, 16, 21–22, 26–30, 34, 83, 94, 100, 102, 112, 114, 178, 190, 191–194, 201, 206, 212, 215, 228
  analogical, 22
  cosmological, 22
  demonstrative, 22
  metaphysical, 165–168, 170, 175
  moral, 114
  physical, 163–165, 168
  practical, 22–24, 26, 192, 215
  teleological, 10, 127, 152, 154, 158–159, 163, 168, 173, 176–178
  theoretical, 22–24

reproduction, 50n17, 51–56, 61–62, 66, 199, 207–208, 210–211, 232–233
Revelation, book of, 116
Richardson, Kara, 7–9

Scheiner, Christof, 165
Schelling, Friedrich, 217
Scholastic philosophy, 8, 105, 111, 123, 178
science, 7, 159, 168, 170, 173, 176, 178, 182, 265, 276–277
  biological, 238, 261, 278n52
  divine, 91
  early modern, 10, 70n25, 150–153, 156–157, 160–161, 177–178, 187–188
  mechanical, 167
  natural, 41n3, 60, 92, 173, 208, 260
  philosophy of, 218
  theoretical, 24
scientific revolution, 10
Scotus, John Duns, 97, 101, 109n36, 111–114
Shakespeare, William, 180n2, 185
Sidney, Sir Philip, 13, 180–185
  Astrophil and Stella, 180–185
  Defence of Poesy, 86, 181–184
Socrates, 5, 15–18, 20–21, 24, 27–29, 32–34, 110n41
sonnets, 183
Spinoza, Baruch, 9–11, 124, 133n27, 136, 139–151, 177, 186–188, 212, 226, 244
  critique of teleology, 139–149
Suárez, Francisco, 95n11, 127n10, 141n54, 178
subjectivity. *See* teleology: subjectivism about

Talmud, 123–126, 137
teleology
  and aesthetic experience, 205–207
  anthropocentric, 35–37, 48n14, 124, 128–129, 134–135, 141
  in Aristotle, 35–38, 39–63
  in Avicenna, 71–89
  biological, 152–161, 177 (*see also* Harvey, William)
  Boyle's defense of, 161–169

teleology (*cont.*)
  causal role of, 4–9, 12, 14–17, 18–20, 24
  Christian, 13, 116–122
  in Cimabue's Apocalypse murals, 116–122
  concept of, 1–2, 5
  in contemporary philosophy, 255–278
  cosmic, 35–37
  craft model, 29–32, 34–35, 37, 55–57
  critique of, 139–149, 151 (*see also* Spinoza: critique of teleology)
  divine, 141–149, 152, 161–176, 228
  and ethics, 103–115
  eudaimonistic, 104, 106, 110–114 (*see also* eudaimonism)
  and explanation, 7, 9–11, 20, 57, 90–91, 146, 151, 178 (*see also* explanation: teleological)
  extrinsic, 2–11, 38, 42, 50, 74, 78, 93–94, 99, 211–212, 220, 224, 227–235
  in Galen, 64–70
  and goodness, 6–9, 126–127, 247–248
  in Hegel, 219–248
  and history, 214–218, 246–248
  human, 141–148
  immanent, 11–12, 41–42, 49–50, 176, 194, 219–248
  and intentionality, 2–12, 42, 97–100, 143, 147–148, 210, 226–229
  intrinsic, 2–12, 40, 92, 95
  and jazz, 249–254
  in Jewish philosophy, 123–149
  in Kant, 186–218, 221–225
  in the later Middle Ages, 90–115
  as a method in philosophy, 190–199
  natural, 11, 24, 37–52, 57, 63, 76, 101, 132, 148, 221, 223–225, 233, 238, 248–249, 253 (*see also* Aristotle: and natural teleology)
  naturalizing of, 268–277
  in Plato, 14–38
  in poetry, 180–185 (*see also* Sidney, Sir Philip)
  primary, 49–50, 57
  in religion, 214–218
  scope of, 3, 5, 8, 100n23, 124, 168
  secondary, 49–50, 53n, 58
  species, 35
  subjectivism about, 11–13, 199–201, 229
theology, 91, 116, 200, 204, 208, 210
  Christian, 116
  Judaic, 124–127
  natural, 177
  physico- (*see* teleology: in Kant)
Tristano, Lennie, 252, 254

Ulanov, Barry, 13, 249–254

Vesalius, 69–70
vision, 27–31, 65, 165
Vrba, Elisabeth, 263n20, 268–270

Wolff, Christian, 188, 194–195
Wright, Larry, 264–266

Xenophon, 183

Young, Lester, 254

Zohar, 136, 139n47
zoogony, 44